Crosswalk Coach for the Common Core State Standards, English Language Arts, Grade 4

Coach™®

Triumph Learning®

Crosswalk Coach for the Common Core State Standards, English Language Arts, Grade 4
311NA
ISBN-13: 978-0-7836-7878-8

Cover Image: © Veer/Image Source Photography

Triumph Learning® 136 Madison Avenue, 7th Floor, New York, NY 10016

© 2011 Triumph Learning, LLC
Coach is an imprint of Triumph Learning®

Printed in the United States of America.

10 9 8 7 6 5

Frequently Asked Questions about the Common Core State Standards

What are the Common Core State Standards?

The Common Core State Standards for mathematics and English language arts, grades K–12, are a set of shared goals and expectations for the knowledge and skills that will help students succeed. They allow students to understand what is expected of them and to become progressively more proficient in understanding and using mathematics and English language arts. Teachers will be better equipped to know exactly what they must do to help students learn and to establish individualized benchmarks for them.

Will the Common Core State Standards tell teachers how and what to teach?

No. Because the best understanding of what works in the classroom comes from teachers, these standards will establish *what* students need to learn, but they will not dictate *how* teachers should teach. Instead, schools and teachers will decide how best to help students reach the standards.

What will the Common Core State Standards mean for students?

The standards will provide a clear, consistent understanding of what is expected of student learning across the country. Common standards will not prevent different levels of achievement among students, but they will ensure more consistent exposure to materials and learning experiences through curriculum, instruction, teacher preparation, and other supports for student learning. These standards will help give students the knowledge and skills they need to succeed in college and careers.

Do the Common Core State Standards focus on skills and content knowledge?

Yes. The Common Core State Standards recognize that both content and skills are important. They require rigorous content and application of knowledge through higher-order thinking skills. The English language arts standards require certain critical content for all students, including classic myths and stories from around the world, America's founding documents, foundational American literature, and Shakespeare. The remaining crucial decisions about content are left to state and local determination. In addition to content coverage, the Common Core State Standards require that students systematically acquire knowledge of literature and other disciplines through reading, writing, speaking, and listening.

In mathematics, the Common Core State Standards lay a solid foundation in whole numbers, addition, subtraction, multiplication, division, fractions, and decimals. Together, these elements support a student's ability to learn and apply more demanding math concepts and procedures.

The Common Core State Standards require that students develop a depth of understanding and ability to apply English language arts and mathematics to novel situations, as college students and employees regularly do.

Will common assessments be developed?

It will be up to the states: some states plan to come together voluntarily to develop a common assessment system. A state-led consortium on assessment would be grounded in the following principles: allowing for comparison across students, schools, districts, states and nations; creating economies of scale; providing information and supporting more effective teaching and learning; and preparing students for college and careers.

Table of Contents

			Common Core State Standards

Common Core State Standards Correlation Chart

Common Core State Standard	Grade 4	Crosswalk Coach Lesson(s)
Reading Standards for Literature		
Key Ideas and Details		
RL.4.1	Refer to details and examples in a text when explaining what the text says explicitly and when drawing inferences from the text.	1
RL.4.2	Determine a theme of a story, drama, or poem from details in the text; summarize the text.	2
RL.4.3	Describe in depth a character, setting, or event in a story or drama, drawing on specific details in the text (e.g., a character's thoughts, words, or actions).	3
Craft and Structure		
RL.4.4	Determine the meaning of words and phrases as they are used in a text, including those that allude to significant characters found in mythology (e.g., Herculean).	34
RL.4.5	Explain major differences between poems, drama, and prose, and refer to the structural elements of poems (e.g., verse, rhythm, meter) and drama (e.g., casts of characters, settings, descriptions, dialogue, stage directions) when writing or speaking about a text.	5
RL.4.6	Compare and contrast the point of view from which different stories are narrated, including the difference between first- and third-person narrations.	4
Integration of Knowledge and Ideas		
RL.4.7	Make connections between the text of a story or drama and a visual or oral presentation of the text, identifying where each version reflects specific descriptions and directions in the text.	
RL.4.9	Compare and contrast the treatment of similar themes and topics (e.g., opposition of good and evil) and patterns of events (e.g., the quest) in stories, myths, and traditional literature from different cultures.	6
Range of Reading and Level of Text Complexity		
RL.4.10	By the end of the year, read and comprehend literature, including stories, dramas, and poetry, in the grades 4–5 text complexity band proficiently, with scaffolding as needed at the high end of the range.	1–6
Reading Standards for Informational Text		
Key Ideas and Details		
RI.4.1	Refer to details and examples in a text when explaining what the text says explicitly and when drawing inferences from the text.	7, 8
RI.4.2	Determine the main idea of a text and explain how it is supported by key details; summarize the text.	8
RI.4.3	Explain events, procedures, ideas, or concepts in a historical, scientific, or technical text, including what happened and why, based on specific information in the text.	9
Craft and Structure		
RI.4.4	Determine the meaning of general academic and domain-specific words or phrases in a text relevant to a grade 4 topic or subject area.	10
RI.4.5	Describe the overall structure (e.g., chronology, comparison, cause/effect, problem/solution) of events, ideas, concepts, or information in a text or part of a text.	11
RI.4.6	Compare and contrast a firsthand and secondhand account of the same event or topic; describe the differences in focus and the information provided.	12

Common Core State Standard	Grade 4	Crosswalk Coach Lesson(s)
Reading Standards for Informational Text *(continued)*		
Integration of Knowledge and Ideas		
RI.4.7	Interpret information presented visually, orally, or quantitatively (e.g., in charts, graphs, diagrams, time lines, animations, or interactive elements on Web pages) and explain how the information contributes to an understanding of the text in which it appears.	14
RI.4.8	Explain how an author uses reasons and evidence to support particular points in a text.	13
RI.4.9	Integrate information from two texts on the same topic in order to write or speak about the subject knowledgeably.	15
Range of Reading and Level of Text Complexity		
RI.4.10	By the end of year, read and comprehend informational texts, including history/social studies, science, and technical texts, in the grades 4–5 text complexity band proficiently, with scaffolding as needed at the high end of the range.	7–15
Foundational Skills		
Phonics and Word Recognition		
RF.4.3	Know and apply grade-level phonics and word analysis skills in decoding words. a. Use combined knowledge of all letter-sound correspondences, syllabication patterns, and morphology (e.g., roots and affixes) to read accurately unfamiliar multisyllabic words in context and out of context.	31
Fluency		
RF.4.4	Read with sufficient accuracy and fluency to support comprehension. a. Read on-level text with purpose and understanding. b. Read on-level prose and poetry orally with accuracy, appropriate rate, and expression on successive readings. c. Use context to confirm or self-correct word recognition and understanding, rereading as necessary.	1–15
Writing Standards		
Text Types and Purposes		
W.4.1	Write opinion pieces on topics or texts, supporting a point of view with reasons and information. a. Introduce a topic or text clearly, state an opinion, and create an organizational structure in which related ideas are grouped to support the writer's purpose. b. Provide reasons that are supported by facts and details. c. Link opinion and reasons using words and phrases (e.g., *for instance, in order to, in addition*). d. Provide a concluding statement or section related to the opinion presented.	16
W.4.2	Write informative/explanatory texts to examine a topic and convey ideas and information clearly. a. Introduce a topic clearly and group related information in paragraphs and sections; include formatting (e.g., headings), illustrations, and multimedia when useful to aiding comprehension. b. Develop the topic with facts, definitions, concrete details, quotations, or other information and examples related to the topic. c. Link ideas within categories of information using words and phrases (e.g., *another, for example, also, because*). d. Use precise language and domain-specific vocabulary to inform about or explain the topic. e. Provide a concluding statement or section related to the information or explanation presented.	17

Common Core State Standard	Grade 4	Crosswalk Coach Lesson(s)
	**Writing Standards** *(continued)*	
	**Text Types and Purposes** *(continued)*	
W.4.3	Write narratives to develop real or imagined experiences or events using effective technique, descriptive details, and clear event sequences. a. Orient the reader by establishing a situation and introducing a narrator and/or characters; organize an event sequence that unfolds naturally. b. Use dialogue and description to develop experiences and events or show the responses of characters to situations. c. Use a variety of transitional words and phrases to manage the sequence of events. d. Use concrete words and phrases and sensory details to convey experiences and events precisely. e. Provide a conclusion that follows from the narrated experiences or events.	18
	**Production and Distribution of Writing**	
W.4.4	Produce clear and coherent writing in which the development and organization are appropriate to task, purpose, and audience. (Grade-specific expectations for writing types are defined in standards 1–3 above.)	16–18
W.4.5	With guidance and support from peers and adults, develop and strengthen writing as needed by planning, revising, and editing. (Editing for conventions should demonstrate command of Language standards 1–3.	19
W.4.6	With some guidance and support from adults, use technology, including the Internet, to produce and publish writing as well as to interact and collaborate with others; demonstrate sufficient command of keyboarding skills to type a minimum of one page in a single sitting.	19
	**Research to Build and Present Knowledge**	
W.4.7	Conduct short research projects that build knowledge through investigation of different aspects of a topic.	20
W.4.8	Recall relevant information from experiences or gather relevant information from print and digital sources; take notes and categorize information, and provide a list of sources.	20
W.4.9	Draw evidence from literary or informational texts to support analysis, reflection, and research. a. Apply grade 4 reading standards to literature (e.g., "Describe in depth a character, setting, or event in a story or drama, drawing on specific details in the text [e.g., a character's thoughts, words, or actions]."). b. Apply grade 4 reading standards to informational texts (e.g., "Explain how an author uses reasons and evidence to support particular points in a text").	
	**Range of Writing**	
W.4.10	Write routinely over extended time frames (time for research, reflection, and revision) and shorter time frames (a single sitting or a day or two) for a range of discipline-specific tasks, purposes, and audiences.	16–18

Common Core State Standard	Grade 4	Crosswalk Coach Lesson(s)
	Language Standards	
Conventions of Standard English		
L.4.1	Demonstrate command of the conventions of standard English grammar and usage when writing or speaking.	
	a. Use relative pronouns (*who, whose, whom, which, that*) and relative adverbs (*where, when, why*).	22–23
	b. Form and use the progressive (e.g., *I was walking; I am walking; I will be walking*) verb tenses.	21
	c. Use modal auxiliaries (e.g., *can, may, must*) to convey various conditions.	21
	d. Order adjectives within sentences according to conventional patterns (e.g., *a small red bag* rather than *a red small bag*).	22
	e. Form and use prepositional phrases.	24
	f. Produce complete sentences, recognizing and correcting inappropriate fragments and run-ons.	25
	g. Correctly use frequently confused words (e.g., *to, too, two; there, their*).	26
L.4.2	Demonstrate command of the conventions of standard English capitalization, punctuation, and spelling when writing.	
	a. Use correct capitalization.	27
	b. Use commas and quotation marks to mark direct speech and quotations from a text.	28
	c. Use a comma before a coordinating conjunction in a compound sentence.	28
	d. Spell grade-appropriate words correctly, consulting references as needed.	27
Knowledge of Language		
L.4.3	Use knowledge of language and its conventions when writing, speaking, reading, or listening.	
	a. Choose words and phrases to convey ideas precisely.	29
	b. Choose punctuation for effect.	28
	c. Differentiate between contexts that call for formal English (e.g., presenting ideas) and situations where informal discourse is appropriate (e.g., small-group discussion).	29
	Language Standards *(continued)*	
Vocabulary Acquisition and Use		
L.4.4	Determine or clarify the meaning of unknown and multiple-meaning words and phrases based on *grade 4 reading and content*, choosing flexibly from a range of strategies.	
	a. Use context (e.g., definitions, examples, or restatements in text) as a clue to the meaning of a word or phrase.	30
	b. Use common, grade-appropriate Greek and Latin affixes and roots as clues to the meaning of a word (e.g., *telegraph, photograph, autograph*).	31
	c. Consult reference materials (e.g., dictionaries, glossaries, thesauruses), both print and digital, to find the pronunciation and determine or clarify the precise meaning of key words and phrases.	32

Common Core State Standard	Grade 4	Crosswalk Coach Lesson(s)
Language Standards (continued)		
Vocabulary Acquisition and Use (continued)		
L.4.5	Demonstrate understanding of figurative language, word relationships, and nuances in word meanings. a. Explain the meaning of simple similes and metaphors (e.g., *as pretty as a picture*) in context. b. Recognize and explain the meaning of common idioms, adages, and proverbs. c. Demonstrate understanding of words by relating them to their opposites (antonyms) and to words with similar but not identical meanings (synonyms).	33 34 32
L.4.6	Acquire and use accurately grade-appropriate general academic and domain-specific words and phrases, including those that signal precise actions, emotions, or states of being (e.g., *quizzed, whined, stammered*) and that are basic to a particular topic (e.g., *wildlife, conservation*, and *endangered* when discussing animal preservation).	10

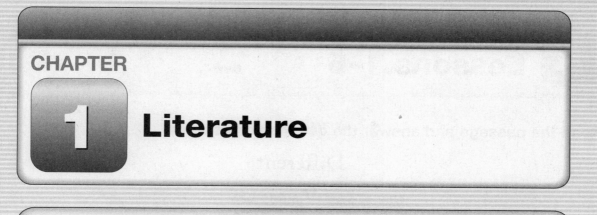

CHAPTER

1 Literature

1 Diagnostic Assessment for Lessons 1–6

Read the passage and answer the questions that follow.

Different

Three animal families—deer, fox, and skunk—lived in a forest. One day, the young deer, the young fox, and the young skunk were playing near the stream that ran through the forest. Their parents had told them to stay out of the stream because it had a strong current. It was on the bank of the stream that they met another young animal.

They had never seen an animal like this before. He had large front teeth and a big, flat tail. They approached him cautiously.

"I'm a fawn," said the young deer. "What kind of animal are you?"

"I'm a beaver," he answered.

"I knew you weren't a fox," said the fox. "I know all the other foxes in this forest. Why haven't we ever seen you before?"

"My family just moved to this forest," said the beaver.

"Where are you going to live?" asked the skunk.

"We don't have a house yet," the beaver said. "We have to build one."

"Don't build it next to mine!" said the fawn.

"Or mine!" added the fox.

"Or mine!" said the skunk.

"Why not?" the beaver asked. "Why don't you want me living near you?"

"Because you're different," said the fawn.

"You look strange," added the fox.

"You're not like us," finished the skunk. "We won't play with you."

The three friends scampered away, leaving the beaver staring after them.

"I couldn't play with you anyway," he called out. "I have to help my mom and dad build our house." But by now they couldn't hear him.

Soon the beaver family was hard at work. They used their sharp front teeth to cut down small trees. Then they dragged the trees into the stream. The swift current didn't bother them because beavers are very good swimmers. They piled the trees up and filled in the spaces with mud. Soon, they had built a dam across the stream. Because of the dam, a pond formed. Now, instead of a stream with a dangerous current, the forest had a pond with water that was still and calm.

The beavers built their home in the middle of this pond. Like the dam, their home was made of trees, sticks, and mud. It didn't take very long for the beaver family to finish and settle into their new home.

That very day, the fawn, the fox, and the skunk returned to the stream for the first time since the day they had met the beaver.

"What happened?" wondered the fawn. "The stream has turned into a pond."

"We did that," said the beaver, popping out of the water.

"How?" asked the fox.

"My family built a dam across the stream. Now the water is still."

"Is it safe to play in?" asked the skunk.

"Yes, because it doesn't have a current anymore," the beaver told them.

The fawn picked a stick up with its teeth, walked to the edge of the stream, and dropped the stick into the water. Instead of being swept away by the current, as it would have been only a few days ago, the stick just floated, barely moving at all. There was no current to sweep it away.

The three animals looked at the stick in the water. Then they looked at one another with wide-open eyes and mouths. Suddenly, they scampered away, leaving the beaver staring after them. But this time, they weren't running away from the beaver. They were running to ask their parents if they could play in the pond.

Soon, all three families returned. The animals' parents stood by the pond and studied the floating stick. It bobbed gently in the water, but stayed in one place.

By now, the beaver's parents had come out of their lodge and were standing next to him.

"Welcome to the forest," the fawn's father said.

"Thanks for turning the dangerous stream into a safe pond," said the fox's mother.

"Let us know if we can do anything for you in return," said the skunk's parents.

"Can we swim in the pond?" the young animals all shouted at once. Their parents nodded, and the young animals were soon splashing about in the water.

"Hey, beaver!" called out the fawn. "Come play with us!"

1. Which detail from the passage shows that the three animals are amazed at the calm water?

   A. "There was no current to sweep it away."

   B. "Then they looked at one another with wide-open eyes and mouths."

   C. "They were running to ask their parents if they could play in the pond."

   D. "The three animals looked at the stick in the water."

2. Which sentence BEST summarizes the passage?

   A. A beaver and his family make new friends by turning a dangerous stream into a safe pond.

   B. A fawn, fox, and skunk are mean to a beaver and run back to their families.

   C. A beaver and his family drag sticks across a fast-moving stream to build a home.

   D. A fawn, fox, and skunk run to their parents to ask permission to go swimming.

3. Which word BEST describes the beaver in the passage?

   A. wise

   B. honest

   C. hardworking

   D. brave

4. Which point of view is used in the passage?

   A. first-person

   B. second-person

   C. third-person limited

   D. third-person omniscient

Read the passage and answer the questions that follow.

The Magpie's Nest

One autumn long ago, in a lovely forest, the air turned very cool and crisp quite early in the season. All the different birds of the forest looked around at the changing leaves. Then they studied their own nests. Most of them had spent a very lazy summer eating bugs and berries, and they hadn't paid much attention to the condition of their homes. Their nests were drafty, and some had terrible leaks.

The birds had a meeting one afternoon and agreed that they would go and ask the magpie for advice on fixing up their nests. The magpie was a rather dull bird, and she wasn't usually included in the summer playing and fun in the forest. In fact, she hadn't even been invited to the meeting where it was agreed that she would be asked to help the others! But she had a very fine nest.

The next day, the birds flew to the magpie's nest. They all admired her nest, cooing and flattering her. Not only was her nest beautiful, they insisted, but it was also durable enough to stand up to wind and rain. Only a very smart and talented bird could make such a nest!

The magpie waited patiently. She knew the other birds just wanted her to tell them what they should do. But in the end, she decided that it would be best if all the birds knew how to build a proper nest. So, she gathered them around and said, "Please, I know how much trouble some of you have listening to others. I know how hard it is to sit still while there are so many bugs out there waiting to be chased. But it is important that you listen to everything I have to tell you—before you go to work on your nests."

"Absolutely, Ms. Magpie!" the birds all cried. "You have our undivided attention!"

"Very well," the magpie continued. "First you need to get some mud and make a round cake with it."

"Oh," said the thrush. "Is that all? I can do that!" And she flew away to build her mud nest. This is still how thrushes make their nests today.

"No, no, there's more!" the magpie cried. "Next, you need to get some twigs and place them around in the mud."

"Oh, anybody can do that!" said the blackbird, and he flew away. Even today, blackbirds have nests made only of mud and twigs.

The magpie was becoming rather annoyed, but she continued anyway. "The next step is to add some more mud over the twigs."

"Why, a child could do that!" hooted the owl, who noisily flapped away to make a nest. Even today, if you look at an owl's nest, you can see that it is made out of some twigs and two layers of mud.

"After the second layer of mud, wrap some more twigs around the outside," the exasperated magpie added, holding her wing to her forehead.

"Okay, boss! I'm on it!" said the sparrow. And to this day, the sparrow makes exactly that kind of nest.

"Next," said the magpie, sitting down wearily, "you add some soft grass to the inside to sit on."

"Grass—got it!" said the starling, who sped off to make a rather nice nest, but not as nice as the magpie's. Even today, this is how starlings make their nests.

The magpie was about to give her final instruction when she realized there were no birds left. She was muttering to herself as she fluffed a layer of soft feathers in her elegant nest. "Fine," she said. "That's the last time I'll ever help those silly creatures!"

Never again would she agree to help the other birds build nests. That is why, today, all of the different birds make different kinds of nests.

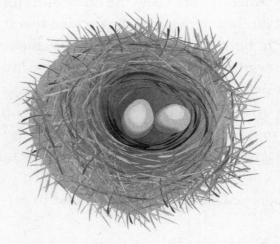

5. What is the MOST LIKELY reason the birds ask for the magpie's help with their nests?

   A. They realize winter is coming soon.

   B. They admire and respect the magpie.

   C. They hope to move in with the magpie.

   D. They need help gathering more food.

6. Which BEST states the theme of the story?

   A. Forests are cold and lonely places.

   B. You have to work hard to make friends.

   C. If you ask for advice, you must be polite and listen.

   D. Seasons will change no matter what.

7. According to the story, which bird listens the longest to the magpie's instructions?

   A. the starling

   B. the owl

   C. the blackbird

   D. the thrush

8. Why does the magpie offer to help the other birds?

   A. She wants them to like her.

   B. She wants them to stop bothering her all the time.

   C. She wants to help them learn about nest building.

   D. She wants to trick them into working on her nest.

Use "Different" and "The Magpie's Nest" to answer questions 9–10.

9. Compare and contrast the two stories. Are the themes alike or different? Use details from both stories to support your answer.

_____

_____

_____

_____

_____

_____

_____

_____

_____

10. Compare the beaver and the magpie. Explain how these characters are different or alike.

_____

_____

_____

_____

_____

_____

_____

_____

_____

Read the poem and answer the questions that follow.

Daisies
by Frank Dempster Sherman

At evening when I go to bed
I see the stars shine overhead;
They are the little daisies white
That dot the meadow of the Night.

5   And often while I'm dreaming so,
Across the sky the Moon will go;
It is a lady, sweet and fair,
Who comes to gather daisies there.

For, when at morning I arise,
10   There's not a star left in the skies;
She's picked them all and dropped them down
Into the meadows of the town.

11. In which stanza does the poet describe the moon?

    A. stanza 1

    B. stanza 2

    C. stanza 3

    D. stanzas 1 and 2

12. Which line from the poem shows which syllables are stressed?

    A. At <u>evening</u> <u>when</u> I <u>go</u> to <u>bed</u>

    B. <u>At</u> evening when <u>I</u> go <u>to</u> bed

    C. At <u>evening</u> when I <u>go</u> to <u>bed</u>

    D. <u>At</u> evening <u>when</u> I <u>go</u> to <u>bed</u>

1 Story Details

RL.4.1, RL.4.10, RF.4.4.a

Getting the Idea

When you read a story, you get information about people, places, and things. Stories tell about characters, such as what they do, where they live, and what they look like. A **detail** is a specific piece of information. Details help you to understand the things contained in stories. The chart below shows some different types of story details.

Type of Story Detail	Example
names of places and characters	Mario visited his aunt in Austin, Texas.
dates and time	The storm arrived on Tuesday evening.
descriptions of places	Yellow sunflowers grew in the grassy field.
things characters say and do	Keisha shouted, "Let's play tag!"
things the narrator tells you	Jake was the best player on the team.
facts in a story	He reminded her of our first president, George Washington.

To find the details in a story, it is often helpful to ask yourself some questions after reading. For example, read the following paragraph.

Eva put on her blue coat, grabbed her knapsack, and rushed out the front door. It was 7:45 A.M. She and her mom walked as quickly as they could. Ten minutes later, Eva arrived at Bellmore Elementary School for her first day of fourth grade.

By asking yourself the following questions, you can find the details in the story. What is the girl's name? *Eva*. What is the color of her coat? *Blue*. What time is it when she leaves her house? *7:45 A.M.* Where is she running to? *Bellmore Elementary School*. What grade is she in? *Fourth grade*. The author uses many kinds of details to help you understand the people, places, and things in the story.

The details in the story about Eva tell you even more. They support larger ideas that are not directly stated in the story. When you use details in the story along with your own knowledge and experience to figure out things for yourself, you make an inference. An **inference** is an educated guess about something that *most likely* or *probably* is true. For example, the passage says that Eva rushed out the front door and ran as fast as she could. Based on those details and your own experience, you can infer that she is late for school. You also read that she grabbed her coat. You can use that detail to infer that it is probably chilly outside.

Another way to better understand a story is to make a simple diagram. A **web** is a diagram that shows an important story idea and the details that help you to understand that idea. The web below is about Dorothy, a character in *The Wizard of Oz*.

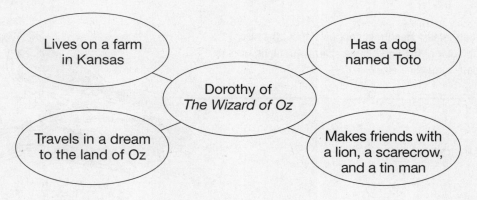

The details are shown in the four outer circles. Each detail gives you a piece of information about Dorothy, such as where she lives and where she travels in her dream. A web can be used for all types of details—characters, places, and events. A web will help you sort and organize information from a story. Seeing the details in a diagram can also help you make inferences about what you read.

Thinking It Through

Read the following sentences, and then answer the questions that follow.

Javier stood quietly and watched a small sparrow land on the branch of a magnolia tree. The brown-and-white bird tilted its head back and began to whistle a beautiful song.

What does the sparrow look like? What is the sparrow doing?

_____

_____

_____

_____

_____

_____

 What details does the author give about the size and color of the bird? Is the sparrow in flight, or is it doing something else?

Coached Example

Read the passage and answer the questions.

As a child, Rochelle would sit in the living room and listen to her mother play the piano every evening. She began to take lessons as a teenager. She would practice two hours every day after school. For the first hour, she would practice her music scales. For the second hour, she would practice learning songs. Rochelle loved the smooth feel of the piano keys beneath her fingers. Each of the eighty-eight black-and-white keys had its own special sound. At night, she would often fall asleep listening to recordings of music by her favorite composers, Mozart and Beethoven. Rochelle liked to dream that, one day, she would play just like the pianists on the recordings.

1. Rochelle will MOST LIKELY continue to practice every day because

   A. she knows she can be a world-famous pianist.

   B. she loves everything about piano playing.

   C. she wants to be a better pianist than her mother.

   D. it helps her relax and fall asleep at night.

   HINT What inference can you make about Rochelle's interest in practicing the piano? Look for the answer choice that makes the most sense.

2. Which detail shows that Rochelle is dedicated to playing the piano?

   A. Rochelle loves the feel of the piano keys.

   B. Rochelle's piano has eighty-eight keys.

   C. Rochelle practices the piano every day.

   D. Rochelle loves to listen to Mozart.

   HINT Which detail supports the idea that Rochelle works hard to learn how to play the piano?

Use the Reading Guide to help you understand the passage.

Reading Guide

Read the first sentence of the passage carefully. Are there any details that describe the season?

Which detail in the passage describes something about the ant's body?

Look at details the author uses to describe how the dove feels. How does the dove feel about the drowning ant?

Which detail tells how the ant saves the dove's life?

The Dove and the Ant

One fall day, an ant stopped by a stream to get a drink of fresh water. Suddenly, a gust of wind came down from the sky and blew the ant into the stream. The ant struggled to stay afloat as the flowing stream swept him along. He paddled as mightily as he could with his six strong legs, but then he began to sink. Luckily, a white dove perched in a tree saw the ant sinking fast. She pitied the drowning ant and flew down to the edge of the stream. As the ant passed by, she reached out her wing.

"Grab hold, dear ant!" called the dove. The ant reached out and crawled onto the dove's wing. Soon the ant was back on dry land.

"I could never thank you enough!" said the ant to the dove. "I hope I can someday return the favor."

A few days later, the ant returned to the stream for another drink. He spied a hunter nearby pointing his bow and arrow into the trees. The ant looked up and saw that the hunter was about to shoot the dove. Quickly, the ant bit the man's foot and made him miss his aim. By doing that, the ant saved the dove's life.

Answer the following questions.

1. What time of year does the passage take place?

    A. summer

    B. spring

    C. winter

    D. fall

2. How does the dove help the ant in the passage?

    A. She teaches the ant how to swim.

    B. She gets the ant some water to drink.

    C. She protects the ant from the wind.

    D. She reaches out her wing to the ant.

3. Which detail from the passage tells that the ant is in trouble?

    A. He looks up into the trees.

    B. He struggles to stay afloat.

    C. He sees a hunter on the shore.

    D. He returns to the stream.

4. Which sentence from the passage BEST helps you know where the passage takes place?

    A. "The ant struggled to stay afloat as the flowing stream swept him along."

    B. "As the ant passed by, she reached out her wing."

    C. "The ant looked up and saw that the hunter was about to shoot the dove."

    D. "By doing that, the ant saved the dove's life."

5. What does the ant say in the passage? How do his words help you to understand his character?

    _____

    _____

    _____

    _____

    _____

    _____

2 Summarize

RL.4.2, RL.4.10, RF.4.4.a

Getting the Idea

One way to better understand a text—and to explain to others what the text is about—is to summarize what you have read. A **summary** is a brief description of a longer work, such as a story, poem, or novel. A summary can also be used for other types of writing, such as a drama. A **drama** is a play that is performed on stage.

A summary states only the most important ideas and details. If you were summarizing a movie, you would not list every single event or mention every character's name. You would tell only about the important characters and events. Read this story. As you read, think about how to summarize it.

Yesterday, my dad and I drove to the beach to try out our new dragon kite. The sun was shining, and big clouds drifted across the breezy sky. Gulls circled and squawked overhead. We assembled the kite on the sand. "Here you go, son," Dad said as he handed me the roll of string attached to the kite and lifted the kite into the air. The red-and-black dragon rose into the sky. I held on tightly as the kite zigzagged back and forth. Suddenly, a gust of wind snapped the kite from the string. We watched our flying dragon grow smaller and smaller as it drifted out of sight.

You could summarize the story as follows:

A father and son lose their kite when the wind snaps it from its string.

This is a good summary because it tells you the main idea and important details of the story. Less important details, such as the weather, the gulls, or the color of the kite, do not belong in the summary.

Theme

When you write a summary of a story, you must look for the most important ideas and details. Summarizing can also help you to figure out a story's theme. The **theme** is the central idea or message of a story. Some stories state their themes directly. For example, in fables and fairy tales, the theme usually appears at the end as a moral, or lesson that the author wants to teach.

However, not all stories have themes that are directly stated as morals. Some themes take a bit of work to discover. As with summarizing, to determine a story's theme, first identify the most important characters, events, settings, and ideas. Then look for a common idea or message that connects these parts. You may ask questions as you are reading to help you. For example:

- What are the main qualities of the characters? (honesty, intelligence, selfishness, humor)
- How do these qualities affect the events in the story?
- What are the actions of the characters?
- How do these actions affect the outcome of the story?
- Does the setting, or where the story takes place, affect the events of the story? How?

Read the following poem.

> The robin wakes before the sun
> And circles fast the muddy field;
> While lazy others snooze away,
> He finds his tasty morning meal.

A good summary of the poem would be: A robin finds his food in the early morning.

The theme, or main message, of the poem is: The early bird is the one who catches the worm.

Notice how the summary and theme are related. They express a similar idea.

Thinking It Through

Read the following drama, and then answer the question that follows.

The curtain opens to show the crafts workshop in a community center. Mr. Anand's pottery class has begun. Six students sit at their pottery wheels.

PABLO: (*cups his hands around a moist mound of clay, which is spinning on the wheel*) I ruined it again! Every time I try to lift up the sides, I knock it out of shape.

MR. ANAND: (*walks over to Pablo and puts his hands on the spinning clay*) You're moving your hands too quickly. Take your time. Feel the shape you want to achieve.

PABLO: (*puts his hands back on the mound of spinning clay*) Wow, slowing down really works. This vase is going to be a nice height and perfectly smooth.

Write a 1–2 sentence summary of this drama. What is the theme of this drama?

_____

_____

_____

_____

_____

HINT A drama is written in dialogue, which is the words the actors speak. As you summarize this drama, choose only the most important details. Think about how Pablo's actions affect the outcome of the drama.

Coached Example

Read the poem and answer the questions.

The Guide

James walked around a bend of shore,
What lay ahead was known no more.

Strange faces shaped in windy clouds;
Dark feathers circling, cawing loud.

Two shells he spied beached side by side
And pleaded each to be his guide.

The small one had lived but a year
And whispered nothing in his ear.

The old one spoke of distant lands
And returned James to familiar sands.

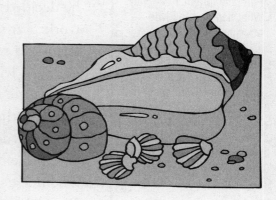

1. Which sentence BEST summarizes the poem?

    A. James looks at birds circling in the sky.

    B. James watches the clouds changing shape.

    C. James listens to the sound of the ocean in a shell.

    D. James finds a shell that helps him find his way home.

    HINT   What are the main events that take place in the poem?

2. Which sentence BEST states the theme of the poem?

    A. With age comes knowledge and experience.

    B. The wind is a powerful force.

    C. Some shells last longer than other shells.

    D. Getting lost is fun and exciting.

    HINT   Why is the old shell able to help James?

Use the Reading Guide to help you understand the passage.

Reading Guide

Read paragraph 1 carefully. What happens to Clyde after the Civil War?

The rancher loans Big Clyde money. What does this detail tell you about Clyde's character?

Which sentences from the passage best tell you about the theme?

Big Clyde Makes Good

Big Clyde got his first job at a mill. After a few years, he decided to leave the mill and head west. While there, he worked at several different jobs. Then he returned home to become a soldier and fight in the Civil War. When the war ended, Clyde moved out west again and became a cowboy on a cattle ranch. He was one of the best cowhands on the ranch. Other cowboys admired his lassoing and herding skills. Clyde taught them many new cow-herding tricks. Then one day, during a stampede, his horse threw him off. The horse's hoof stepped on Big Clyde's foot. After that, Big Clyde walked with a limp.

Clyde became the camp cook on cattle drives. He developed a special way of seasoning smoked meat and basting it with sauce. He also created a number of tasty desserts made from simple ingredients like molasses and honey. When he became too old to ride with the cattle drives, he stayed at the ranch and tried new ways of cooking.

The rancher lent Clyde money to set up an inn, where he fed guests. The inn made Clyde and his children rich. Clyde always said, "Good luck and bad luck are the salt and pepper of life. With the right amount of both, you can make good barbecue."

Answer the following questions.

1. Which sentence BEST summarizes paragraph 1 of the passage?

   A. Clyde walked with a limp after hurting his foot in an accident.

   B. Clyde became a talented cowboy after fighting in the Civil War.

   C. Clyde impressed other cowboys with his lassoing and herding skills.

   D. Clyde's horse threw him to the ground during a stampede.

2. Which detail should NOT be included in a summary of the passage?

   A. Clyde became a camp cook.

   B. Clyde made desserts from molasses and honey.

   C. Clyde worked as a cattle rancher.

   D. Clyde opened a successful inn.

3. What is the main idea of paragraph 2?

   A. Meat can be seasoned in special ways.

   B. Camp cooks work hard.

   C. Clyde smoked and basted meat.

   D. Clyde was a creative cook.

4. Which sentence BEST states the theme of the passage?

   A. Cooks make a lot of money.

   B. Fighting in wars is dangerous.

   C. Hard times can turn into good ones.

   D. People should try many different jobs.

5. What is a good summary of the passage? Write your summary below.

_____

_____

_____

_____

_____

3 Elements of Fiction

RL.4.3, RL.4.10, RF.4.4.a

Getting the Idea

Fiction is writing that describes made-up people and events. Fiction includes stories, fables, fairy tales, poems, dramas, and novels. Just as an artist uses things like shapes and colors to create a painting, a writer uses a number of elements to create a work of fiction. Character, plot, and setting are the main elements of fiction.

Characters are the main actors in a story. They can be people, animals, or other creatures. Like people in real life, characters in stories have inner qualities or **character traits**. A character might be funny or serious, brave or cowardly, selfish or generous. Sometimes an author will directly describe a character's traits. Other times you must look at details, such as what a character says, does, or thinks, to figure out what he or she is like as a person. For example:

> "Next Tuesday is soccer tryouts," Coach Breyer announced at the end of gym class. "The competition will be tough."

> Alex pumped his fist in the air and dribbled his soccer ball back to the locker room. "I can't wait for those tryouts," he thought to himself.

The author does not say that Alex is very confident, but you can figure it out from the way he pumps his fist in the air. He seems eager to try out for the team.

Characters also have **motivations**, or reasons for the ways they act. Specific details provide clues about a character's motivation. Read this example.

> Each day, after school, Julie studied her multiplication tables. She thought of how proud she would feel if she got an A on the upcoming math test.

Julie's motivation for studying is that she wants to get an A on the math test. And the reason she wants an A is so that she can feel proud.

Plot is the series of events that happen in a story. A plot begins with a period of rising action. **Rising action** refers to the events in a story that lead to a conflict. A **conflict** is a problem that the main character must solve. Some stories contain more than one conflict. The **climax** is when the conflict reaches its most exciting point. It is when the character is just about to solve the problem. The final part of the plot is the resolution. A **resolution** is how the conflict or problem is solved.

Read the following passage.

> Max made a sharp turn on his skateboard as he neared the top of the hill. Suddenly, one of the wheels popped off. Max tried to balance on the wobbling board as he sped downhill. He was just about to crash into a fence when he jumped off the board and landed on soft grass.

During the rising action, Max turns and a wheel pops off his skateboard. The conflict is Max's effort to keep his balance. The climax is when Max is just about to crash. And the resolution is when Max lands on the grass.

Setting is where and when a story takes place. The setting might be stated directly, or you may have to figure it out from the details in the story. Settings may change as the story unfolds.

> The sound of the crashing waves grew fainter as I walked on. Soon the shells and pebbles gave way to the dry crunch of pine needles beneath my feet. All around, wind hissed through the branches.

It is not directly stated in the passage, but you can guess from the details that the narrator is walking from the seashore into a forest.

Thinking It Through

Read the following passage, and then answer the question that follows.

All afternoon, Louis paddled his oar against the rough waters of the river. His arms and back ached. Finally, he turned to his brother Pete in the back of the canoe. "Can you give me some help for a change?" Louis asked.

"What?" Pete said, lifting his headphones from his ears as he looked up from reading his comic book.

"Never mind," Louis said, shaking his head as he paddled on.

How would you describe Pete's character?

_____

_____

_____

_____

_____

HINT   At the end of the story, Louis shakes his head. What does this detail tell you about how he feels?

Coached Example

Read the passage and answer the questions.

Jamar lifted his violin to his chin, and then he grinned. He had never felt better prepared for a concert. The air hummed with the sounds of people taking their seats in the auditorium. From where he sat on stage, he could hear the audience rustling behind the thick velvet curtain. Jamar tried not to notice Oscar, who was sitting next to him. Oscar's twitching had started to get on Jamar's nerves. If Oscar had practiced as he should have, he'd have nothing to worry about. "Boy, I'll be glad when this is over," Oscar whispered. Jamar ignored him. He looked at his sheet music and waited for the band leader's signal to begin.

1. Where does this passage take place?

   A. in a classroom

   B. in an auditorium

   C. at a park

   D. on a roof

   HINT Which details tell you about the setting of the passage?

2. What is Jamar's motivation for ignoring Oscar?

   A. He doesn't want to get in trouble.

   B. He doesn't hear him.

   C. He wants to annoy him.

   D. He wants to focus on his playing.

   HINT What does Jamar do after ignoring Oscar?

Use the Reading Guide to help you understand the passage.

Reading Guide

Where are Marla and Teddy playing and studying?

Which events lead up to Marla and Teddy making a bet?

In paragraph 5, Teddy says, "I'm not too concerned." What character trait does this detail reveal about him?

The Night Before

Marla had been studying for hours, and her eyelids felt heavy. The science test that she was taking the next day was very important, so she wanted to go over everything one more time. Unfortunately, her brain was no longer cooperating. She knew she needed a break.

Downstairs, Teddy sat playing video games. Teddy had to take the same science test. Though he was Marla's twin brother, Teddy did not share her love of studying. In fact, Teddy hated to study, and his grades showed it. Marla came in and asked what he was doing.

"I'm studying," Teddy joked.

"I can't believe you," Marla said. "You know the test tomorrow is really important, right?"

"Important to you," Teddy said. "I'm not too concerned. I bet I do better than you on the test."

"It's a bet," Marla answered. "The winner has to do the other's chores for a week."

Marla and Teddy shook hands. With that, Marla grabbed a pack of crackers from the kitchen and returned upstairs.

The next day, she went into the test feeling confident. For the next few days, she waited excitedly to find out her grade. When she got an A, she knew she had earned it, just as Teddy had earned his F and the prize of doing all her chores for a week.

Answer the following questions.

1. Which word BEST describes Marla?

   A. clever

   B. honest

   C. responsible

   D. humorous

2. Which sentence from the story describes the climax of the story?

   A. "Unfortunately, her brain was no longer cooperating."

   B. "Downstairs, Teddy sat playing video games."

   C. "Marla and Teddy shook hands."

   D. "For the next few days, she waited excitedly to find out her grade."

3. Which of the following is part of the setting?

   A. a pack of crackers

   B. a kitchen and a staircase

   C. a science test

   D. weekly chores

4. The rising action in the story is when

   A. Marla questions and challenges her brother.

   B. Teddy fails the science test.

   C. Marla grabs a pack of crackers from the kitchen.

   D. Teddy plays video games.

5. Describe the conflict in the story, and tell how it is resolved.

   _____

   _____

   _____

   _____

4 Point of View

RL.4.6, RL.4.10, RF.4.4.a

Getting the Idea

When you read a story, someone is *telling* it to you. A **narrator** is the person who tells the story. **Point of view** is the perspective, or view, from which the narrator tells the story. Most stories are told in either first-person or third-person point of view.

In **first-person** point of view, the narrator is a character in the story. The words *I* and *we* are used. Read this example.

> I walked onto the pitcher's mound and faced the batter. He took a couple of practice swings and then looked straight at me, waiting for the pitch. As soon as I threw the ball, I knew it would be a strike. He swung and missed as the ball sailed right over the plate!

The narrator is a character (the pitcher) and is represented by the word *I*.

Second-person point of view is rarely used in fiction. Here, the narrator speaks directly to the reader, making you part of the passage. Read this example.

> Open the box and remove the fan. Be sure to take off the plastic wrap before you plug in the machine.

In **third-person** point of view, the narrator tells the story without actually being in it. The story uses words such as *he, she, it,* and *they*. When the narrator knows only the thoughts and feelings of a single character, the point of view is **third-person limited**. Read this example.

> Robby felt scared as the *Santa Maria* heaved back and forth in the stormy waves. He knew Captain Jones had calmly steered the ship through worse storms. Still, he felt uneasy, and he sensed the other passengers were also afraid.

The narrator is outside of the story. He knows only the thoughts and feelings of Robby. Those of the other characters—Captain Jones and the passengers—are told only through Robby's eyes.

In some stories, the narrator knows about all of the characters' thoughts and feelings. This is called **third-person omniscient** point of view. Read this example.

> Dexter lay in bed. He wanted to go outside and play in the snow, but he had a cold. His mother asked him to drink some orange juice. She was glad he was resting. She hoped he would feel better in the morning.

Again, the narrator is outside of the story. But this time, he knows the thoughts and feelings of *all* of the characters—both Dexter and his mother. Notice that the narrator uses the words *he* and *she*.

Comparing and contrasting the point of view from which different stories are told can change how you think about the narrator and characters. A story told from first-person point of view gives you a very personal look at a character's (the narrator's) thoughts and feelings. However, it is only the way one character views the story. A story told in third-person point of view might seem less personal, but you may get a broader view of the characters.

The chart below shows the different points of view and their features.

First-Person	Third-Person Limited	Third-Person Omniscient
Told by one character in the story	Told by narrator outside of the story	Told by narrator outside of the story
Narrator is *I*, *me*, *we*, *us*	Narrator uses *he*, *she*, *it*, *they*, and *them*	Narrator uses *he*, *she*, *it*, *they*, and *them*
Narrator relates personal view	Narrator knows thoughts and feelings of single character	Narrator knows thoughts and feelings of all characters

Thinking It Through

Read the following passage, and then answer the question that follows.

I felt scared as I inched toward the edge of the diving board. The pool below seemed so far away. I took a deep breath and closed my eyes. I had done this a hundred times before, and I knew that I needed to stay calm. I raised my arms over my head, bent down, and sprung off of the board. For a moment, I felt nothing as I fell through the air. Then I plunged into the pool with a loud splash and rose back to the surface with a wide smile.

Which point of view is used in the passage? Explain how this point of view helps you to understand the thoughts and feelings of the diver.

_____

_____

_____

_____

_____

HINT The narrator uses the word *I* in the passage. What does this tell you about the point of view?

Coached Example

Read the passages and answer the questions.

Cutting Wood

"Good day to make a fire," Grandpa said, looking out the window at the gray winter sky. "I'll need to cut some wood."

"Can I help?" I asked.

"Sure, Calvin," he said. "You're old enough now to handle a saw."

We grabbed our coats and walked to the garage. I felt excited when he handed me a saw and a pair of gloves. I had wanted to learn how to use a saw for some time. We walked to the woodpile outside. Grandpa placed a log on an old stump, which he used as a sort of worktable. He moved the saw back and forth across the log. Soon, the sawed half dropped to the ground.

"Now you try," he said, placing another log on the stump and handing me the saw. I pressed the blade on the log tried to push the saw. The blade jerked and jammed in the wood.

"I can't do it," I said, feeling my excitement turn to disappointment.

"You're trying too hard," Grandpa said. "Let the tool do the work."

I relaxed my grip on the handle, and sure enough, the saw moved easily through the wood. When the log fell in half, I felt proud. "I did it!" I said.

Fishing at Night

Ned led the way through the dunes to the ocean. He knew that his grandson, Anthony, had never been to the shore at night, and he wanted to make sure that he didn't get lost on the way.

The full moon hung low over the ocean as they reached the water's edge. Ned tied a hook to Anthony's line and put on a piece of bait. He enjoyed teaching Anthony new things and felt that his grandson really loved spending time with him. He baited his own line and showed Anthony how to cast out beyond the waves. He watched Anthony struggle with his first few casts, but knew that he would get the hang of it.

A few hours later, Ned waded into the surf to net Anthony's first fish. As he handed Anthony the beautiful sea trout from the net, he remembered the excitement of catching his first fish many years ago.

He watched Anthony hold the fish up in the moonlight. He knew that his grandson would remember this day for the rest of his life.

1. Which point of view is used in "Cutting Wood"?

   A. first-person

   B. second-person

   C. third-person limited

   D. third-person omniscient

   HINT The words give you clues to the point of view. Which word is used to represent the narrator in "Cutting Wood"? Who is telling the story?

2. Which statement BEST describes the similarity between the narrators of the stories?

   A. Both narrators are characters in the stories.

   B. Both narrators tell mostly about one character's feelings.

   C. Both narrators watch the story events from outside of the stories.

   D. Both narrators know about the thoughts and feelings of all the characters.

   HINT In third-person limited, the narrator has limited knowledge of the characters' thoughts and feelings.

3. Write how Anthony feels at the end of "Fishing at Night," using the first-person point of view.

   _____

   _____

   _____

   _____

   _____

   HINT What words might Anthony use to express his feelings about catching the fish?

Lesson Practice

Use the Reading Guides to help you understand the passages.

Identify the words that represent the narrator in the passage.

Is the narrator a character in the story or someone outside of the passage?

How does the point of view help you understand the passage?

Show Time

I watched with excitement as family members and relatives filed into the auditorium. Tonight was the dance recital. At last, I would get to show off all my hard work. I hoped everything would be perfect.

My dance class was doing a routine using large wooden boxes. Each dancer had to balance on top of a box and do different steps. It wasn't an easy routine, but I'd practiced it at home many times.

The first part of the show went smoothly. Then came the part with the boxes. We all stood in line, each girl on her own box, facing the audience. For my next move, I needed to place one foot on the box next to mine. At the same time, I needed to keep my other foot on my own box. It was an easy move, I always thought.

I looked out at the audience, head up, with a big smile. Oops! While my head was up, I didn't look at where I was going. I missed my partner's box and slipped! Suddenly, I was standing on the stage floor.

My face was red with embarrassment. But I remembered what our dance teacher had told us: "If you make a mistake, keep dancing so the audience will not notice." I did my best to follow her advice and finished the routine without making any more mistakes. My family said I did a great job.

Does the narrator know about the feelings of all the characters?

Which character is the narrator telling the reader mostly about?

Is the narrator represented by the word *I*? What does this tell you about the point of view?

The Audition

Anita woke up with a start. Today was her audition for the Youth Symphony Orchestra. She bounced out of bed and ran to take a shower.

At breakfast, her mother asked, "Are you ready?"

Anita didn't answer as she sat down. She didn't feel hungry, but her teacher, Mr. Jackson, told her it was important to eat today. As Anita ate, she thought about her mother's question.

Her clothes were ready. The Symphony's Web site said to wear nice clothes that were comfortable to perform in. Anita had chosen the blue dress she had gotten for her sixteenth birthday last year.

Her music was ready. She had chosen four pieces by her favorite composer, Chopin. The Web site said that people auditioning didn't have to memorize their music, but Anita knew all of her music by heart.

Her mind was ready. The audition would last from five to eight minutes. "Don't think about the time," Mr. Jackson had told her. "Just think about the music. Let it flow through you. That's what Chopin would have done."

Anita had applied to the Youth Orchestra online last month. Before she sent her application, she had asked Mr. Jackson, "Do you really think I'm good enough?"

He had given her a big smile. "Anita Hernandez, you're the hardest-working student I have. You have enormous musical talent. You're going to be absolutely great!"

Thinking back on that now, Anita grinned and looked up at her mother. "Yes, Mama. I'm ready."

Answer the following questions.

1. Which point of view is used in "Show Time"?

   A. first-person

   B. second-person

   C. third-person limited

   D. third-person omniscient

2. Who is the narrator of "The Audition"?

   A. Anita

   B. Anita's mother

   C. Mr. Jackson

   D. someone outside of the story

3. Which BEST describes the narrator of "Show Time"?

   A. a character in the story

   B. someone who tells about the feelings of all of the characters

   C. a person who is not in the story

   D. someone represented by the word *her*

4. Which point of view is used in "The Audition"?

   A. first-person

   B. second-person

   C. third-person limited

   D. third-person omniscient

5. Which story gives a more personal view of the main character? Explain your answer.

_____

_____

_____

_____

5 Understanding Poetry and Drama

RL.4.5, RL.4.10, RF.4.4.a

Getting the Idea

Prose, poetry, and drama are different kinds of writing. In **prose**, one sentence follows another. Sentences are grouped in paragraphs. Examples of prose include chapter books and newspaper articles. **Poetry** is written in lines. Lines are grouped in **stanzas**, or **verses**.

The paragraph and poem below both tell about the same topic. What differences do you see?

Prose	Poem
Last night, I tried to finish my math assignment on the couch. I was having a hard time concentrating because all I could hear was the sound of my dog snoring.	Papers strewn about my lap, A dog's snoring fills the room, Making the earth tremble. Soon it's nine o'clock, The time continues to pass. Will my homework be ready For tomorrow's class?

Poets use the sounds of words in creative ways. For example, many poems include rhyme. Words that **rhyme** end with the same sound. The rhyming words in a poem often appear in a pattern at the ends of lines. In the poem below, *green* and *between* rhyme.

> I'm **glad** the **sky** is **paint**ed **blue**,
> And the **earth** is **paint**ed **green**,
> With **such** a **lot** of **nice** fresh **air**
> All **sand**wiched **in** be**tween**.

A poem also has a **rhythm** created by the stressed and unstressed syllables in the poem. If there is a pattern to the rhythm, the pattern is called **meter**. Read the poem aloud. The stressed syllables are shown in bold print. In this poem, almost every other syllable is stressed. Lines 1 and 3 each have four stressed syllables, and lines 2 and 4 each have three stressed syllables. This pattern gives the poem its rhythm.

Like a short story or novel, a **drama** tells a story. It includes characters, a setting, and a plot. However, a drama is written so that people can put on a play. It begins with a **cast of characters** that lists the characters who appear in the play. It includes a description of the **setting**. This description tells the director, set designers, and actors what the stage should look like. A drama includes stage directions and dialogue. The **stage directions** are written in *italic* print. They tell the actors what to do. **Dialogue** is the words the actors speak.

A **scene** is a part of a drama. Read this drama about unfinished homework and a snoring dog.

CAST OF CHARACTERS
Ruben
Mom
Tag, the family dog

Scene One
In dim lights, we can see a living room. On one end of the couch, Tag, a dog, is curled up asleep. On the other end sits Ruben, in his pajamas. Paper is scattered around him, and a textbook is open. The snoring of the dog and the ticking of a clock grow louder and louder until Ruben speaks.

RUBEN: (*to himself*) If only Tag would stop snoring! Then maybe I would be able to think straight.

The snoring of the dog and the ticking of the clock can still be heard, but more softly. Mom enters. She is wearing pajamas.

MOM: Ruben! Why are you still up? It's getting late.

RUBEN: (*pushing his book and papers to the floor*) I can't figure out this math homework!

Thinking It Through

Read the following poem, and then answer the question that follows.

excerpted from

Songs of Innocence
by William Blake

Piping down the valleys wild,
Piping songs of pleasant glee,
On a cloud I saw a child,
And he laughing said to me:

"Pipe a song about a Lamb!"
So I piped with merry cheer.
"Piper, pipe that song again;"
So I piped: he wept to hear.

What characteristics of poetry can you find in this poem? Give three examples.

_____

_____

_____

_____

 Read the poem aloud. Do you hear any rhymes? Do you hear a beat, or rhythm?

Coached Example

Read the drama and answer the questions.

CAST OF CHARACTERS
Jenny
Tanya

Scene One

The backdrop shows a meadow with hills and trees. Jenny enters pulling a wagon holding a giant pumpkin. Tanya enters and meets Jenny in the center of the stage.

TANYA: Jenny, where on Earth did you find that pumpkin?

JENNY: (*grinning with pride*) In my garden!

TANYA: You mean you grew that thing?

JENNY: I sure did! And I'm taking it to Grandma's house. Now that I've grown the biggest pumpkin that Hillsdale has ever seen, we're going to bake the biggest pumpkin pie that Hillsdale has ever seen.

TANYA: Ooh! I want to see that! And then I want to eat it!

The two girls exit together.

---

1. The setting of this scene could BEST be described as

   A. a city sidewalk.

   B. Grandma's kitchen.

   C. the country.

   D. a schoolyard.

    The description of the setting is given before the dialogue.

2. How does Jenny feel about the pumpkin?

   A. proud

   B. frightened

   C. embarrassed

   D. curious

    Read the stage directions as well as the dialogue.

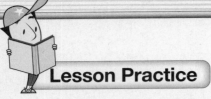

Lesson Practice

Use the Reading Guide to help you understand the poem.

Reading Guide

The lines of this poem are grouped into stanzas. How many stanzas does the poem have?

Do you see any words that rhyme in stanza 1?

Read stanza 1 aloud. How many beats do you hear in each line? Do you hear the pattern of the rhythm?

Which words rhyme in stanza 2? Do you see a pattern to the rhymes in the poem?

excerpted from

The Gardener

by Robert Louis Stevenson

The gardener does not love to talk,
He makes me keep the gravel walk;
And when he puts his tools away,
He locks the door and takes the key.

5   Away behind the currant row
Where no one else but cook may go,
Far in the plots, I see him dig
Old and serious, brown and big.

He digs the flowers, green, red and blue,
10   Nor wishes to be spoken to.
He digs the flowers and cuts the hay,
And never seems to want to play.

Silly gardener! summer goes,
And winter comes with pinching toes,
15   When in the garden bare and brown
You must lay your barrow down.

barrow: wheelbarrow

Answer the following questions.

1. Which version shows which syllables are stressed in line 2?

    A. He <u>makes</u> me <u>keep</u> the <u>gravel</u> walk

    B. <u>He</u> makes <u>me</u> <u>keep</u> the <u>gravel</u> <u>walk</u>

    C. <u>He</u> makes <u>me</u> keep the gravel <u>walk</u>

    D. He <u>makes</u> me <u>keep</u> the gravel <u>walk</u>

2. Which words from the poem do NOT rhyme?

    A. walk, away

    B. row, go

    C. blue, to

    D. brown, down

3. Which stanza tells where the gardener digs?

    A. stanza 1

    B. stanza 2

    C. stanza 3

    D. stanza 4

4. The speaker thinks that the gardener

    A. works too hard.

    B. is too old.

    C. would rather be a cook.

    D. likes winter better than summer.

5. What does the speaker think that the gardener should do? Give examples from the poem.

_____

_____

_____

_____

_____

_____

Lesson Practice

Use the Reading Guide to help you understand the drama.

Reading Guide

What does the description of the setting tell you about where this scene takes place?

What does the dialogue tell you about the characters?

What do the stage directions tell you about the characters' actions?

The Race

CAST OF CHARACTERS

Luis

Anna

Scene One

The curtain opens to show a bike path with trees, shrubs, wildflowers, and a park bench. A teenage boy and girl enter from stage right. They are both wearing T-shirts, athletic shorts, and running shoes. They are breathing as if they have just stopped running.

LUIS: That was a good run! You've really improved!

ANNA: (*laughs*) You're just saying that because you're my kind big brother.

LUIS: When have I ever said anything to you just to be nice?

ANNA: (*laughs again*) That's true. (*She sits down on the bench and begins to untie the laces of one of her shoes.*) But still, I'm really worried about the race.

LUIS: What for? The race is only three miles long. You run farther than that all the time. And anyway, your goal is to finish, not to win.

ANNA: (*She pulls off her shoe and pulls a stone out of it.*) For one thing, Mom and Dad will be there. For another thing, anything could happen. (*She holds up the stone.*) I could get another stone like this in my shoe! I could trip and fall and break my leg!

LUIS: You could trip and fall and break your leg crossing the street, too. Why worry about everything that could go wrong?

ANNA: (*sighs*) Why are you always right?

Answer the following questions.

1. The setting of this scene is MOST LIKELY

    A. in a big city park or the country.

    B. in a gym.

    C. at Luis and Anna's house.

    D. at the beach near a lake or the ocean.

2. Which of the following is a line of stage directions?

    A. You're just saying that because you're my kind big brother.

    B. *She sits down on the bench and begins to untie the laces of one of her shoes.*

    C. The race is only three miles long.

    D. I could get another stone like this in my shoe!

3. How does Luis think that Anna should feel about the race?

    A. He thinks she should be scared because she needs to practice more.

    B. He thinks she should tell their parents that she is not going to run.

    C. He thinks she should tell everyone that she is going to win.

    D. He thinks she should not worry about the race.

4. Why does Anna take off her shoe?

    A. She wants to put on a different pair of shoes.

    B. She is joking around with Luis.

    C. She needs to take a stone out of the shoe.

    D. She has decided to stop running.

5. Write two lines of dialogue to continue this scene.

    _____

    _____

    _____

    _____

    _____

6 Compare and Contrast Literature

RL.4.9, RL.4.10, RF.4.4.a

Getting the Idea

When you think about the ways that passages are alike and different, you compare and contrast. When you **compare**, you look for ways in which passages are alike. When you **contrast**, you look for ways in which they are different.

When you compare and contrast, pay attention to the plot, or the series of events in a story. Look at the setting, too. Does one story take place in the city and one in the country? And of course, look at the characters. Are there similarities or differences in the appearance or personality of the characters? What problem does each character have to solve?

Theme is another basis for comparison. A **theme** is the central idea of a story. Often, it is a lesson about life. Take the story "Cinderella," for example. This fairy tale is told around the world. If you were to compare two different Cinderella stories, you would find that they share similar themes. These are: *Good things come to those who wait* and *Kindness is usually rewarded*. However, you would soon see that the stories differ in several ways.

Read this passage from a classic version of "Cinderella" that most American readers know.

> Cinderella wore old, tattered clothes, while her stepmother and stepsisters had lovely clothes and lived comfortably. But no matter how mean her stepmother and stepsisters were, Cinderella was always cheerful. Even the little animals loved to be near her. She made friends with the mice and birds, and sewed outfits for them to wear.

Now read this passage from "Yeh-Shen," a version of the story that is told in China.

> The stepmother did not like Yeh-Shen, for she was more beautiful and kinder than her own daughters. She gave Yeh-Shen the worst jobs to do. Yeh-shen's only friend was a fish with golden eyes. Each day, the fish came out of the water to be fed by Yeh-Shen. The young girl had little food for herself, but she was always willing to share with her friend the fish.

A good way to compare and contrast the passages is with a Venn diagram, like the one below.

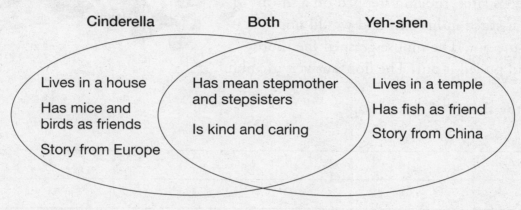

Cinderella   Both   Yeh-shen

Lives in a house

Has mice and birds as friends

Story from Europe

Has mean stepmother and stepsisters

Is kind and caring

Lives in a temple

Has fish as friend

Story from China

In this Venn diagram, the differences between the stories are shown in the outer parts of the circles. The similarities are shown in the overlapping middle part. Readers of this story in America and China—and in many other countries, too—will learn about a kind young girl who, despite her difficulties, finds true happiness. Although the specific details of the stories differ, the themes are the same.

Thinking It Through

Read the following passage, and then answer the question that follows.

A lion used his big paw to catch a mouse. The mouse was afraid of the lion. He promised the lion that if he were set free, he would someday repay the lion. The lion laughed at him. How could a mouse ever help him? He was amused, so he let the mouse go. Many weeks later, the lion stepped on a thorn that stuck in his paw and would not come out. The mouse grasped the thorn and pulled it out. The lion was very thankful.

What is the theme of this passage?

_____

_____

_____

_____

HINT   What lesson do you think the lion learned from his experience with the mouse?

Coached Example

Read the passages and answer the questions.

Santosh's Elephant

The sun was just beginning to rise over the small village where Santosh lived. Santosh woke up with a nervous feeling in his stomach. He walked out the door of his house and headed slowly toward the forest nearby. When he arrived at the clearing, he stood there for a few moments and wiped the sleep from his eyes. While he had helped his father wash and feed the elephants many times, today would be his first time riding one by himself. He knew his father and other villagers would be traveling with him. Still, for some reason, Santosh felt anxious about the journey. Was he skilled enough to handle an elephant? His palms were moist, and there was a lump in his throat. He looked up at the female elephant that he would be riding behind his dad through the twisting jungle trail that lay ahead. She seemed to loom over him, larger than any animal he had ever seen.

A Mountain Journey

Kayla watched the sun's rosy crown peek over the low, rolling hills to the west. The day promised to be bright and clear. As she walked to the stables from her house, her heart beat more quickly than usual. Yesterday, her two older brothers had gone camping in the mountains. Today, she was going to meet up with them at a lookout point about two miles from the family's ranch. It would be the first time she took her horse on a ride off the sprawling ranch by herself. Kayla was pleased that her parents trusted her to make the trip, and she couldn't wait to begin the adventure. As she led her horse from the stable, a big smile spread across her face. She took a small map of the route from her pocket and studied it for a few minutes. Then she took a deep breath and got on her horse. She was ready to go.

1. The themes of these passages are similar because they both involve

   A. spending time outdoors.

   B. experiencing something for the first time.

   C. traveling far from home on your own.

   D. taking care of large animals.

   HINT The theme is the central idea of a story. Notice how Santosh and Kayla each react to what is planned for the day.

2. How does Santosh differ from Kayla?

   A. Santosh is young, while Kayla is old.

   B. Santosh feels excited, while Kayla feels bored.

   C. Santosh feels nervous, while Kayla feels confident.

   D. Santosh often rides by himself, while Kayla never does.

   HINT Look for specific details that show how each character reacts to what is planned for the day. Pay attention to the descriptive words that the author uses.

3. While these passages are set in different places, they have some things in common. Compare and contrast them, using specific details in your answer.

   _____

   _____

   _____

   _____

   _____

   _____

   _____

   HINT Look for details that describe where the story takes place, the feelings and actions of the characters, and the events of the plot.

Lesson Practice

Use the Reading Guides to help you understand the passages.

Reading Guide

How does Akande respond to his wife's suggestion?

Why does Akande think it is alright to bring a cup of water to the feast?

What do you think went through Akande's mind after seeing that the lamps would not light?

The Chief's Feast
based on a fable from Nigeria

One day, a village chief announced a great midnight feast. He asked that each guest bring a cup of oil to light the many lamps arranged around the garden. Akande wanted to attend, but he had no oil to bring.

His wife suggested that he buy some oil. Akande replied, "Why would I spend my own money to attend a feast that is free?"

Akande thought, "If hundreds of people were to pour their oil into the chief's pot, could my one cup of water spoil all that oil?"

The day of the feast came. Everyone gathered at the chief's house. There was music and dancing. As each man entered the chief's house, he poured the contents of his cup into a large earthen pot. Akande poured his water into the pot and then greeted the chief.

When all the guests had arrived, the chief ordered his servants to fill the lamps with the oil. Akande was impatient. His mouth watered for the feast. At the chief's signal, just before darkness fell, the lamps were ordered to be lit. Everyone was surprised that no lamp would light. For each guest had thought that his one cup of water would not spoil a large pot of oil. And like Akande, each had brought water instead of oil. As the guests quietly ate their food in the darkness, they realized just what had happened.

The Judge's Decision
a fable from Turkey

Look for clues that tell you what each character is like. How do they behave throughout the passage?

What do you learn about the beggar by the end of the passage? What about the innkeeper?

Read each passage again, paying special attention to the theme of each one.

In the ancient city of Ankara, a beggar was given a piece of bread, but nothing to put on it. Hoping to get something to go with his bread, he went into a nearby inn and asked for some food. The innkeeper turned him away with nothing. Under the darkening sky, the beggar saw an open door and sneaked into the inn's kitchen. There he saw a large pot of soup cooking over a fire. He held his piece of bread over the steaming pot, hoping to capture a bit of flavor from the good-smelling steam.

Suddenly, the innkeeper grabbed him by the arm and accused him of stealing soup.

"I took no soup," said the beggar. "I was only smelling the steam."

"Then you must pay for the smell," answered the innkeeper.

The poor beggar had no money, so the angry innkeeper dragged him before the judge.

The judge, a man named Hodja, heard the innkeeper's complaint and the beggar's explanation.

"So, you demand payment for the smell of your soup?" asked Hodja after the hearing.

"Yes!" insisted the innkeeper.

"Then I myself will pay you," said Hodja. "And I will pay for the smell of your soup with the sound of money."

Hodja drew two coins from his pocket. He then rang them together loudly, put them back into his pocket, and sent the beggar and the innkeeper each on his own way.

Answer the following questions.

1. Both passages share a similar

    A. setting.

    B. theme.

    C. set of characters.

    D. unhappy ending.

2. How are Akande and the innkeeper alike?

    A. They have bad tempers.

    B. They are hungry.

    C. They like to steal.

    D. They want something for nothing.

3. Both passages have characters that are trying to

    A. trick someone else.

    B. embarrass someone else.

    C. share knowledge with others.

    D. learn an important lesson.

4. How are the two passages MOST different from each another?

    A. Akande has money, while the beggar has none.

    B. Akande learns his lesson, while the beggar does not.

    C. "The Chief's Feast" takes place in modern times, while "The Judge's Decision" takes place in ancient times.

    D. "The Chief's Feast" takes place indoors, while "The Judge's Decision" takes place outdoors.

5. Why do Akande and the innkeeper act the way they do? What lesson do you think each man learned?

    _____

    _____

    _____

    _____

    _____

1 Cumulative Assessment for Lessons 1–6

Read the passage and answer the questions that follow.

excerpted and adapted from

The Secret Garden
by Frances Hodgson Burnett

When Mary Lennox was sent to Misselthwaite Manor to live with her uncle, everybody said she was the most disagreeable-looking child ever seen. It was true, too. She had a little thin face and a little thin body, thin light hair and a sour expression. Her hair was yellow, and her face was yellow because she had been born in India and had always been ill in one way or another. Her father had held a position under the English government and had always been busy and ill himself. And her mother had been a great beauty who cared only to go to parties and amuse herself with happy people. She had not wanted a little girl at all, and when Mary was born, she handed her over to the care of an Ayah (a nanny). The Ayah was made to understand that if she wished to please the Mem Sahib (Mary's mother), she must keep the child out of sight as much as possible.

When Mary was a sickly, fretful, ugly little baby, she was kept out of the way. And when she became a sickly, fretful, toddling thing, she was kept out of the way also. She never remembered seeing anything but the faces of her Ayah and the other native servants. They always gave Mary her own way in everything, since the Mem Sahib would be angry if she was disturbed by her daughter's crying.

By the time she was six years old, she was as mean and selfish a little girl as ever lived. The young English governess who came to teach her to read and write disliked her so much that she gave up the job within three months. When other governesses came to try to fill it, they always went away in a shorter time than the first one. So if Mary had not chosen to really want to know how to read books, she would never have learned her letters at all.

One frightfully hot morning, when she was about nine years old, she awakened feeling very upset. She became more upset when she saw that the servant who stood by her bedside was not her Ayah.

"Why did you come?" Mary said to the strange woman. "I will not let you stay. Send my Ayah to me."

The woman looked frightened, but she only stammered that the Ayah could not come. When Mary threw herself into a passion and beat and kicked her, she looked only more frightened and repeated that it was not possible for the Ayah to come to Missie Sahib (Mary).

There was something mysterious in the air that morning. Nothing was done in its regular order, and several of the native servants seemed missing. Those whom Mary saw slunk or hurried about with ashy and scared faces. But no one would tell her anything, and her Ayah did not come. She was actually left alone as the morning went on, and at last, she wandered out into the garden and began to play by herself under a tree. She pretended that she was making a flower bed. She stuck big scarlet hibiscus blossoms into little heaps of earth, all the time growing more and more angry and muttering to herself the things she would say and the names she would call her Ayah when she returned.

1. Which word BEST describes Mary?

   A. worried

   B. angry

   C. happy

   D. moody

2. Which point of view is used in the passage?

   A. first-person

   B. second-person

   C. third-person limited

   D. third-person omniscient

3. Which detail from the passage shows that Mary probably does not have many friends?

   A. "There was something mysterious in the air that morning."

   B. "But no one would tell her anything, and her Ayah did not come."

   C. "One frightfully hot morning, when she was about nine years old, she awakened feeling very upset."

   D. "She had a little thin face and a little thin body, thin light hair and a sour expression."

4. Which sentence BEST summarizes the passage?

   A. A young girl's mother leaves her at home alone.

   B. A rich young girl is mean to people and learns that no one likes her.

   C. A bossy little girl becomes upset when she finds her nanny is missing.

   D. A young girl wakes up to find herself alone and goes outside to plant flowers.

Read the passage and answer the questions that follow.

excerpted and adapted from

Little Lord Fauntleroy

by Frances Hodgson Burnett

The Captain had a small house on a quiet street, and his little boy was born there. His wife was very sweet, and their little boy was like both her and his father. Though he was born in so quiet and cheap a little home, it seemed as if there never had been a more fortunate baby.

In the first place, he was always well, so he never gave anyone trouble. In the second place, he was so sweet and charming that he was a pleasure to everyone. And in the third place, he was so beautiful to look at that he was quite a picture. Instead of being a bald-headed baby, he started in life with soft, gold-colored hair. It curled up at the ends, and went into loose rings by the time he was six months old. The boy had big brown eyes and long eyelashes and a darling little face. And his legs were so sturdy that at nine months, he suddenly learned to walk.

His manners were so good, for a baby, that it was delightful to meet him. He seemed to feel that everyone was his friend. When anyone spoke to the boy when he was in his carriage on the street, he would give the stranger a sweet, serious look and follow it with a lovely, friendly smile. This meant that there was not a person in his neighborhood who was not pleased to see him and speak to him. Not even the grocery man at the corner, who was thought to be the meanest creature alive. Every month of his life, the boy grew more handsome and interesting.

When the boy was old enough to walk out with his nanny, he would drag a small wagon about. He wore a big white hat set back on his curly yellow hair. The boy was so handsome and strong and rosy that he attracted everyone's attention. His nanny would come home and tell his mamma stories of the ladies who had stopped their carriages to look at and speak to him. And how pleased they were when the boy talked to them in his cheerful way, as if he had known them always.

His greatest charm was this cheerful, fearless way of making friends with people. I think it arose from his having a very confident nature and a kind heart. It made him very quick to understand the feelings of those about him. Perhaps this had grown on him, too, because he had lived so much with his father and mother, who were always loving and considerate and tender. He had never heard an unkind word spoken at home; he had always been loved and caressed and treated tenderly, and so his childish soul was full of kindness and warm feelings. He had always heard his mamma called by pretty, loving names. So he used them himself when he spoke to her. He had always seen that his papa watched over her and took great care of her, and so he learned, too, to be caring toward her.

5. People on the street are nice to the boy because he is

   A. friendly and kind.

   B. lonely and quiet.

   C. needy and demanding.

   D. worried and sad.

6. What detail from the story BEST tells the reader where the story takes place?

   A. The boy lives in a small house on a quiet street.

   B. The boy has brown eyes and long eyelashes.

   C. The nanny tells stories about people who speak to the boy.

   D. The boy visits the grocery man on the corner.

7. The boy speaks sweetly with his mother because

   A. he wants her to spend more time with him.

   B. he sees others acting nicely toward her.

   C. he doesn't know how to be mean to others.

   D. he hopes for gifts in return for his kindness.

8. Which BEST states the theme of the passage?

   A. Be grateful for what you have.

   B. It is best to think things through.

   C. Good things come to those who wait.

   D. Treat others as you would like to be treated.

Use "The Secret Garden" and "Little Lord Fauntleroy" to answer questions 9–10.

9. Compare the characters of Mary and the boy. Explain how they are different or alike.

    _____

    _____

    _____

    _____

    _____

    _____

    _____

    _____

10. Compare and contrast the two passages. Are the themes alike or different? Use details
    from both passages to support your answer.

    _____

    _____

    _____

    _____

    _____

    _____

    _____

Read the poem and answer the questions that follow.

My Little Neighbor
by Mary Augusta Mason

My little neighbor's table's set,
And slyly he comes down the tree,
His feet firm in each tiny fret
The bark has fashioned cunningly.

5   He pauses on a favorite knot;
Beneath the oak his feast is spread;
He asks no friend to share his lot,
Or dine with him on acorn bread.

He keeps his whiskers trim and neat,
10   His tail with care he brushes through;
He runs about on all four feet—
When dining he sits up on two.

He has the latest stripe in furs,
And wears them all the year around;
15   He does not mind the prick of burs
When there are chestnuts to be found.

I watch his home and guard his store,
A cozy hollow in a tree;
He often sits within his door
20   And chatters wondrous things to me.

11. Which line from the poem shows which syllables are stressed?

    A. He <u>does</u> not <u>mind</u> the <u>prick</u> of <u>burs</u>

    B. <u>He</u> does <u>not</u> mind <u>the</u> prick of <u>burs</u>

    C. He <u>does</u> not <u>mind</u> the prick <u>of</u> burs

    D. <u>He</u> does <u>not</u> mind <u>the</u> prick <u>of</u> burs

12. In which stanza does the poet talk about the squirrel's appearance?

    A. stanza 1

    B. stanza 2

    C. stanza 3

    D. stanza 5

CHAPTER

2 Informational Texts

2 Diagnostic Assessment for Lessons 7–15

Read the passage and answer the questions that follow.

Mark Twain: Master of American Literature

Mark Twain is one of the world's most famous authors. He was born Samuel Clemens on November 30, 1835, in a small town in Missouri. About four years later, the Clemens family moved to Hannibal, Missouri, on the banks of the Mississippi River. Hannibal was a growing port city. It was a frequent stop for steamboats arriving from New Orleans or St. Louis. Samuel Clemens liked to describe Hannibal as *drowsing*. He thought of the town as a place that was sleepy and never fully awake. In Hannibal, where he lived for ten years, Samuel and his friends watched the steamboats come and go every day. He vividly recalled those days for his readers in such books as *The Adventures of Tom Sawyer* (1876), *Life on the Mississippi* (1883), and *The Adventures of Huckleberry Finn* (1885).

In 1847, when Samuel was not yet a teenager, his father died. Soon after, Samuel left school to become a printer's apprentice for a local newspaper—this was his first experience with the newspaper business and writing. Later, he moved to St. Louis, Missouri, where he worked as a printer. He also traveled to New York and Philadelphia during this time, where he wrote for a number of newspapers.

In 1857, Clemens moved back to Missouri where he began a new career as a riverboat pilot on the Mississippi River. Clemens became a pilot's apprentice, or "cub," for the well-known pilot Horace Bixby. Over the next two years, Clemens became familiar with the length of the river between St. Louis and New Orleans. He eventually earned his own pilot's license. He would also take his famous pseudonym, or pen name, from his experience working on the river. *Mark twain* is a riverboat pilot's term that means two fathoms—or 12 feet. When the water was mark twain—12 feet deep—it was safe to <u>navigate</u>.

Clemens believed he would never need another career. But all riverboat traffic along the Mississippi stopped in 1861, when the Civil War began. Clemens's career as a riverboat pilot ended. The trips of early 1861 were the last he would ever make. The steamboat business never recovered. Clemens went up the river as a passenger on the last steamboat to make the trip from New Orleans to St. Louis. He would have been quite sad had he known that his days as a riverboat pilot were over.

"I loved the profession (job) far better than any I have followed since," Clemens later said, "and I took a measureless pride in it."

Clemens headed out for the West in the summer of 1861, in search of a new career. Silver had recently been discovered in Nevada, and along with many others, Clemens hoped to become rich. When he did not, Clemens started writing for local newspapers again. He went to San Francisco in 1864. Around this time, he began using the pen name Mark Twain. This was when he first realized he wanted to be an author.

In 1870, Clemens married Olivia Langdon. He had published his first book, *The Innocents Abroad*, the year before. In all, Mark Twain wrote 28 books along with numerous short stories and letters.

Mark Twain died on April 21, 1910. People around the country were saddened. Newspapers wrote, "The whole world is mourning." By that time, Samuel Clemens was no longer a private citizen. He had become Mark Twain, one of the best authors the United States ever produced.

Mark Twain Timeline

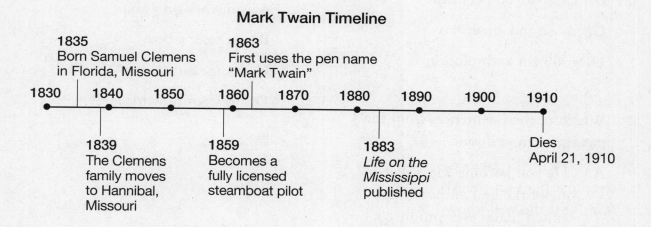

1835
Born Samuel Clemens in Florida, Missouri

1863
First uses the pen name "Mark Twain"

1830 — 1840 — 1850 — 1860 — 1870 — 1880 — 1890 — 1900 — 1910

1839
The Clemens family moves to Hannibal, Missouri

1859
Becomes a fully licensed steamboat pilot

1883
Life on the Mississippi published

Dies
April 21, 1910

1. What is the main idea of this passage?

   A. Mark Twain and Samuel Clemens were the same person.

   B. Mark Twain wrote many books.

   C. Mark Twain lived a long and interesting life.

   D. Mark Twain was from Missouri.

2. What is the MAIN text structure the writer uses in this passage?

   A. chronological order

   B. compare and contrast

   C. cause and effect

   D. problem and solution

3. Which of these sentences from the passage is an opinion?

   A. "He had become Mark Twain, one of the best authors the United States ever produced."

   B. "He eventually earned his own pilot's license."

   C. "When he did not, Clemens started writing for local newspapers again."

   D. "Hannibal was a growing port city."

4. How does the timeline help readers to better understand the passage?

   A. It gives readers information that the passage does not.

   B. It lists all the books that Mark Twain ever published.

   C. It provides a fact for every year of Mark Twain's life.

   D. It provides the exact dates when certain events occurred in Mark Twain's life.

5. What does the word *navigate* mean?

   A. to work on a ship

   B. to steer a boat

   C. to measure water

   D. to learn how to sail

Read the passage and answer the questions that follow.

excerpted and adapted from

Life on the Mississippi
by Mark Twain

The Boys' Ambition

When I was a boy, there was but one lasting ambition among my friends in our village on the west bank of the Mississippi River. That was, to be a steamboat pilot. We had ambitions of other sorts, but they were only brief. When a circus came and went, it left us all burning to become clowns. Now and then, we had a hope that we could be pirates. These ambitions faded out, but the ambition to be a steamboat pilot always remained.

Once a day, a ship arrived from St. Louis, and another from Keokuk. Before these events, the day was filled with anticipation. After them, the day was a dead and empty thing. Not only the boys, but the whole village, felt this. After all these years, I can still picture that old time now, just as it was then. The town is "drowsing" in the sunshine of a summer's morning. The streets are empty, or pretty nearly so—one or two clerks are sitting in front of the stores, asleep. The great Mississippi—the magnificent Mississippi—is rolling its mile-wide tide along, shining in the sun. Then a film of dark smoke appears. A worker cries out, "S-t-e-a-m-boat a-comin'!"

A Cub-Pilot's Experience

The *Paul Jones* was now bound for St. Louis. My pilot, Mr. Bixby, agreed to teach me the Mississippi River from New Orleans to St. Louis for five hundred dollars, payable out of my first wages. I undertook the project of "learning" twelve or thirteen hundred miles of the great Mississippi with the easy confidence of youth. If I had really known what I was about to require of myself, I would not have had the courage to begin. I thought that all a pilot had to do was to keep his boat in the river. I did not think that that could be much of a trick, since the river was so wide.

The boat backed out from New Orleans at four in the afternoon, and it was "our watch" until eight. Mr. Bixby "straightened her up," and steered her along past the other boats. Then he said, "Here, take her. Shave those steamships as close as you'd peel an apple."

I took the wheel, and felt my heartbeat quicken. It seemed to me that we were about to scrape the side off every ship in the line, we were so close. I held my breath and began to claw the boat away from the danger. I had my own opinion of the pilot who had known no better than to get us into such danger, but I was too wise to express it. In half a minute, I had a wide margin of safety between the *Paul Jones* and the ships. And within ten seconds more I was shoved aside in disgrace. And Mr. Bixby was going into danger again and criticizing me for my lack of courage. I was stung, but I had to admire the easy confidence with which my chief loafed from side to side of his wheel. Mr. Bixby trimmed the ships so closely that disaster always seemed near.

When he had calmed down a little, he told me that the easy water was close ashore and the fast-moving current was outside. Therefore, we must hug the bank going upstream to get the benefit of the easy water. And we must stay well out going downstream to take advantage of the outside current. In my own mind, I decided to be a downstream pilot and leave the upstreaming to people with no common sense.

6. How did Samuel Clemens MOST LIKELY feel about his pilot, Mr. Bixby?

   A. a combination of wonder and love

   B. a combination of dislike and annoyance

   C. a combination of fear and respect

   D. a combination of loyalty and trust

7. According to the passage, what happened just BEFORE Mark Twain took the wheel of the boat for the first time?

   A. Mr. Bixby said, "Here, take her."

   B. Mark Twain's heart started pounding.

   C. Mr. Bixby commented on Mark Twain's lack of courage.

   D. Mr. Bixby calmed down.

8. Which is the BEST summary of the whole passage?

   A. A young boy dreams of becoming a steamboat pilot.

   B. A young man travels from New Orleans to St. Louis.

   C. A young boy grows up on the Mississippi.

   D. A young man fulfills his childhood dream of becoming a steamboat pilot.

9. The passage from *Life on the Mississippi* is a primary source. What other primary sources could you use to find out more about Mark Twain?

   _____

   _____

   _____

   _____

   _____

Use "Mark Twain: Master of American Literature" and "Life on the Mississippi" to answer question 10.

10. Compare the two passages. How does information in the second passage give you a better understanding of information in the first passage?

_____

_____

_____

_____

_____

_____

_____

_____

_____

7 Text Details

RI.4.1, RI.4.10, RF.4.4.a

Getting the Idea

When you read **nonfiction**, you learn factual information about people, places, and things. Think about the many types of information contained in textbooks, encyclopedias, and newspaper articles. Informational texts tell about people, animals, plants, and many other things—what they are, what they do, what they look like. Details are specific pieces of information in a passage. They help you understand what the passage is about. Details can be descriptions, names, dates, and even actions.

All informational texts contain details. The chart below shows some of the different kinds of details you should look for when reading nonfiction.

Type of Text Detail	Example
names of people and places	Abraham Lincoln was born in Hardin County, Kentucky.
dates and time	Lincoln was born on February 12, 1809.
descriptions of places	Lincoln's family moved to a part of Indiana that had many bears and other wild animals.
things people say and do	In his Gettysburg Address, Lincoln said that "government of the people, by the people, for the people, shall not perish from the earth."
facts	Abraham Lincoln was the sixteenth president of the United States.

One way to identify important details in a text is by asking yourself questions after you read. Read this passage.

> In 1541, the Spanish explorer Hernando de Soto became the first European to see the Mississippi River. More than a hundred years later, the French explorer René-Robert de La Salle led an expedition to the Mississippi River. La Salle claimed all the land bordered by the great river for King Louis XIV of France and named the area Louisiana.

Now, think about what you just read. There are several questions you could ask to help you understand the passage. For example, how did Louisiana get its name? The passage tells you it was named after King Louis XIV. Was this the first time Europeans had been in the area? The answer is no. The passage says that Hernando de Soto, an explorer from Spain, was the first European to see the Mississippi River. As you can see, the writer uses many types of details in the passage to help you understand what happened, who was involved, and when things occurred.

Some of the details in the passage support ideas that are not mentioned specifically. Using text details and your own prior knowledge to make a guess is called making an **inference**. For example, the writer did not state the exact date of La Salle's expedition to the Mississippi, but enough information is given for you to make a reasonable guess at the date. The writer says that de Soto explored in 1541, and that La Salle explored more than a hundred years later. So, you can infer that La Salle made his journey around the middle of the 1600s.

Here's another inference to try. The writer says that Hernando de Soto was the first European to see the Mississippi. You already know that Native Americans lived all over North America before the Europeans arrived. The writer does not say it, but you can infer that Native Americans were living where de Soto explored, and that he most likely met some of them. By putting all the text details together and making inferences, you can get a fuller picture of what the passage is about.

Thinking It Through

Read the following passage, and then answer the question that follows.

Michigan and Florida are in different parts of our country. Florida is in the south. It is warm in most of Florida most of the year. Sometimes it is very hot. This allows farmers to grow crops such as oranges and coconuts. Michigan is in the north. It has four seasons with great ranges in temperature. It is hot in the summer, and cold and snowy in the winter. Autumn is a beautiful time in Michigan. The leaves on the trees change colors and then fall to the ground. Many fruits are grown in Michigan from spring to fall, such as blueberries, apples, and cherries.

The passage states that Michigan and Florida have different weather. How does the climate affect what grows in these areas? Use details from the text to support your answer.

_____

_____

_____

_____

_____

 What does the author write about the weather in each state, and the seasons during which certain crops can grow?

Coached Example

Read the passage and answer the questions.

Some sea creatures are among the world's greatest travelers. Pacific salmon are hatched in rivers, but they return to the sea to grow to full size. After a few years, they journey hundreds of miles to return upstream to the place where they were born. There, they hatch eggs.

The European eel travels even farther and goes in the opposite direction. Unlike the salmon, which hatch in freshwater rivers, this eel comes to life in the salt water of the northern Atlantic Ocean. The very young eels travel 4,000 to 5,000 miles to Europe. They take two years to make the trip. In the freshwater of European rivers, they grow slowly. It can take them thirty years to grow to full size! When they are ready to hatch eggs of their own, they make the journey across the Atlantic in the other direction.

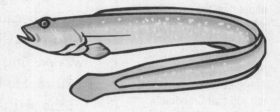

1. What sentence from the passage BEST supports the idea that Pacific salmon are among the world's "greatest travelers"?

    A. "The very young eels travel 4,000 to 5,000 miles to Europe."

    B. "After a few years, they journey hundreds of miles to return upstream to the place where they were born."

    C. "When they are ready to hatch eggs of their own, they make the journey across the Atlantic in the other direction."

    D. "In the freshwater of European rivers, they grow slowly."

    HINT Read the text closely, keeping in mind that you are looking for detailed information about salmon.

2. The European eel MOST LIKELY lays its eggs in

    A. European rivers.

    B. Pacific rivers.

    C. salt water.

    D. freshwater.

    HINT Use details in the passage to infer where the eels most likely end up when it is time for them to lay their eggs.

Use the Reading Guide to help you understand the passage.

Reading Guide

Read paragraph 1 of the passage carefully. Are there any details that describe when Grandma Moses was born?

Which details tell something about how the art collector might have affected Grandma Moses's life?

Read the last paragraph. Are there any details that tell you that Grandma Moses was still painting in the final year of her life?

Grandma Moses: A Great American Artist

Grandma Moses was born Anna Robertson in Greenwich, New York, in 1860. As a child, she loved to draw. At the age of 12, Anna left home to work as a maid on a farm. When she was 27 years old, she married Thomas Moses, who worked on the same farm.

As she got older, Anna took up embroidery. At the age of 76, because of arthritis, she gave up embroidery and began to paint. Two years later, in 1938, an art collector who was passing through her town saw some of her paintings in a store. He bought them all for $3 to $5 each. Then he went to the artist's home and bought more.

In 1939, Grandma Moses showed her paintings in an exhibition of new artists at the Museum of Modern Art in New York City. An exhibition devoted to her paintings was held in 1940.

By 1943, there was a huge demand for her artwork. A self-taught artist, Grandma Moses worked from memory, portraying a way of farm life she knew from experience. She painted her New England landscapes from the top down. As she said, "First the sky, then the mountains, then the hills, then the trees, then the houses, then the cattle, and then the people."

During her life, Grandma Moses painted more than 1,000 pictures, 25 of them after her 100th birthday. Grandma Moses died in 1961. She was 101 years old.

Answer the following questions.

1. According to the details in the passage, Grandma Moses was born in

   A. 1860.

   B. 1939.

   C. 1940.

   D. 1961.

2. Which detail from the passage tells why Grandma Moses started painting?

   A. She lived to be 101.

   B. She had her first one-woman show in 1940.

   C. She got arthritis and could not embroider.

   D. She liked to paint New England landscapes.

3. How did the art collector change Grandma Moses's life?

   A. He taught her how to paint.

   B. He brought her to a doctor.

   C. He told her that she should go to art school.

   D. He bought all her paintings.

4. Which detail from the passage describes Grandma Moses's landscape painting methods?

   A. She painted from left to right.

   B. She painted from right to left.

   C. She painted from the top down.

   D. She painted from the bottom up.

5. How do you know that Grandma Moses enjoyed painting up until the end of her life?

   _____

   _____

   _____

   _____

8 Main Idea, Supporting Details, and Summary

RI.4.1, RI.4.2, RI.4.10, RF.4.4.a

Getting the Idea

The **main idea** of a passage is what the passage is mostly about. It is the most important point that a writer makes in the article. The main idea can often be stated in one sentence. For instance, the main idea in a paragraph about bicycle safety may be to wear a helmet.

Recognizing main ideas is important. To figure out the main idea of a text, it is often helpful to ask questions. For example, you might ask yourself: What point does the writer focus on most? Are any points repeated? Are any points stressed with strong language?

Writers need more than a main idea to make their point about a topic. A **supporting detail** is a fact, example, or other piece of information that strengthens or backs up the main idea. Think about the paragraph about bicycle safety. If the main idea of a paragraph is to wear a bicycle helmet, a supporting detail might be that bicycle helmets are designed to protect riders' heads.

Read this passage. Then try to figure out the main idea and supporting details.

> The manta ray is one of the most graceful animals in the ocean. Although it is very large—about 20 feet across at the widest point—it gets around easily. With its large, triangular wings, the manta ray can move fast. It pushes itself through the water easily. When other sea creatures try to attack it, it rarely gets caught. The manta ray travels smoothly and safely through the sea.

Making a diagram is a good way to identify the main idea and supporting details. Look at this diagram about the manta ray. The main idea is at the top, and the supporting details are below it.

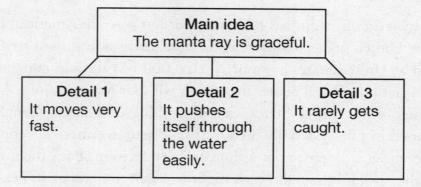

Summary

Another way to understand informational texts is to summarize what the author has written. Your **summary** should state only the main idea and the most important supporting details. Read this passage.

> Population is all the people living in a certain area. The world's population is uneven. Some places, such as the United States, are densely populated. That means a lot of people live there. The climate makes it easy for people to live and work. Other places are less populated and have few people. One example is northern Canada. The cold climate makes it difficult for people to live there.

Here is a good summary of the passage.

> The world's population is uneven. Some places have a lot of people, while other places have fewer people.

When you read, first look for the main idea, and then look for the important details. The title of a passage might give you a clue to the main idea, so that is a good place to start.

Thinking It Through

Read the following passage, and then answer the question that follows.

Since its creation, radio has had an important place in American life. Today, the United States has more radio broadcast stations than any other country. The United States has more than 6,000 FM stations and almost 5,000 AM stations. Brazil comes in second, with far fewer stations. Many people think of the United States when they think of radio. Although radio was first used in England, daily broadcasting began in America. People now in their seventies still remember a time before television. Back then, families would gather around the radio each night to listen to news or stories.

What is the main idea of this passage?

_____

_____

_____

 HINT Reread the first sentence of the passage. Does the rest of the passage support it? Try to state the main idea of the passage in one complete sentence.

Coached Example

Read the passage and answer the questions.

Libraries are amazing places. Every library has books on thousands of subjects. Each book is full of information, and each piece of information is something to learn. In fact, some people call libraries temples of learning. People can learn about almost anything at the library. Music fans can learn about different kinds of music. Farmers can learn about planting crops. Doctors can learn about medicine. Lawyers can learn about the law. Each book has its place on a shelf. This is because libraries are extremely well organized. Libraries also have helpful and knowledgeable librarians on staff. These librarians are there to answer readers' questions and to help solve problems. It's easy to see why so many people, young and old, like to spend time at the library.

1. The main idea of this passage is

    A. libraries have many books.

    B. libraries are well organized.

    C. libraries are amazing places.

    D. each book has its place.

    HINT Look for a big, general idea, rather than a small detail.

2. Which statement from the passage is a supporting detail?

    A. "Every library has books on thousands of subjects."

    B. "In fact, some people call libraries temples of learning."

    C. "Libraries are amazing places."

    D. "It's easy to see why so many people, young and old, like to spend time at the library."

    HINT Supporting details strengthen the passage's main idea.

Use the Reading Guide to help you understand the passage.

Reading Guide

Underline the main idea in the passage.

What did babies and adults both do while they slept?

Remember that a good summary gives the main message of a passage.

Eugene Aserinsky and the Dreaming Brain

Have you ever wondered what happens to our brains during sleep? Do our brains just shut off and rest throughout the night, or do they remain active?

In 1953, a scientist named Eugene Aserinsky asked these same questions. To find the answers, he decided to do an experiment. He closely observed a number of babies during sleep to see if their eyes moved beneath their lids. He noticed the babies had very slow eye movements when they first fell asleep. Then he noticed something very interesting. At certain times during sleep, the babies' eyes began to move very rapidly. They seemed to move as if the baby was awake and playing outside. Eugene called these periods of sleep "Rapid Eye Movement," or "R.E.M." for short.

Aserinsky then decided to try the same experiment with adults. He found the same thing. Adults also had rapid eye movements. These movements lasted between three minutes to nearly an hour. Aserinsky decided to awaken the adults when their eyes were moving rapidly. He asked them what they were seeing. The adults reported that they were dreaming. Aserinsky also awakened the adults when there was no eye movement. During these times, the adults did not report any dreams.

This experiment showed that sleep has different stages. During some stages, the brain is active. During others, it is not. Before Aserinsky's discovery, scientists believed that sleep had only one stage. Aserinsky forever changed the world's view of sleep.

Answer the following questions.

1. Aserinsky watched various subjects sleep because he wanted to know

   A. why people sleep for hours at a time.

   B. what happens while people are asleep.

   C. what people dream about while sleeping.

   D. why people sleep without dreaming.

2. According to the passage, babies and adults

   A. have very different sleep patterns.

   B. do not dream while asleep.

   C. both experience Rapid Eye Movement.

   D. have slow eye movements when dreaming.

3. What is the main idea of this passage?

   A. Babies dream more than adults.

   B. People always dream while sleeping.

   C. Scientists want to know what happens when people sleep.

   D. The human brain has different stages of activity when asleep.

4. What caught Aserinksy's attention when watching babies sleep?

   A. He noticed that they did not move much.

   B. He watched their eyes move as if they were playing.

   C. He found that they slept without dreaming.

   D. He did not see any movement beneath their eyelids.

5. Write a brief summary of the passage in your own words.

   _____

   _____

   _____

   _____

9 Relationships between Events

RI.4.3, RI.4.10, RF.4.4.a

Getting the Idea

Most of the informational passages you read are written in a certain order, or sequence. For example, take the events leading up to America becoming an independent country. Our country's first conflict with Britain came before the second event for a reason, and the second event came before the third event for a reason. Finally, the problems became so great that America declared its independence from Britain.

Chronology is another word for historical sequence. When history writers put events into **chronological order**, they are placing those events in the order in which they happened. But listing a series of events in chronological order is not enough—it is only telling the reader what happened. To truly teach the reader something about history, the writer should also tell *why* something happened.

Read this passage.

> Yellowstone was our country's first national park. Congress passed a bill creating it in 1872. Then, Congress opened more parks in other areas of our country. People saw that an agency was needed to run the park system. The National Park Service was created in 1916.

The paragraph tells the events that led up to the creation of the National Park Service. The events are in chronological order. The paragraph also tells you why the National Park Service was needed.

Events in a science text are related to each other in a similar way. They must also happen in a certain sequence, or order. Read about the process of photosynthesis on the following page.

Green plants make their own food using a process called photosynthesis. First, plants take in sunlight. Plants use the energy from the sun to break down the water and carbon dioxide. The plant also takes in water from the soil and carbon dioxide from the air. Plants use the sugar as food. Finally, they release the oxygen into the air. Then, these materials are put together in a new way to make sugar and oxygen.

Sound confusing? That's because the steps in the process are out of order. The sequence needs to be fixed in order for the text to make sense. The plant needs to take in water and carbon dioxide *before* it can break them down. And if you see the word *finally*, it signals an event that should come last. Time-order words such as *first, next, then,* and *finally* can help you understand the sequence of events.

Now read the correct version of the passage.

Green plants make their own food using a process called photosynthesis. First, the plant takes in sunlight. The plant also takes in water from the soil and carbon dioxide from the air. Next, plants use the energy from the sun to break down the water and carbon dioxide. Then, these materials are put together in a new way to make sugar and oxygen. Plants use the sugar as food. Finally, they release the oxygen into the air.

Now the passage makes sense. You can understand the steps in the process. Pay attention to the order of events and steps in a process when you read about history or science. Doing so will help you to better understand what you read.

Thinking It Through

Read the following passage, and then answer the question that follows.

Many Native American groups in North America planted Three Sisters gardens. The "three sisters" were corn, beans, and squash. These three crops were planted together in the same small plot of earth to help them grow. This "cooperation" among crops is still used today. First, corn seeds are planted in a small mound. When the corn is about 6 inches high, it is time to plant the beans. About a week after the beans have sprouted, it is time to plant the squash. The corn provides a stalk for the beans to climb up. And the beans provide nutrients, or food, for the soil. As the squash grows, its leaves spread out, which prevents weeds from competing for the available nutrients and sunlight.

Which of the vegetables should be planted first? Why?

_____

_____

_____

_____

HINT   What do the beans need for support?

Coached Example

Read the passage and answer the questions.

In 1920, Earle Dickson was working for a medical supplies company called Johnson & Johnson. Dickson's new wife, Josephine, was just learning how to cook. She often cut her fingers while making meals. So, Earle came up with a plan. He got some tape and gauze and a pair of scissors. He cut small rectangles of gauze and stuck them on pieces of tape. After that, whenever Josephine got a cut, she could easily use a ready-made bandage.

Soon after making his homemade bandages, Dickson showed them to the managers at his company. They liked the idea so much that by 1921, they were selling the bandages. They also promoted Dickson to vice president of the company. By 1924, Johnson & Johnson was manufacturing boxes of "Band-Aids" for Americans to buy and keep in their medicine cabinets.

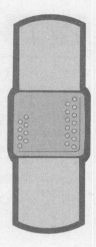

1. What did Earle Dickson do right before showing the bandages to Johnson & Johnson?

   A. He became vice president.

   B. He came up with a plan.

   C. He cut pieces of gauze and put them on tape.

   D. He taught his wife how to cook.

   HINT Look for clue words that help you figure out the sequence of events.

2. Why did Earle Dickson decide to make bandages at home?

   A. He couldn't get them at work.

   B. His wife frequently cut herself.

   C. He wanted to impress his co-workers.

   D. He was working on various inventions.

   HINT Review the passage for details on why Dickson came up with the idea.

Use the Reading Guide to help you understand the passage.

The Chunnel

The Channel Tunnel, or "Chunnel," is a unique railway tunnel. It is 31.4 miles long—and 24 miles of it are underwater!

The idea behind the Chunnel was first thought of around 1802. England and France wanted to figure out a quick way to travel between the two countries without having to take a boat. Engineers thought of digging a tunnel beneath the English Channel, the sea that separates England from France. Construction workers started to dig into the earth, but no real progress was made. The project lay quiet for years.

Then, in 1984, the undersea railway project reopened. England and France hoped private companies would work together to pay for the huge cost to build the Chunnel. Many companies were interested. They knew a tunnel would provide a cheaper way to move goods than by ship, airplane, or truck. The Eurotunnel Group, a group of 200 banks and companies, was formed. The group gave England and France their blueprints for the Chunnel. By 1986, England and France gave the Eurotunnel Group their approval. Two years later, construction finally began.

The Chunnel took 15,000 workers seven years to complete. On May 6, 1994, the queen of England and the president of France held an opening ceremony for the Chunnel. The Chunnel is considered one of the seven wonders of the modern world. High-speed trains carry vehicles, equipment, and people. Nearly seven million passengers take the two-hour journey from London to Paris and Belgium every year.

Answer the following questions.

1. People first hoped the Chunnel could be built because they wanted

   A. a fun way to travel.

   B. an easy way to get to France.

   C. a way to travel besides by boat.

   D. a cheap way to move goods.

2. According to the passage, what happened BEFORE 1984?

   A. The Chunnel was on hold.

   B. The Chunnel was half finished.

   C. The money for the Chunnel was collected.

   D. The governments gave approval for the Chunnel.

3. Why did so many companies want the Chunnel built?

   A. Travel by boat was slow.

   B. Moving goods would be less expensive.

   C. Building the Chunnel was cheaper than a new road.

   D. Airplanes had not yet been invented.

4. What happened LAST?

   A. Construction workers began to dig.

   B. The Eurotunnel Group was formed.

   C. An opening ceremony was held.

   D. 15,000 workers constructed the Chunnel.

5. Explain how dates in the passage helped you understand how long it took between major events in the construction of the Chunnel.

   _____

   _____

   _____

   _____

   _____

10 Reading in the Subject Areas

RI.4.4, RI.4.10, L.4.6, RF.4.4.a

Getting the Idea

When you are reading a textbook, you will probably come across words you do not know. Each subject you study in school—science, social studies, history—uses its own special keywords and terms. Often, new terms will appear in bold print or highlighted another way. That means that you can find the word's meaning in the book's **glossary**. A glossary is a section at the back of a textbook that includes an alphabetical list of all the new words in that book and their definitions.

Read the following passage.

> During the Revolutionary War in America, **muskets** were not very accurate. American and British soldiers stood in long lines and fired large numbers of lead balls at one another. Army leaders hoped that the deadly shots would make holes in the enemy line.

The word *muskets* appears in bold print. That means it will be defined in the book's glossary. For example, the entry might look like this:

musket a heavy shoulder gun carried by foot soldiers

Sometimes, you may come across a word you do not recognize that is not in bold print. That means it is not in the glossary. So, you can use a **dictionary** to look for a definition. Think of a dictionary as a huge glossary, containing many more words. Often a dictionary will list the definitions for all the different meanings of a word, whereas a glossary might have only the definition that fits the meaning of the word as it is used in a book.

Sometimes, a word can have more than one meaning, depending on the kind of text where it is used. In a science book, the word *conductor* means a material that electricity flows through easily. In a text about music, a conductor is a person who leads an orchestra.

Here's another example from a science textbook.

> Igneous rocks are produced by heat or by a volcano. Igneous rocks can be classified by their texture and **composition**. Many kinds of igneous rocks contain the minerals quartz and plagioclase.

Now read this passage from a language arts textbook.

> Learning how to write a thoughtful **composition** can be a difficult process. However, if you follow all the steps and you understand what you are supposed to do, composition writing can be simple and fun.

The word *composition* appears in both passages, but it does not have the same meaning in both. Using the context in which the word appears in each passage, you should be able to choose which definition is the right one in each case. Look at the dictionary entry below.

> **com·po·si·tion** *noun* **1.** the act or process of composing **2.** the general makeup of a material **3.** a piece of writing, especially a school exercise in the form of an essay **4.** a written piece of music

Using what you know, which definition tells you what *composition* means as used in the science passage? The answer is definition 2. Definition 3 tells you what the same word means in the language arts passage.

Thinking It Through

Read the following passage, and then answer the questions that follow.

       The Oregon-California Trail was an important part of American history. The trail was a 2,000-mile route from Missouri to Oregon and California that allowed the early <u>pioneers</u> to travel to the western United States. The first large wave of pioneers followed the trail in 1843, when roughly 1,000 settlers made the journey at one time.

What does the word <u>pioneers</u> mean in this passage? Where would you look in a textbook containing this passage to find out?

_____

_____

_____

HINT   Which words in this passage help you understand the meaning of the word *pioneers*?

Coached Example

Read the passage and answer the questions.

Clouds start with warm, moist air near Earth's surface. The moisture in the air is in the form of water vapor, or water in the gas state. The warm air rises. As the air rises, it cools.

High in the sky, the air becomes so cool that the water vapor <u>condenses</u>, or changes from a gas to a liquid. The water vapor forms tiny droplets of liquid water. If the air is very cold, the water vapor forms ice crystals. Clouds are made up of billions of droplets or ice crystals, sometimes both.

<u>Cloud droplets</u> form around tiny specks of dust or soot. Cloud droplets are too tiny to fall to Earth. For rain to fall, larger, heavier drops of water must form in clouds. Raindrops form when droplets bump into each other and stick together. It takes millions of droplets to make one raindrop.

1. When water changes from a gas to a liquid, it is called

   A. freezing.

   B. condensation.

   C. melting.

   D. crystallizing.

   HINT Find the keywords *gas* and *liquid* in the passage. What does the passage say about them?

2. Cloud droplets do not fall as rain because they are too

   A. hard.

   B. large.

   C. small.

   D. sticky.

   HINT Reread the description of how cloud droplets form.

Use the Reading Guide to help you understand the passage.

Reading Guide

Look at the underlined word in paragraph 1. Information in paragraphs 1 and 3 will help you understand its meaning.

What kind of information is being described in paragraph 2?

Think about the word *colony*. Would it have another meaning in a history book?

Amazing Honeybees

Humans have kept honeybees for thousands of years. In modern times, <u>beekeeping</u> isn't just a popular hobby, it is a major industry. Honeybees pollinate plants. This helps the plants to produce seeds. We harvest many of these plants for food.

A hive can have up to 30,000 bees in the winter. In the summer, there can be as many as 80,000 bees living in one hive! That's a remarkable number of bees! There is only one queen bee for each bee <u>colony</u>. The queen bee is the master of the hive, and all the bees follow her lead. The queen can lay 2,000 eggs a day. Most of the eggs will grow into <u>worker bees</u>. They take care of the hive. Each worker bee has a specific job. Some become nursemaids and take care of the babies. Others have jobs such as food finders, hive builders, or guards. Some of the eggs will grow into <u>drone bees</u>. They mate with the queen been and will become the fathers of future baby bees. Bees work together to keep the hive functioning smoothly.

When beekeepers work with bees, they must wear special clothing. This <u>protective clothing</u> helps prevent bee stings. Beekeepers wear a helmet with a strong net that is pulled down over the face. They always wear jackets with long sleeves to protect the arms. Bees can also climb up unprotected legs. Most beekeepers use pieces of string to tie the bottoms of their pants around their ankles.

Answer the following questions.

1. Look at the dictionary entry below.

   col·o·ny *noun* **1.** a group of people who settle in a new land **2.** a group of the same kind of animals or plants that live together **3.** a territory that has been settled by people from another country and is ruled by that country **4.** a group of people having the same interests

   Which definition tells you what <u>colony</u> means as used in the passage?

   A. definition 1

   B. definition 2

   C. definition 3

   D. definition 4

2. Which of the following is NOT a job of a worker bee?

   A. guarding the hive

   B. laying eggs

   C. taking care of babies

   D. building the hive

3. What does the word <u>beekeeping</u> mean?

   A. keeping bees as pets

   B. selling beehives

   C. raising and caring for bees as a business

   D. running an industry

4. The drone bees

   A. mate with the queen.

   B. guard the queen.

   C. lead the other bees in the hive.

   D. leave the hive in winter.

5. What is protective clothing? Which words in the passage help you understand its meaning?

   _____

   _____

   _____

   _____

Use the Reading Guide to help you understand the passage.

Reading Guide

Look at the underlined words in paragraph 1. What do you think the words mean in this passage?

In paragraph 2, notice the words and sentences around the words *nomadic* and *bison*. Which clues help you understand the meaning of each word?

If this passage were in a textbook, the underlined words would be defined in the glossary at the back of the book.

The Plains Indians

The Plains Indians lived in the area of the United States known as the Great Plains. These Native American groups had a strong connection to the land—a connection so deep that it was felt throughout every part of their culture. The people had to gather, grow, or hunt all their food. Some groups farmed the land and grew crops such as beans, maize, and pumpkins.

The people were nomadic, moving constantly as they collected wild fruits and vegetables and hunted wild animals. They followed herds of bison across the plains. Bison are large, strong, and fast, so they were not easy to hunt. But they were valuable because they provided most of a tribe's basic needs: food, clothing, and shelter. The Plains Indians never killed more bison than they needed. They were grateful for the bison and used every part of it—nothing was wasted. The meat was eaten. The skin was used to make shelter, clothing, shields, shoes, and pouches. Bison fat was turned into soap.

Because the Plains Indians moved all the time, they needed a type of shelter that could be put up and taken down quickly. They built a tepee by leaning long poles together and covering the poles with bison skin. A fire was built in the center of the tepee. There was a hole at the top of the teepee to let the smoke out. The hole could be moved depending on which way the wind was blowing.

Answer the following questions.

1. Look at the dictionary entry below.

    cul·ture *noun* **1.** an interest in the arts, such as music and painting **2.** the growth of bacteria in a laboratory for scientific purposes **3.** the beliefs and way of life of a group of people **4.** the process of growing new kinds of animals or plants

    Which definition tells you what <u>culture</u> means as used in the passage?

    A. definition 1

    B. definition 2

    C. definition 3

    D. definition 4

2. What is maize?

    A. a kind of animal

    B. something to eat

    C. a piece of clothing

    D. an item used for travel

3. What does the word <u>nomadic</u> mean?

    A. hard-working

    B. quiet

    C. staying in one place

    D. moving from place to place

4. The bison provided the Plains Indians with

    A. shelter and clothing.

    B. long poles for shelter.

    C. food, clothing, and shelter.

    D. hunting tools.

5. What is a tepee? Which words in the passage help you understand its meaning?

    _____

    _____

    _____

    _____

11 Text Structures

RI.4.5, RI.4.10, RF.4.4.a

Getting the Idea

When you read, it is helpful to understand how the writer arranges the information. The way an article or passage is organized is called its **text structure**. There are a number of ways in which writers can organize information.

Chronological Order

Chronological order is the order, or sequence, in which events happen. History texts are often written using chronology. Read the following passage.

> New Mexico has an interesting history. First, Native Americans lived in the area now known as New Mexico. Then, in the late 1500s, the region was ruled by Spain. Next, in the early 1800s, the region became part of Mexico. After that, it came under U.S. control. Finally, in 1912, New Mexico became our forty-seventh state.

Notice the keywords such as *first, then, next, after,* and *finally*. They help you track the events. The dates not only help you to understand the sequence, but also how much time passed between each event.

Compare and Contrast

When you **compare**, you show how things are alike. When you **contrast**, you show how things are different. Read the following passage.

> Oranges and apples are alike in several ways. They are both fruits, and they both have seeds inside and grow on trees. Apples have a skin that you can eat, but oranges have a rind that you cannot eat. Oranges and apples grow in different climates. Orange trees grow in warmer states like Florida, while apples grow in cooler states like Washington.

The keywords *alike, both, but,* and *different* help you to understand the similarities and differences between the fruits. Other keywords you may see are *like, unlike, while, either, same, although,* and *opposite*.

Cause and Effect

A **cause** is why something happens. An **effect** is what happens as a result of a cause. For example, if you accidentally drop a glass and it falls to the floor, the glass will break. The cause is dropping the glass. The effect is the glass breaking. Read the following passage.

> The scientist Isaac Newton was the first person to explain why tides occur. Tides are the rises and falls of large bodies of water, such as oceans. Tides are caused by the moon's gravity. The gravitational pull of the moon causes the oceans to bulge out toward the moon.

Science texts often use cause and effect to explain *why* things happen in nature. Look for keywords such as *why, cause, because, therefore, as a result*, and *effect*.

Problem and Solution

Problem and solution is a text structure in which the problem, or issue, is presented first. Then, the writer tells how the problem was solved. Read the following passage.

> Central Park, in New York City, was built in the mid-1800s. Over the years, the park began to decline. By the 1970s, Central Park had become dirty and unsafe. Part of the problem was that the city did not have enough money to run the park. Then, in 1980, a group of citizens formed the Central Park Conservancy. The group raised private funds to restore the park and keep it in beautiful condition.

The writer starts off by telling you the problem: the decline of the park. Then you learn how a group of concerned citizens solved the problem.

Thinking It Through

Read the following passage, and then answer the question that follows.

      Dolphins and porpoises are alike in many ways. Both are mammals that live in the ocean. They have a similar body shape, including a tail fluke. Both animals breathe through a blowhole at the top of their body. But there are many differences between these creatures. Porpoises are smaller than dolphins. Dolphins are usually about 6 to 12 feet long, while most porpoises are only about 4 to 7 feet long. A dolphin's nose is often described as a pointed "beak." But a porpoise's nose is shorter and rounder, more like a snout. The teeth of a porpoise are flat, while dolphin teeth are usually shaped like cones.

What is the text structure of this passage? Use examples from the passage to explain your answer.

_____

_____

_____

HINT The passage focuses on two kinds of animals. Look for keywords that give you a clue to the text structure.

Coached Example

Read the passage and answer the questions.

Many years ago, the Colorado River flooded almost every spring. In the late 1800s, farmers had settled the land along the lower Colorado River. The floods caused major damage every year. This was a big problem for the farmers who worked near its banks. People tried to control the river. They built irrigation canals and levees to control the water. Nothing worked.

In the early 1900s, the U.S. government found a solution. It would build a dam on the river. This huge structure would stop the flooding and help create a year-round water supply for the people in the area. The government announced in 1931 that the dam would be built. The dam would be 726.4 feet high. The Hoover Dam was completed in 1935. It is located along the border of Arizona and Nevada.

---

1. In this passage, the MAIN text structure the writer uses is

    A. chronological order.

    B. problem and solution.

    C. comparison.

    D. cause and effect.

    HINT What situation is described in the beginning of the passage? What do you learn later in the passage?

2. How did the government finally stop the Colorado River from flooding every spring?

    A. It built a dam.

    B. It built an irrigation canal.

    C. It built new farms nearby.

    D. It built a bridge.

    HINT Reread the passage. Which solution finally worked?

Use the Reading Guide to help you understand the passage.

Look for cause and effect keywords that help you understand the reasons leading up to the Boston Tea Party.

How do the dates in the passage help you follow the order of events?

A passage can have more than one text structure. When you read about history, you learn what happened, when it happened, and why it happened.

The Boston Tea Party

The Boston Tea Party was a major event in our country's history. It is a symbol of the American Revolution.

Massachusetts was still a British colony in 1773. That year, the British government passed the Tea Act. The law said only one British company, the East India Company, could sell tea to the colonies. Americans would have to buy that tea—and they'd have to pay a tax on it, too! Many colonists were so angry, they flatly refused to buy the British tea.

The East India Company lost a lot of money because the colonists would not buy their tea. Still, the British continued to send tea to the colonies. Three British tea ships docked in Boston Harbor in 1773. Many colonists wanted the tea sent back. They did not want to pay any taxes. But the British demanded payment.

The Americans stood up for their rights. On the night of December 16, 1773, around 100 men boarded the three ships. Many belonged to a group called the Sons of Liberty. Some were dressed as Native Americans. The men worked quietly. They dumped 342 crates of tea into the harbor. About 45 tons of tea was thrown overboard. This event was called the Boston Tea Party.

The British government passed new laws the following year to punish Massachusetts. These were called the Intolerable Acts. The word *intolerable* means "very difficult to live with or accept." One act banned the loading of any ships in Boston Harbor.

Answer the following questions.

1. What is the MAIN text structure the writer uses in this passage?

   A. chronological order

   B. compare and contrast

   C. cause and effect

   D. problem and solution

2. What was the main cause of the Boston Tea Party?

   A. the Intolerable Acts

   B. the Tea Act

   C. the lack of tea

   D. the American Revolution

3. What was one effect of the Boston Tea Party?

   A. the Intolerable Acts

   B. the Tea Act

   C. the colonists' refusal to buy British tea

   D. the formation of the East India Company

4. Which event happened LAST?

   A. Colonists boarded three ships docked in Boston Harbor.

   B. The British government said only the East India Company could sell tea to the colonies.

   C. Colonists dumped 45 tons of tea into the Boston Harbor.

   D. Colonists formed a group called the Sons of Liberty.

5. Choose a text structure that the writer uses in the passage. Use examples from the passage to show how this text structure is used.

   _____

   _____

   _____

   _____

   _____

   _____

   _____

12 Primary and Secondary Sources

RI.4.6, RI.4.10, RF.4.4.a

Getting the Idea

Sources are materials that provide information. You use sources to gather facts and details about topics you wish to learn or write about.

A **primary source** was written at the time of an event by someone who was there. A primary source is also called a firsthand account. For example, a letter from a soldier who fought in a war is a primary source. The soldier is writing about things he personally experienced. An autobiography is another example. Benjamin Franklin told the story of his life in his autobiography. Other examples are diary entries, interviews, quotes (a person's exact words), and eyewitness accounts. One way to identify a primary source is to look for the word *I*. This word means that the writer of the source is reporting his or her own thoughts and experiences.

Read this passage.

> When I arrived at the scene, about fifteen people had already gathered near the half-beached whale. Two scientists waded into the water, trying to lead the 30-foot creature off the bottom and back out to sea. After two hours, the whale began to flap its tail and fins. The scientists gave it a final push, and off it went.

The passage is an eyewitness account by a newspaper reporter (*I*) on the scene. The reporter is telling about an event that he or she actually observed or witnessed. Therefore, it is a primary source.

Not all primary sources are written works. A photograph can also be a primary source, since it gives direct information about something. Because primary sources are original accounts, their information is usually accurate and reliable.

A **secondary source** is an account of an event that was *not* witnessed by the writer. In fact, the writer most likely used information from several primary sources to write his or her account. Secondary sources are useful and important, but they are one step further away than primary sources are from the events they describe. Some examples of secondary sources are encyclopedia articles, magazine articles, textbooks, and biographies.

Read this passage.

> Kay Harris moved to Greenlawn, New York, in 1996. She took a daytime job in an art supply store. During this time, Kay developed an interest in painting. After work, she would stay up all night painting in her kitchen. Her paintings showed bold splashes of lines and colors. Kay told her friends and family that she was painting images from her imagination. For the next five years, Kay created over one thousand paintings.

In this secondary source, the writer is not an eyewitness to the events described. The writer simply gives information collected from primary sources. The writer may have interviewed people who knew Kay Harris or read other accounts of Kay Harris, such as her personal diary. Because secondary sources often collect information from more than one primary source, they can be good general sources of information.

The chart below shows examples of primary and secondary sources.

Primary Sources	Secondary Sources
eyewitness account	textbook
diary entry	encyclopedia article
interview	magazine article
quote	book review
autobiography	biography
letter	almanac
photograph	atlas

Thinking It Through

Read the following passage, and then answer the questions that follow.

On May 29, 1953, Edmund Hillary and Tenzing Norgay became the first people to climb Mount Everest, the tallest mountain in the world. Many adventurers had attempted to climb Everest before, but none had reached the top. Hillary and Norgay planned their climb very carefully. They had the support of a great team, and they also used the best equipment. All of these things helped them to succeed.

Edmund Hillary once said, "People do not decide to be extraordinary. They decide to accomplish extraordinary things." He proved this on Mount Everest. It was truly an amazing achievement.

Does this source provide mainly primary or secondary information? Explain. What part of the source is a primary source?

_____

_____

_____

_____

_____

Coached Example

Read the passages and answer the questions.

Interview with Rusty Williams

Interviewer: When did you begin playing the guitar?

Williams: My father gave me a guitar for my sixth birthday. It was love at first sight. I've been playing ever since.

Interviewer: Who was your first guitar teacher?

Williams: His name was Ronnie Jones. He was a fine teacher and showed me all of the basics. After Ronnie, I studied with Brian Wall and Debbie Ray. They taught me how to play blues and jazz. After that, I learned by listening to records.

Interviewer: Who are some of your favorite guitarists?

Williams: Well, I would say Jimi Hendrix, for sure. I also love Joe Pass.

Interviewer: What are your plans for this year?

Williams: I'm playing ten concerts in Texas and California. Then, I'm recording some new songs I've written for my upcoming album, *Blues Out West*.

Interviewer: Good luck with those new songs. I'm a fan, so I can't wait to hear them!

Williams: Thanks!

Rusty Williams

Born on August 15, 1928, in Hazlehurst, Mississippi

American guitarist, singer, and composer who combines jazz and blues to create a unique guitar style

Rusty Williams began playing guitar at age six after receiving a guitar from his father as a present. Williams studied with local guitarists in his youth. He then began listening to the records of Jimi Hendrix and Joe Pass. His first song, *Trembling Blues*, used many of Hendrix's guitar styles. Later, Williams developed his own style, which is a mix of blues and jazz. His album, *Blues Out West*, has sold over one million copies since it was released in 2008.

1. The first passage is a primary source because it

   A. tells about a famous person.

   B. uses a person's actual words.

   C. contains historical facts.

   D. provides useful information.

   HINT Look for words such as *I* to figure out whether a source is primary or secondary.

2. How are the two passages alike?

   A. Both provide an account of someone's life.

   B. Both report eyewitness events.

   C. Both include quotes from famous people.

   D. Both are based on secondary sources.

   HINT What is the topic of both passages?

3. Which passage could have been used as a source for the other passage? Explain.

   _____

   _____

   _____

   _____

   _____

   _____

   HINT Which source reports experiences in Williams's own words? What makes that source valuable to someone writing about him?

Lesson Practice

Use the Reading Guides to help you understand the passages.

Reading Guide

What is the topic of this passage?

Look for words in the passage that give you a clue to whether it is a primary or secondary source.

Where would this passage most likely be found?

excerpted and adapted from

Ralph Waldo Emerson's Essay of May 9, 1862

Henry David Thoreau was born in Concord, Massachusetts, on July 12, 1817. He graduated from Harvard College in 1837. He worked briefly at a pencil-making factory. Soon after, he began his endless walks and many studies. Each day, he learned about some new plant or animal or creature in nature.

In 1845, he built himself a small house on the shores of Walden Pond. He lived there two years alone, growing a garden, chopping wood, and studying nature.

No truer American lived than Thoreau. He loved his country deeply. He had more common sense and wisdom than most people.

Mr. Thoreau loved the fields, hills, and waters of his native town, and he made them known and interesting both to fellow Americans and to people all over the world.

He knew the country like a fox or a bird, and passed through it as freely on paths of his own. He knew every track in the snow or on the ground, and what creature had taken this path before him.

His interest in a flower or a bird lay very deep in his mind. He sensed everything around him, almost as if he had an extra pair of eyes or ears. He saw things closely, as if under a microscope. His memory was a photograph of all he saw and heard. Every bit of nature was a thing of beauty to him.

Who is reporting the events in this passage?

What does the word *I* tell you about this source?

Is the author of this passage directly observing nature? Is he using his personal observations to describe what he sees?

excerpted and adapted from

The Journal of Henry David Thoreau

The surface of the water reflects the sparkling light of the sun. The red maples will blossom in a day or two. A couple of large ducks fly low over the water. At first, I see patches of white underneath, but that is just the bright light of the sun bouncing off the water. The black ducks rise at once high in the sky. They often circle about to gather their troops.

The golden-brown tassels of the alder trees hang down from their branches. The tassels are very rich in color now. One or two buttercup flowers on Lee's Cliff, fully out, surprise me like a flame bursting from the ground. I see the white and yellow lily flowers are also blooming. There are two kinds of elm trees that grow here: the common elm and the slippery elm. The common elm has all of its new leaves out and open. The slippery elm will open its new leaves in about two days of pleasant weather.

As I was going along the road by Meadow Mouse Brook, I saw a great bird on the oaks. It was just starting to lift off. It was mostly a dirty white with broad wings with black tips and black on other parts. I am not sure whether it was a white-headed eagle or a fish hawk. It rose and circled, flapping several times, till it got under way. Then, it moved off steadily in its flight over the woods northwest.

Answer the following questions.

1. Information in the first source could BEST be used for

    A. writing a report about Thoreau's life.

    B. learning about Thoreau's personal feelings.

    C. writing an eyewitness account of Thoreau.

    D. gathering quotes made by Thoreau.

2. The second source provides the reader with

    A. details from an interview.

    B. general information.

    C. historical facts.

    D. personal observations.

3. Which statement BEST describes how the two sources are similar?

    A. Both explain or describe primary sources.

    B. Both describe the scene of an event.

    C. Both provide information about a specific person.

    D. Both gather information from secondary sources.

4. Which statement BEST describes how the two sources differ?

    A. Only the second source describes direct observations.

    B. Only the second source uses other sources.

    C. Only the second source gives accurate information.

    D. Only the second source could be used to learn more about a topic.

5. Which passage could have been used as a source for the other passage? Explain.

_____

_____

_____

_____

13 Opinion and Evidence

RI.4.8, RI.4.10, RF.4.4.a

Getting the Idea

Authors of informational texts make claims about many things. A **claim** is a statement that something—an idea, event, or observation—is true. For example, an author states: "Babe Ruth was the most talented baseball player of all time." The author is stating this idea as if it is true. However, it may or may not actually be true.

An **opinion** is a personal belief that cannot be proven true. No one can *prove* that Babe Ruth was the best baseball player; some people may disagree. When stating an opinion, authors often use words like *good, bad, pleasant, awful,* and *should* to express their feelings. Authors may also use phrases such as *I think, I believe,* and *in my view* to let you know that they are stating a personal opinion. Read this passage.

> Bigelow Park is the most beautiful park in our state. Its wildlife, lakes, and bike paths are more wonderful than any other park has to offer. It also has the best swimming pool and roller-skating rink. There is no better way to spend an afternoon than at Bigelow Park.

Words such as *better, best, most, beautiful,* and *wonderful* tell you that the author is stating opinions. These are the author's own feelings about Bigelow Park, and no one else's. Read the chart below.

Examples of Opinions
The dinner that Ted cooked tasted awful.
I feel that my mom made the right decision.
People should exercise every day to stay healthy.
In my view, the umpire made a bad call.

Authors use evidence to back up their claims. **Evidence** is information used to support a point or claim. One effective type of evidence is fact. A **fact** is a statement that is always true. Unlike an opinion, you can prove a fact in an encyclopedia or other reliable source. See how evidence affects the claim about Babe Ruth:

> Babe Ruth was the most talented baseball player of all time. In 1927, he hit 60 home runs in a single season, a record that lasted for 34 years. When he retired in 1935, Ruth had hit a total of 714 home runs. This major-league record lasted for 39 years.

The facts about the home runs and records are powerful evidence. They can be verified in a book. Together, they make the author's opinion about Babe Ruth believable and strong.

Another type of evidence writers use is an eyewitness account. An **eyewitness account** is someone's firsthand description of an event. For example:

> The tornado was the worst storm that ever hit Norwood. "I've never seen a storm damage so many houses," said Mayor Peter Olson.

The writer uses an eyewitness account (Peter Olson's statement) to support his claim about the tornado.

Finally, a writer could use expert opinion. **Expert opinion** is the opinion of an expert or someone who knows a great deal about a topic. For example:

> Rainforests are valuable places that should be protected. Scientists at Costa University say that our planet would suffer greatly if the rainforests were cut down.

The writer uses an expert opinion (the opinion of scientists) to support the claim that rainforests should be protected.

Thinking It Through

Read the following passage, and then answer the questions that follow.

Riding a bicycle without a helmet is dangerous. In 2007, nearly 52,000 people were injured in bicycle accidents. More than 60 percent of serious bicycle injuries are head injuries.

What claim does the writer make? What kind of evidence does the writer use to support this claim?

_____

_____

_____

_____

_____

HINT A claim is often stated at the beginning of a passage. Do you see information in the passage that can be proved?

Coached Example

Read the passage and answer the questions.

Seagulls are annoying birds. They are a nuisance and a pest to everything around them. Have you ever heard their squawking and crying? It's enough to drive a person crazy. They are even annoying to look at. Their feathers are messy and their splotchy grey and brown color is ugly.

Last week at the beach, I saw an entire flock of seagulls attacking a man and woman who were eating lunch. They waved and yelled at the diving gulls. The gulls kept diving at them. The screaming birds stole their french fries and hamburgers. When the gulls were finished with their stolen meal, they picked from the garbage pails and littered the beach with trash. This is not the first time I've seen this happen.

1. Which sentence from the passage is an opinion?

   A. "Seagulls are annoying birds."

   B. "The screaming birds stole their french fries and hamburgers."

   C. "The gulls kept diving at them."

   D. "This is not the first time I've seen this happen."

    Which answer choices describe events that actually happened? Which answer tells how the writer feels?

2. What kind of evidence does the author use in the passage?

   A. expert opinion

   B. scientific facts

   C. eyewitness account

   D. personal views

    The writer tells about his experience at the beach.

Use the Reading Guide to help you understand the passage.

Reading Guide

Look at paragraph 1. What does the writer claim about highways?

Opinions express an author's feelings or beliefs about something.

Note that Carl Yates works for the National Highway Service.

Highway Problems

Highways have changed the way Americans live. While highways may have improved travel in some ways, they have also caused many problems.

Highways are bad for the environment. Today, more than 244 million cars travel on our highways. Cars burn gasoline for their fuel. Burning gasoline creates air pollution. An average car burns 581 gallons of gasoline each year. Now, think about those 244 million cars traveling on our highways. Think about all of the gasoline they are burning. Do you get the picture? Highways create pollution.

Highways are dangerous. Cars travel at high speeds on highways, and it is easy for accidents to happen. Carl Yates, who studies highways for the National Highway Service, explains that highway traffic offers drivers little room or time to react to mistakes. Yates also points out that many highways have poor road surfaces and lack proper safety signs. This also causes accidents, he says.

Highways are noisy and upsetting. For example, last week I was stuck in traffic for three hours on a local highway. Drivers were honking their horns and flashing their lights. The air was filled with the smell of car exhaust. The noise and smell gave me a headache for hours. This happens often when I travel on highways. I like highways when they are empty, which is never!

Answer the following questions.

1. Which sentence from paragraph 2 is an opinion?

   A. "Highways are bad for the enviroment."

   B. "Cars burn gasoline for their fuel."

   C. "Today, more than 244 million cars travel on our highways."

   D. "An average car burns 581 gallons of gasoline each year."

2. What kind of evidence does the writer use in paragraph 2?

   A. expert opinion

   B. firsthand account

   C. facts

   D. personal beliefs

3. The writer mentions Carl Yates in paragraph 3 to

   A. support a claim.

   B. provide facts.

   C. retell an account.

   D. express a feeling.

4. What kind of evidence does the writer use in paragraph 4?

   A. personal views

   B. eyewitness account

   C. proven facts

   D. judgments

5. What is the writer's claim in paragraph 4? What kind of evidence could the writer add to paragraph 4 to strengthen this claim?

   _____

   _____

   _____

   _____

   _____

14 Charts, Diagrams, and Timelines

RI.4.7, RI.4.10, RF.4.4.a

Getting the Idea

Authors of informational texts often use graphics to convey information. **Graphics** are visual tools such as charts, graphs, diagrams, and timelines. These visuals help you to better understand a text; they may even give you extra information that is not in the text.

A **chart** is a graphic that organizes information. Look at the chart below. It uses columns and rows. An author might use this chart about different countries in an article comparing countries of the world.

Country	Capital	Flag Colors	Language
Sweden	Stockholm	blue, yellow	Swedish
France	Paris	blue, white, red	French
Poland	Warsaw	red, white	Polish

Each column of the chart has a **heading** in bold print at the top. The headings tell you what the information in each column is about. To find the capital of France, go to the "Country" column, find France, and then follow the row to the "Capital" column.

A **diagram** is a simple drawing with labels to make something easier to understand. A diagram may show the different parts of an object. For example, an author might use the diagram on the right to help you to better understand a text that describes the different fins of a fish. They help the fish to swim.

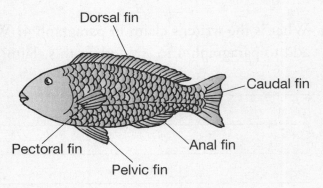

Dorsal fin

Caudal fin

Anal fin

Pelvic fin

Pectoral fin

The fish moves its tail (caudal) fin back and forth to move forward in the water. The dorsal and anal fins, at the top and bottom of the fish, help the fish keep its balance as it swims. And the pectoral and pelvic fins help the fish to steer.

A diagram may also show how something works, how to put something together, or how to play a game. For example, an article that tells about an eruption of a volcano might include this diagram about how volcanoes work:

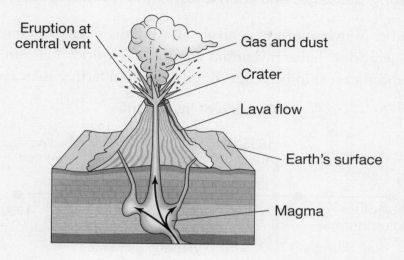

Look closely at the diagram. It shows how magma beneath the surface of Earth rises up and causes a volcano to erupt. You can read a description of a volcano in a text, but seeing it in a diagram helps you to understand the process even more.

Another kind of graphic tool is a timeline. Authors writing about history and science often use a **timeline** to show the dates when important events happened. Timelines make it easy for you to see the order in which events take place. For example, an author writing about dinosaurs might include the following timeline to show when different dinosaurs lived.

Dinosaur Timeline

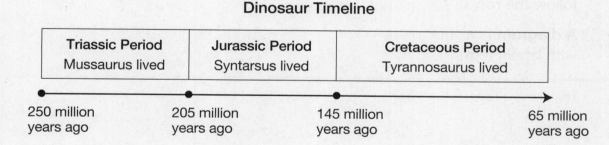

Time (millions of years) is shown at the bottom of the timeline. The names of the time periods and dinosaurs appear above. Most timelines show time moving from left to right, or past to recent.

Thinking It Through

Read the following passage, and then answer the question that follows.

A number of inventions were created during the nineteenth and twentieth centuries. These inventions changed the world. The automobile, airplane, and rocket ship helped us travel faster and farther than ever before.

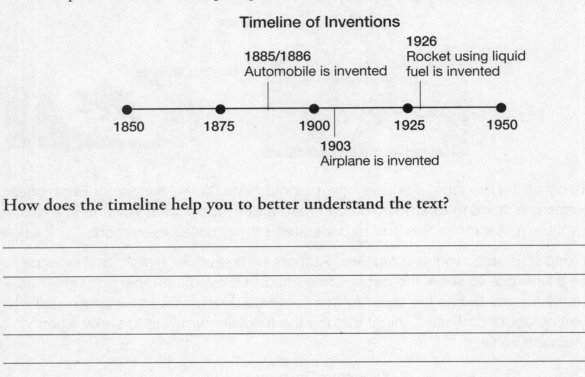

Timeline of Inventions

1885/1886
Automobile is invented

1926
Rocket using liquid fuel is invented

1850   1875   1900   1925   1950

1903
Airplane is invented

How does the timeline help you to better understand the text?

_____

_____

_____

_____

_____

HINT   Look at the dates on the timeline. Are those dates also in the text? Which invention came first? Which came next?

Coached Example

Read the passage and answer the questions.

Most ants live in nests. It is the job of the worker ants to build the nest. The worker ants dig tunnels below the earth. The tunnels lead to rooms called chambers. Each chamber of the nest has its own special purpose. One chamber is built especially for the queen. Another is built for her to lay her eggs. Other chambers are used for storing food. Newborn ants have their own nursery chamber. A single ant nest may be home to millions of ants!

Ant Nest

Food storage

Resting room

Egg room

Nursery

Queen's room

---

1. What additional information can a reader learn by looking at the diagram?

   A. Ant nests have tunnels.

   B. Some ant nests are built underground.

   C. Ant nests have resting chambers.

   D. Some ant nests are built as mounds.

    Look at the different types of rooms labeled in the diagram.

2. The diagram BEST helps readers understand

   A. the role of the ant queen.

   B. the kinds of food ants eat.

   C. the design and purposes of an ant nest.

   D. the way ant nests differ from other nests.

   HINT What kind of information does the diagram mainly provide?

Use the Reading Guide to help you understand the passage.

Reading Guide

Read the passage carefully and look at the chart. Do you see any connections?

In the chart, notice the headings in the columns *Year Invented* and *Purpose*. Read each row for information.

Why do you think the author included this chart?

Ben Franklin: Inventor and Problem Solver

Ben Franklin was a famous inventor and problem solver. He had a lot of good ideas. One of his best was the volunteer fire company.

There was a big fire in Philadelphia, and many buildings burned down. So Franklin decided to organize a fire company. He did not have money to pay people, so he asked people to volunteer. Thirty men said that they would help. In 1736, the Union Fire Company began.

Whenever there was a fire, these men would stop what they were doing. They would get together and put the fire out.

Today, there are volunteer fire companies all over the world. They help people every day. This is just one example of Franklin's good ideas.

Benjamin Franklin's Inventions

Invention	Year Invented	Purpose
armonica	1762	a musical instrument made of glass
bifocals	1784	glasses that allow the wearer to see at a distance and up close
Franklin stove	1742	a stove that uses less fuel than a fireplace and prevents fires
lightning rod	1752	a rod that prevents lightning from hitting a house and causing fire
odometer	1775	a device that measures how many miles a vehicle has traveled

Answer the following questions.

1. According to the chart, what was Franklin's LAST invention?

   A. armonica

   B. bifocals

   C. Franklin stove

   D. lightning rod

2. Other than the volunteer fire company, what else did Franklin think up that prevented fires?

   A. odometer and armonica

   B. lightning rod and odometer

   C. bifocals and armonica

   D. Franklin stove and lightning rod

3. Which of the following did Benjamin Franklin invent FIRST?

   A. lightning rod

   B. odometer

   C. Franklin stove

   D. armonica

4. The information in the chart shows that Benjamin Franklin

   A. had different skills and interests.

   B. worked for the fire department.

   C. was a famous musician.

   D. traveled often.

5. How does the information in the chart help you to better understand the passage?

   _____

   _____

   _____

   _____

   _____

   _____

   _____

15 Compare and Contrast Informational Texts

RI.4.9, RI.4.10, RF.4.4.a

Getting the Idea

When you **compare** informational texts, you examine how they are alike. When you **contrast** them, you see how they are different. Comparing and contrasting texts on the same topic often gives you a fuller understanding of it. One text can add to the information given by another text on the same topic.

When comparing and contrasting informational texts on the same topic, pay attention to how the texts are organized. Read these two passages.

> The Battle of the Alamo happened because of a conflict between Texas and Mexico. At the time, Texas belonged to Mexico. Mexico was angry at Texas for taking over their military fort, the Alamo. This caused the Mexican army to attack the fort to try to take it back. The Mexican troops won the battle, but this made Texas fight even harder for its independence.
>
> In February 1836, over a thousand Mexican troops arrived in San Antonio. Twelve days later, the troops attacked the Alamo. They climbed the walls of the fort. Twice, the Texas troops inside the fort pushed them back. The Mexican troops attacked for a third time. They entered the fort and defeated the Texas troops in a terrible battle.

Both passages are about the battle of the Alamo. But the first passage explains the causes and effect of the battle. The second passage tells about the events in chronological order.

You might also read about a topic in which each passage is told from a different **point of view**. You can compare and contrast those as well. Read the two passages on the next page.

Working as a professional diver is exciting. I get to see many different underwater fish and plants. My diving suit and equipment are fun to wear. They keep me safe and warm in the chilly deep sea.

Scuba diving is a method of exploring underwater. A scuba diver wears a diving mask that protects the eyes. A scuba tank is worn to provide air for breathing. Scuba divers wear wet suits to keep warm and swim fins to help move through the water.

The first passage is a personal account. The *I* refers to the diver. The diver gives the reader personal details about his experience underwater. The second passage is not personal. It states facts and gives descriptions of a diving method and diving equipment. Comparing and contrasting the information from both passages gives you a fuller understanding of the topic of diving than if you had only read one of them.

Some texts look at the same topic from a different perspective. **Perspective** is the attitude or feeling of the author toward the topic. Read these two passages.

Dams are helpful. They provide water for farmers. They create new lakes and waterways for boaters. Many dams produce electricity for homes, businesses, and schools.

Cedar Creek Dam caused a lot of flooding. The floodwaters damaged nearby homes, crops, and wildlife habitat. Now, many fishermen can no longer earn enough money to make a living.

If you had only read the first passage, you might think that dams are always helpful. But in the second passage, you learn that dams may have negative effects, too.

Thinking It Through

Read the following passage, and then answer the questions that follow.

Chess is a fun and challenging game. Children and adults throughout the world play chess. Chess players have different ranks. The best chess players are known as grandmasters. Next come masters, and after that, experts. Most chess players agree that you need a lot of natural talent to become a grandmaster.

In 2009, 14-year-old Ray Robson became the youngest American grandmaster ever. He believes that studying the game hard and playing it every day is the best way for a chess player to improve.

Compare and contrast the information in paragraph 2 of the passage to the information in paragraph 1. How is it similar? How is it different?

_____

_____

_____

_____

HINT Look closely at the types of details given in each paragraph. What kind of information do you learn about in each paragraph?

Coached Example

Read the passages and answer the questions.

Being a Geologist

Being a geologist is hard work, but it is a rewarding job. Mostly, I work outdoors. I climb up and down rocks. I chip off samples. I try to learn how rock and mineral formations were created.

Sometimes I work on a team with other geologists. We might spend weeks in an area looking at the different types of rocks and minerals. We often make maps of what we see. For example, we might show where a bed of limestone meets a layer of hard shale. We trace these rock formations through hills and valleys and fields and wherever they go.

Part of my job is also trying to figure out what kinds of rocks, minerals, and other valuable resources are underground. We look for oil as well as the mineral gold.

Indoors, I work in a lab on my computer. I use computer programs to find out how the earth might have shifted to form rocks. It may look like I'm playing a videogame, but this is a real-life game about our planet! Every day, I think how lucky I am to have this job.

The Scratch Test for Mineral Hardness

One way geologists identify minerals is by figuring out their hardness. The scale of hardness goes from 1 to 10. Diamond is the hardest mineral. It is rated 10 on the scale. Talc is the softest mineral. It is rated 1 on the scale. Geologists use a scratch test to rate minerals. If one mineral can scratch another mineral, it is harder than the mineral it scratches.

An easy way to get an idea of a mineral's rating is to scratch it with a material whose rating is already known. For example, your fingernail has a hardness of 2.5. A penny has a hardness of about 3.5. A steel nail or a piece of glass is about 5.5. Scratch the unknown mineral with each of the known materials and see if any leaves a scratch line. If your fingernail leaves a scratch line on the mineral, you know the mineral has a hardness rating of less than 2.5. If the fingernail does not leave a scratch but the penny does, you know the mineral has a hardness rating between 2.5 and 3.5. If only the nail or glass leaves a scratch, the mineral's rating must be between 3.5 and 5.5. If none of the materials leaves a scratch, the mineral has a hardness rating of above 5.5.

1. How are both passages alike?

   A. Both provide step-by-step instructions.

   B. Both contain information about minerals.

   C. Both give a personal point of view about a topic.

   D. Both organize information by cause and effect.

   HINT   What types of materials do geologists study?

2. Which statement BEST describes how the two passages are different?

   A. The passages describe topics that are not related.

   B. The passages contain different types of information about related topics.

   C. The passages show different perspectives of the writers.

   D. The passages describe different ways of performing a similar activity.

   HINT   Pay attention to the kinds of details and descriptions each passage presents

3. Do you think the information in the second passage gives you a better understanding of the information in the first passage? Explain your answer.

   _____

   _____

   _____

   _____

   _____

   _____

HINT   Review the information about point of view. Each passage is told from a different point of view.

Lesson Practice

Use the Reading Guides to help you understand the passages.

What kind of information is contained in this passage?

How is the information in this passage organized?

Does this passage give information about all kinds of trees or just one type of tree?

excerpted and adapted from

How Trees Grow and Multiply
by Charles Lathrop Pack

The trees of the forest grow by forming new layers of wood under the bark. Trees are held upright in the soil by roots that reach to a depth of many feet where the soil is loose. These roots are the supports of the tree. They hold it stiffly in position. They also supply the tree with food. The body of the tree acts as a passageway through which the food and drink are moved to the top, or crown. The crown is the place where the food is digested and the renewal of trees occurs.

After the first year, trees grow by increasing the thickness of the older buds. Increase in height and density of crown cover comes from the development of the younger twigs. New growth on the tree is spread evenly between the wood and bark over the entire plant. Year after year, new layers of wood are formed around the first layers. This first layer finally develops into heartwood. As far as growth is concerned, heartwood is dead material. Its cells are blocked up and prevent the flow of sap. It aids in supporting the tree. The living sapwood surrounds the heartwood.

Each year, one ring of this sapwood develops. This process of growth may continue until the annual layers amount to 50 or 100, or more, according to the life of the tree.

The Bristlecone Pine Tree

Reading Guide

Do both passages share similar topics?

What does the first passage help you to understand about bristlecone pine trees?

Does this passage provide facts or a personal point of view?

Bristlecone pine trees are the oldest trees in North America. They are found in the western states of Nevada, New Mexico, Arizona, California, Utah, and Colorado. The oldest bristlecone pines grow in the Bristlecone Pine Forest in the White Mountains of California. While most bristlecone pines in this forest are around 1,000 years old, some of the trees are over 4,000 years old!

Bristlecone pines live in windy, harsh areas. Each tree has many trunks, each of which is twisted and gnarled. Sand and ice carried by the wind has polished and smoothed the surface of the bristlecone's bark. Dead layers of the bark peel back after damage from storms and fire. This shedding helps keep the trees healthy.

Bristlecone pines grow to a height of about 60 feet. Like other pine trees, bristlecone pines have needles instead of leaves. The needles grow in bunches of five. The bristlecone has dark purple egg-shaped cones. The cones are covered with bristly or prickly scales. This is what gives the tree its name.

The wood of the bristlecone pine is very thick and heavy. Because of this, a bristlecone pine can remain standing for hundreds of years after it has died. Only when its roots have worn away will the bristlecone finally fall.

The single oldest bristlecone pine tree is known as Methuselah. At more than 4,750 years old, this ancient tree has been growing since the time the ancient pyramids of Egypt were being built!

Answer the following questions.

1. Information in the first passage could help readers better understand

    A. how bristlecone pines stand upright in the soil.

    B. why bristlecone pines grow in windy areas.

    C. how bristlecone pines got their name.

    D. why bristlecone pines grow to only 60 feet in height.

2. Which statement BEST describes how both passages are alike?

    A. Both describe past events.

    B. Both give personal points of view.

    C. Both describe a problem and how it was solved.

    D. Both provide information about related topics.

3. What kind of information does the second passage MOSTLY provide?

    A. facts and details

    B. personal account

    C. causes and effects

    D. opinions and beliefs

4. What is one difference between the passages?

    A. The first passage tells about events in chronological order; the second passage tells about causes and effects.

    B. The first passage describes all trees; the second passage describes a particular type of tree.

    C. The first passage describes forests in a positive way; the second passage describes forests in a negative way.

    D. The first passage contains facts and explanations; the second passage tells about personal feelings.

5. Explain whether the information in the first passage gives readers a better understanding of information in the second passage.

_____

_____

_____

_____

2 Cumulative Assessment for Lessons 7–15

Read the passage and answer the questions that follow.

John James Audubon

Many people have painted the birds of America, but John James Audubon is said to be the greatest artist ever to have done so. His famous book, *The Birds of America*, is a collection of 435 paintings. These detailed paintings are considered to be the best. For that reason, people judge other wildlife artists by comparing them to Audubon.

Audubon was born on April 26, 1785, in Les Cayes, Santo Domingo (now Haiti). He was the son of a French sea captain and a servant. His mother died when he was still a baby. In 1789, he was taken to France, where he was raised by his father and stepmother. The young Audubon had a happy childhood. He studied math and geography, but he took a greater interest in nature. He loved birds. He spent hours collecting and drawing birds' nests and eggs.

In 1803, at the age of eighteen, Audubon was sent to America. He managed Mill Grove, his family's farm near Philadelphia. He studied and drew birds there. He also met his future wife, Lucy Bakewell. The couple married in 1808. During that time, Audubon performed one of the earliest experiments with banding birds in North America. He tied strings around the legs of one species of migrating bird. By doing this, he learned that the birds returned to the same places to nest every year.

Audubon spent more than ten years at Mill Grove. Then, he traveled down the Ohio River to Henderson, Kentucky, where he opened a store. Still, he continued to draw birds as a hobby. In 1820, Audubon decided to publish a book of bird illustrations. He began collecting and drawing with that goal in mind. Audubon set off on his quest to draw all of America's birds. He traveled first to the South, bringing along his art supplies and an assistant. He had been working mainly with pastels, but around this time, he began to use more watercolors.

In 1826, Audubon sailed to England in hopes of finding a way to publish his book. He successfully showed his work at the Royal Institution in Liverpool. He soon began his project of creating life-size, dramatic portraits of American birds. These portraits showed the birds as they appeared in real life, eating or flying. Audubon traveled back and forth between England and the United States many times over the next few years.

His work, *The Birds of America*, contained 435 hand-colored pictures. It showed a portrait of every bird then known in the United States. Most people were used to seeing birds shown simply, against a blank background. Some people objected to Audubon's use of dramatic poses and settings. Yet his attempt to show birds as they actually looked in the wild was very important. Today, Audubon's colorful paintings are widely admired. Art lovers appreciate their liveliness and realistic qualities.

Audubon had spent eighteen years searching for and observing the birds, creating his book, and selling it to subscribers. After that huge effort, he traveled across the United States a few more times in search of birds. Some say that he saw more of the North American continent than anyone else had before. During his lifetime, he discovered twenty-five new species of birds. He also produced a version of *The Birds of America* that was made up of illustrations that were reduced in size. This book was quite successful. It allowed the artist to retire in comfort. Now famous, Audubon spent his last years in New York City. He died there on January 27, 1851, at the age of sixty-five.

John James Audubon had no relationship with the Audubon Society, an organization that bears his name today. But the name *Audubon* is still connected with birds and nature conservation all over the world.

Some Birds Painted by Audubon

Bird	Appearance	Where It Lives in North America	Interesting Fact
Ivory-billed woodpecker	black and white streaks, red crown, long white bill	southeastern and south central American states	It is the largest woodpecker in North America.
Bald eagle	dark brown body, white head and tail	most of North America	Its name comes from *piebald*, meaning "spotted" or "patchy," which is how bald eagles look when young.
California condor	triangular patches of white on undersides of wings	Southern California, Arizona	It is one of the largest birds in the world.
Brown pelican	brown body, white head, large bill and pouch	southern and Gulf coasts	It is known for its 7-foot wingspan and can live over 40 years.
Barn owl	round face, stubby body, long wingspan	everywhere, except polar and desert areas	It is known for its beautiful plumage and graceful flight.

1. According to the passage, what happened LAST?

   A. Audubon was sent to America.

   B. Audubon moved to New York City.

   C. Audubon was taken to France.

   D. Audubon moved to Kentucky.

2. What is the main idea of this passage?

   A. John James Audubon had no relationship with the Audubon Society.

   B. John James Audubon was America's leading wildlife artist for fifty years.

   C. John James Audubon saw more of the North American continent than anyone else had before.

   D. John James Audubon learned that some birds return to the same nesting sites each year.

3. Both the chart and the passage provide evidence that

   A. Audubon only painted extinct or endangered species of birds.

   B. Audubon won many awards in his lifetime.

   C. Audubon traveled widely to paint different birds.

   D. Audubon was a difficult, unpleasant person.

4. What is the MAIN text structure the writer uses in this passage?

   A. cause and effect

   B. comparison

   C. problem and solution

   D. chronology

Read the passage and answer the questions that follow.

"American White Pelican"

excerpted and adapted from

The Birds of America

by John James Audubon

I feel great pleasure, good reader, in telling you something. Until now, our white pelican has been seen as the same bird as the one found in Europe. But it is quite different. As a result of this discovery, I have honored it with the name of my country. May this splendid bird wander free over its mighty streams.

I first moved to Kentucky more than thirty years ago. At that time, I often saw these birds on the banks of the Ohio River. A few years later, I moved to the town of Henderson. There were so many white pelicans there that I often saw dozens at a time. I found them on a sandbar that protects Canoe Creek Island. During those pleasant days of my youth, how often did I watch them with delight! I think those days have returned to me now. This has allowed me once more to read the scattered notes contained in my treasured journals. Here is one such page:

A hundred large pelicans stand near the sides of the sandbar. They are in small groups. Gorgeous fall colors enrich the leaves of every tree. Their reflections are like fragments of the rainbow. They seem to fill the very depths of the calm and almost sleeping waters of the Ohio River. The red beams of the sun assure me that the Indian summer has started. This happy season is lovely and still. It is also a symbol of the later years of life. To every nature lover, it must be the purest and calmest period of his career.

The full pelicans are patient. They wait for the return of hunger. Should someone chance to watch, one after the other they open their long and broad bills and yawn lazily. Now, the whole length of their largest <u>quills</u> is passed through the bill. At last their feathers are beautifully trimmed. But look! The red beams of the setting sun color the tops of the forest trees. The birds feel the cravings of hunger. To satisfy themselves, they must now work. They rise clumsily on their long legs and waddle heavily to the water. But now, how changed they seem! How lightly they float! They patrol themselves and extend their line. Now, like paddles, their broad feet push them onward.

In another spot, the young birds are dancing in the quiet water. Perhaps in their own way they are bidding farewell to the sun. Or maybe they are seeking something for their supper. There are thousands of them, and they are all happy. The very manner of their joy causes the waters to sparkle. It invites the small fish to come closer, to swim in shallow water. Now the pelicans are aware of their fishy prey. At once, they spread out their broad wings. They press forward with powerful strokes of their feet. They drive the little fishes toward the shore. Then, with the huge pouches under their bills wide open, the pelicans scoop the fishes out and eat them by the thousands.

American white pelican, from *The Birds of America*, by John James Audubon

5. Which is the BEST summary of the passage?

   A. The author remembers a time when he watched a group of pelicans.

   B. The author tells how he discovered a new kind of bird.

   C. The author describes how pelican eat fish.

   D. The author tells about life in Kentucky.

6. Reading through his journals and notebooks, the writer MOST LIKELY feels

   A. sad and lonely.

   B. eager to fight for animal rights.

   C. happy and content.

   D. bored and dissatisfied.

7. Which of the following is a fact from the passage?

   A. "A few years later, I moved to the town of Henderson."

   B. "I feel great pleasure, good reader, in telling you something."

   C. "Gorgeous fall colors enrich the leaves of every tree."

   D. "There are thousands of them, and they are all happy."

8. What does the word <u>quills</u> mean?

   A. beams

   B. feathers

   C. legs

   D. birds

Use "John James Audubon" and "American White Pelican" to answer questions 9–10.

9. Compare the two passages. How does information in the first passage give readers a better understanding of information in the second passage?

    _____

    _____

    _____

    _____

    _____

    _____

10. Which passage could be used as a source for the other passage? Explain.

    _____

    _____

    _____

    _____

    _____

    _____

    _____

CHAPTER

3 Writing

3 Diagnostic Assessment for Lessons 16–20

This passage contains mistakes. Read the passage and answer the questions that follow.

Snowed In

(1) Although the curtains were still closed, Misha could tell it was a bright, sunny day outside. (2) He also knew that it must be very cold. (3) He could hear the sounds of children shouting and laughing. (4) He heard the swishing of their sleds as they zipped down the hill. (5) Misha's dog was named Scout.

(6) Misha looked at his mother. (7) She was standing beside his bed holding a thermometer in her hand. (8) "Did it snow a lot last night?" he asked.

(9) "Yes, more than two feet—which is a new record," she said. (10) "Now open up so I can take your temperature."

(11) The bulb of the thermometer felt icy and slightly bitter under Misha's tongue. (12) Although Misha was sick, the last thing he felt like doing was staying in bed. (13) Now he was getting antsy. (14) His friends was having so much fun! (15) He <u>desperatly</u> wanted to go out and play in the snow, too. (16) He'd been in bed for two whole days.

(17) "Am I still running a fever?" he asked his mother.

(18) "Yes, Misha," his mother said. (19) "I'm sorry to tell you this, but you still have a fever. (20) That means you'll have to stay in bed until you get better."

(21) Misha felt his heart sink. (22) There was nothing in the world more exciting than playing with his friends, but he knew it was out of the question. (23) He pulled the blankets back up over him. (24) He sunk down into his pillows. (25) This was hard.

(26) That evening, Misha ate dinner. (27) He watched a little TV. (28) Then he read a book and fell asleep. (29) Misha awoke the next morning and feels much better. (30) His mother took his temperature just as she had the day before. (31) His curtains were closed. (32) Yet he could hear the children out on the hill, laughing and having fun.

(33) "You don't have a temperature any more," his mother said. (34) "How do you feel?"

(35) "I feel great!" Misha said. (36) "Can I go out and play now?"

(37) "Yes," his mother replied, smiling. (38) "Go out and have fun!"

1. Which sentence does NOT belong in paragraph 1?

   A. He also knew that it must be very cold.

   B. He could hear the sounds of children shouting and laughing.

   C. He heard the swishing of their sleds as they zipped down the hill.

   D. Misha's dog was named Scout.

2. Which sentence is the BEST revision of sentence 29?

   A. When Misha awoke the next morning, he felt much better.

   B. Misha awakes in the morning and feels much better.

   C. Misha was awake in the morning and felt much better.

   D. If Misha awoke the next morning, he felt much better.

3. Which sentence has incorrect subject-verb agreement?

   A. Then he read a book and fell asleep.

   B. His friends was having so much fun!

   C. Misha felt his heart sink.

   D. His mother took his temperature just as she had the day before.

4. What is the correct spelling of the underlined word in sentence 15?

   A. desperately

   B. despertly

   C. desperatelee

   D. desperatelly

5. Which is the BEST way to reorder paragraph 4?

   A. Move sentence 15 before sentence 14.

   B. Move sentence 12 before sentence 11.

   C. Move sentence 16 before sentence 13.

   D. Move sentence 15 before sentence 12.

6. Which of the following is the BEST way to paraphrase sentence 11?

   A. The thermometer felt weird.

   B. The cold bulb of the thermometer tasted bitter.

   C. Misha hates being sick and feels cold.

   D. The thermometer felt cold and tasted bitter in Misha's mouth.

Narrative Prompt

Write a story about a boy (or a girl) who wakes up one day and discovers he has superpowers. Be sure to include characters, a setting, and events in your story. Include description and dialogue to make your story interesting.

Use the checklist below to help you do your best writing.

Does your story

❏ have a situation and characters?

❏ use dialogue and description to develop the story?

❏ have a clear plot?

❏ use good word choice?

❏ have a satisfying ending?

❏ have good spelling, capitalization, and punctuation?

❏ follow the rules for good grammar?

Write your response on the page provided. You may use your own paper if you need more space.

16 Writing Opinions

W.4.1.a–d, W.4.4, W.4.10

Getting the Idea

We write to express our ideas, thoughts, and feelings. An **opinion** is a statement about how you feel about something. Here are some examples of opinions: *Our school needs a new gymnasium. Science is the best subject. Everyone should eat cereal for breakfast.* Each of these statements is a personal belief. They cannot be proven, and other people may disagree with them.

An **argument** is piece of writing that states and defends an opinion. The purpose of an argument is to persuade, or convince, your audience to agree with your opinion.

An effective argument takes a clear position on a topic. You begin by stating your opinion or view in a **position statement**. Suppose you are writing an argument to persuade your school principal to buy new uniforms for the baseball team. Here are two examples of possible position statements for that argument:

Strong Position Statement	Weak Position Statement
Our baseball team's uniforms need to be replaced because they are worn-out and out of style.	I think our baseball team's uniforms sometimes look bad, so the team probably needs new uniforms.

The strong position statement takes a definite stand on the issue. The writing is specific and clear. The weak position statement uses words like *sometimes* and *probably*. The writer does not seem so sure of his opinion.

After writing your position statement, you need to back up it up with reasons that are supported by facts and details. Finally, provide a **concluding statement** to sum up your argument.

Use a graphic organizer to help you plan your essay. An **outline** is a "skeleton" of your essay in list form. In the outline below, the position statement and concluding statement are numbered I and II. You can include as many reasons and details as you want.

I. Our baseball team's uniforms need to be replaced because they are worn-out and out of style.

    A. Uniforms are worn-out.

        1. Some have holes in them.

        2. Some do not fit properly because they are stretched out or shrunken.

    B. Uniforms are out of style.

        1. They do not look like most other teams' baseball uniforms.

        2. The colors of the uniforms do not match the school's colors.

II. If we want to support our baseball team and give them confidence, then they need great new uniforms!

Think about the style of your writing, too. You are trying to convince your audience to agree with your opinion, so remember to write in a formal and respectful tone.

Formal	Informal
Please consider getting us new uniforms this year.	You need to get us cool new duds.

Use **transitions** to achieve a smooth flow of ideas. Use transitional phrases such as *in addition* and *for example* to introduce your reasons and details. Use words such as *first, then, next, however,* and *finally* to connect sentences and paragraphs. That way, your audience will be able to follow your argument more easily.

Finally, carefully proofread your writing. Check for any errors in grammar, spelling, and punctuation, and be sure to correct them.

Coached Example

Read the position statements below. Then rewrite each one so that the positions are clearer to the reader.

> **1.** I think we should get a hamster for a pet, or maybe a bird. I have always wanted a dog, too.

_____

_____

_____

_____

 The writer mentions too many pets. Which pet does the writer really want, and why?

> **2.** I love salad. The cafeteria better give us salad more often.

_____

_____

_____

_____

 This writer does not use a formal style. The audience is probably the principal of the school. How should you write for this kind of audience?

Lesson Practice

Use the Writing Guide to help you understand the passage.

<table>
<tr>
<td>

Writing Guide

The writer's position is clearly stated right away.

Notice the formal language the writer uses. Words such as *please* and *consider* are appropriate for this audience.

Notice how transitional words like *first* and *in addition* connect parts of the writing.

Each paragraph has a strong opening sentence followed by details that support the main idea.

</td>
<td>

Sports for All!

Every student should be required to play a sport. While kids should be allowed to choose the sport they prefer, everyone should play something for at least one season. Some people may think that students who don't like sports should not be required to play, but I think that kids should choose a sport that they like. Please consider making all students join a team. There are so many benefits to sports!

First, playing a sport is a great way to exercise regularly. Exercise is an important part of a healthy lifestyle. Some kids just play video games on the weekends. Sports would help them be more active. Rather than just staying in all day, kids could run around outside and enjoy the fresh air!

In addition, being on a sports team helps build a strong school community. It can be nice to get to know your fellow classmates outside of the classroom. People could make new friends through sports. Usually, students just hang out with the same people every day. Playing a sport forces you to interact with new people.

</td>
</tr>
</table>

Write a concluding statement for this argument.

_____

_____

_____

_____

_____

 HINT What examples does the writer use to support his position? A strong concluding statement should sum up those reasons.

Plan Your Writing

Read the writing prompt, and then plan your response below.

> Think about all the things you like to do in your spare time. Some people play sports. Others play a musical instrument. And some may prefer writing or creating art. Imagine your school is looking for a new after-school activity. Write a letter to your principal in which you propose a new after-school activity. Include reasons, facts, and details that convince the principal to agree with your opinion.

I. Position statement: _____

_____

A. Reason: _____

_____

   1. Detail: _____

_____

   2. Detail: _____

_____

B. Reason: _____

_____

   1. Detail: _____

_____

   2. Detail: _____

_____

II. Concluding statement: _____

_____

Write Your Response

Write your response in the space provided. You may use your own paper if you need more space.

_____

_____

_____

_____

_____

_____

_____

_____

_____

_____

_____

_____

_____

_____

_____

_____

_____

_____

_____

_____

_____

_____

_____

_____

_____

_____

_____

17 Writing Informational Texts

W.4.2.a–e, 4-W.4.4, W.4.10, L.4.6

Getting the Idea

The purpose of an **informational text** is to provide the reader with facts and details about a topic. You read informational texts every day. When you read from your science or social studies textbooks, you are reading informational texts. Newspapers are filled with informational text. You probably also write informational texts in the form of reports for school.

When writing an informational piece, you should begin with a clear statement of your topic, provide facts and details to support that topic, and close with a **concluding statement** about the information you just explained.

One kind of graphic organizer you can use to help you plan your informational writing is a **web**. For example, suppose you were planning to write an informative paragraph about the country of Brazil. Your completed web might look like this:

The main topic is shown in the center circle. The subtopics are categories of information about Brazil—its cities, climate, special events, and landscape. They are connected to the main circle. The outer circles contain details about each subtopic.

Once you have organized your text, it is time to write. You will probably want to add small details as you put your information into sentences. Your **topic sentence** should clearly state what your paragraph is about. For example, if you write "Brazil is an interesting country in South America," details should include the specific kinds of weather and the names of the cities.

In longer informational articles, the text is often divided into sections with bold **headings** that say what the section is about. Each paragraph should have a topic sentence that tells what that paragraph is mainly about. Each sentence that follows should provide information that supports the topic sentence. For example, you can use any of the following:

- Fact: a true statement about something that can be proved
- Detail: descriptive information about a topic
- Quotation: specific words said by someone. The speakers' words are put in quotation marks. For example: President Franklin D. Roosevelt said, "The only thing we have to fear is fear itself."
- Example: something that represents the point you are trying to make. If you were writing about good citizenship, you could include voting as an example.

Connect your facts, details, quotations, and examples with linking words, as shown on the chart below.

If you want to show…	use transitions like…
comparison	similarly, also, like
difference, or contrast	on the other hand, but, however
examples	for example, for instance
more examples	in addition to, as well, further

Try to use the vocabulary, or words, that fit the subject area you are writing about. For example, in science, some words might include *data* or *experiments*. *Data* is information. *Experiments* are tests or trials to prove something. In social studies, some terms might include: *population* (how many people live in a location), *government* (the people running a country or state), *culture*, or *transportation*.

Watch for any mistakes in grammar, spelling, and punctuation. To pass on correct information to your readers, it is best to write it in the clearest way possible.

Coached Example

Read the paragraphs and answer the questions.

> Alligators have long bodies and short legs. Their feet are webbed, which helps them swim. Alligators are fierce hunters who eat only meat.

1.   Write a topic sentence for this paragraph.

_____

_____

_____

  A topic sentence tells what the whole paragraph is about.

> A food chain shows how living things get and use energy. Simple food chains exist in our own backyards. The grass uses the sun's energy to make food. A bird eats grass from the lawn. Then your neighbor's cat eats the bird. Most cats eat fish. That's a food chain!

2.   Which sentence does NOT support the topic sentence of the paragraph?

_____

_____

_____

_____

  Think about what the main idea of the paragraph is. Find the sentence that does not relate to that idea.

Lesson Practice

Use the Writing Guide to help you understand the passage.

Writing Guide

The title of the passage gives you an idea about what the passage will be about.

The writer points out the example of getting a cat or a fish and uses the linking words *for example*.

Words such as *exercise* and *diet* are appropriate for this topic.

Owning a Pet

Many families own pets and enjoy caring for them. The responsibilities of owning a pet are often shared by children and parents. There are some things to keep in mind when you open up your heart and home to a new pet.

First, decide what kind of pet to get. If you live in a small apartment, a large dog that needs room to run around is not the best choice. Dogs need to go on walks. If this is a job that you cannot commit to, then a pet that does not need walking would be better for your lifestyle. For example, a cat, a hamster, or fish are possibilities.

In order for a pet to stay healthy, it needs to get enough exercise. Pets also need the right kind and right amount of food. An animal's diet is usually also based on how large, how active, and how old it is. The wrong diet can make a pet overweight, lazy, or sick.

Most people agree that owning a pet involves a lot of work. But if you ask any pet owners, they will say it is well worth it!

What is the main idea of this informational text?

_____

_____

_____

_____

_____

HINT   Look for the topic sentence at the beginning of the passage.

Plan Your Writing

Read the writing prompt, and then plan your response below.

Choose a place that you like to visit. For example, it could be a relative's house, a park, or someplace farther away that you have been to with your family. Write an informative piece about this place. Tell where it is, what it looks like, and what you do there. Include details about the place to support your writing.

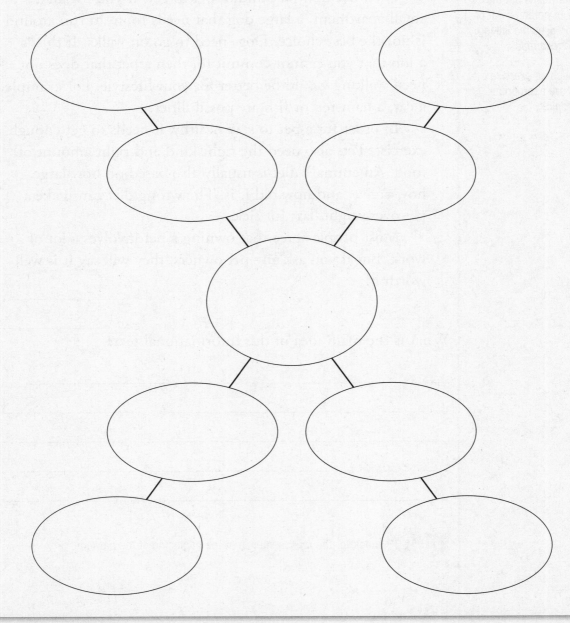

Write Your Response

Write your response in the space provided. You may use your own paper if you need more space.

_____

_____

_____

_____

_____

_____

_____

_____

_____

_____

_____

_____

_____

_____

_____

_____

_____

_____

_____

_____

_____

_____

_____

_____

_____

_____

_____

_____

18 Writing Narratives

W.4.3.a–e, W.4.4, W.4.10

Getting the Idea

The purpose of **narrative text** is to entertain the reader with a story. Every novel or story you have ever read is an example of a narrative text.

When you write a narrative, you use characters, setting, and plot. The **characters** are the people in your story. The **setting** is where and when your story takes place. The **plot** is the series of events that take place in the story.

A plot includes three main parts: the beginning, where you meet the characters and learn the main problem, or conflict; the middle, where the characters try to solve the problem; and the conclusion, the part where the story ends and you see how the characters did or did not solve the problem.

One way to make your story more interesting is to use **descriptions** of the people and places you are writing about. Vivid descriptions appeal to the reader's five senses: touch, taste, smell, sight, and hearing. Here are some examples:

Sense	Description
sight	the lake glittering like a shiny mirror
smell	the sweet aroma of warm apple pie
taste	the salty crunch of a pickle
touch	a sweater as soft as a kitten's fur
hearing	music hammering inside my head

When planning a narrative, remember that a plot usually follows a particular order, or **sequence**. Each event comes after the one before. A helpful graphic organizer for this kind of writing is a flowchart. A **flowchart** shows the order of events in a story from start to finish. A flowchart can be horizontal (left to right) or vertical (top to bottom). Read this flowchart.

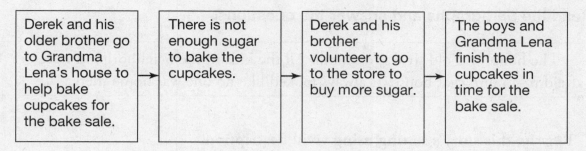

Notice what is written in each box of the flowchart. You can see what happens in each event, or part, of the story. Planning your story on a flowchart first will help you to write it in paragraphs later.

The arrows on the flowchart represent the links from one event to the next. Of course, when you write, you use words instead of arrows to move your narrative along. The chart below shows some sequence words you can use.

Sequence Words	Examples
first, once	Derek and his older brother first went to Grandma Lena's house to help her get ready for the bake sale.
then, next	Then, they realized there wasn't enough sugar for the cupcakes.
finally, at last	Finally, the boys went to the store to buy more sugar.

You can add to your narrative by using dialogue. **Dialogue** is the words that the characters say to each other. Dialogue makes the characters come alive on the page. Notice the use of commas, quotation marks, and capital letters in the following dialogue:

"Would you like a piece of pie?" Grandma asked.

"Yes, please," Derek replied. "Thank you."

Be sure your narrative has a conclusion. This is also called the resolution, where mysteries and problems are solved and all loose ends are tied up.

Coached Example

Read the paragraphs and answer the questions.

> The house was old. It was on a hill. All the kids in the neighborhood were afraid to go into that house. It always looked like no one was home there.

1. Rewrite this story's setting using vivid description.

_____

_____

_____

_____

 Your description should relate to one or more of the five senses: touch, taste, smell, sight, and hearing.

> On Saturday, Sara saw Minh at the park. The girls looked at each other for a long time.
> "I can't believe I haven't seen you all summer!" Minh exclaimed.
> "I know," replied Sara. "What have you been doing these past few months?"

2. Add dialogue to continue the conversation between the characters.

_____

_____

_____

_____

 Put quotation marks around the words each character says. End punctuation should be inside the quotation marks.

Lesson Practice

Use the Writing Guide to help you understand the passage.

Writing Guide

The setting of the story is Keiko's neighborhood. What words help you to know the setting?

What is Keiko's main problem in the story? How does she solve it?

Notice the quotation marks around the characters' spoken words.

Looks Aren't Everything

Keiko looked around nervously. She hadn't seen the big gray dog yet, but it always seemed to show up at some point on her walk home from school.

Everything felt new to her lately. Keiko and her family had recently moved to California from Japan. The kids at school seemed to be from another planet. As she came to her block, Keiko saw her neighbor, Mrs. Landis, wave to her.

"How is school going?" Mrs. Landis asked with a smile.

"Not bad," Keiko began. Then she heard a bark. Her head jerked up, and she saw the big gray dog running toward them. Suddenly, the dog stopped right in front of Mrs. Landis.

"Do you know this dog?" asked Keiko, backing away.

"Oh, yes. Ben's a good dog," said Mrs. Landis. "He wouldn't hurt a fly."

"But he's so big," said Keiko, still staring at the dog.

Mrs. Landis smiled again. "Looks aren't everything, you know. It's what's underneath that really counts. And Ben has a heart of gold. Right, boy?"

Keiko smiled. She hadn't given Ben a fair chance—just like the kids at school. Slowly, she reached out to pet Ben's back. "Hello, Ben. I'm Keiko. It's nice to meet you."

What lesson does Keiko learn at the conclusion of this story?

_____

_____

_____

_____

HINT Keiko's main problem in the story is her fear of the big gray dog. This problem gets solved in the conclusion.

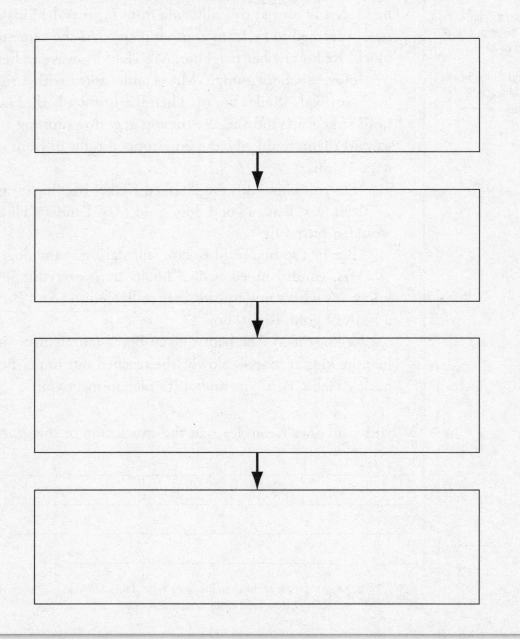

Plan Your Writing

Read the writing prompt, and then plan your response below.

Write a story about a boy or girl who wins a contest. Tell what kind of contest it is. Describe the main character. Tell how the character wins the contest. Finally, tell what happens after the contest is over. What prize does the winner receive? Plan the events in your narrative. Be sure to include description and dialogue to make your story interesting.

Write Your Response

Write your response in the space provided. You may use your own paper if you need more space.

_____

_____

_____

_____

_____

_____

_____

_____

_____

_____

_____

_____

_____

_____

_____

_____

_____

_____

_____

_____

_____

_____

_____

_____

19 Revising, Editing, and Publishing

W.4.5, W.4.6

Getting the Idea

No matter what you write, you should always review your work. **Revising** and editing your writing can make it better. Parents, teachers, older siblings, and even other classmates can often make helpful suggestions. Read this paragraph.

> The weather is cold outside, and I plant seeds in small containers. I make sure they have enough sunlight. They sit in the sun. The seeds sprout and the weather is warm enough. I put the plants in the ground. We have fresh vegetables to eat! Peas are my favorite vegetable. Then I watch them grow.

There are some problems with this paragraph. First, it needs a topic sentence. Some sentences are out of order and repetitive. The paragraph needs transitions to help the reader move from one idea to the next. One sentence does not belong in the paragraph. It also needs a concluding sentence at the end. Read this revised paragraph.

> I grow vegetables in my backyard. While the weather is still cold outside, I plant seeds in small containers. I make sure they have enough sunlight. When the seeds sprout and the weather is warm enough, I put the plants in the ground. Then I watch them grow. By the end of summer, we have fresh vegetables to eat!

The **topic sentence** tells you what the paragraph is about. The sentence *They sit in the sun* has been deleted because it repeats an earlier sentence. Notice the words *while, when, then,* and *by the end.* They connect ideas and help the writing to flow. The last two sentences have been reordered, so the ideas make more sense. The sentence about the peas has been deleted because it does not relate to the main idea. The concluding sentence sums up the ideas in the paragraph. All of these revisions greatly improve the writing.

When you **edit**, you look for mistakes such as words that are not spelled correctly, missing or incorrect punctuation, or errors in grammar.

Spelling can be tricky. Pay attention to plurals. Many nouns form their plurals by adding -s (friend—friends). When pluralizing nouns ending in -s, -z, -x, -sh, or -ch, add -es (gas—gases, fox—foxes, branch—branches). For nouns ending in -y, drop the -y and add -ies (memory—memories). Here are some more words and their plurals: tomato—tomatoes, foot—feet, deer—deer.

When you learn a new word, learn how it is spelled, too. For example, see how these words are spelled: *celebrate, organize, fraction, ingredient, university.* Keep a dictionary nearby when you read or write, so you can look up the correct spelling of unfamiliar words.

Check your punctuation. Sentences should end with a period, a question mark, or an exclamation point. Use quotation marks around a speaker's words.

"Our team won by two points," said Levon.

Subject-verb agreement is an important part of grammar. The **subject** is the person or thing doing the action in a sentence. The **verb** is the action word. If the subject is singular, the verb must be singular. If the subject is plural, the verb must be plural.

Singular: <u>Brad</u> happily <u>hugs</u> his brother.
Plural: <u>Brad and Joe</u> happily <u>hug</u> their brother.

The **tense** of a verb tells you the time in which the action takes place—present, past, or future. Regular past-tense verbs end in -ed. Some past-tense verbs are irregular. They do not end in -ed. Future-tense verbs are paired with the helping verb *will.*

Thinking It Through

Read the following passage, and then answer the question that follows.

One unusual pizza topping is macaroni and cheese. It is a favorite in Wisconsin. Another type is mashed potatoes. This topping is often eaten in Brazil. Perhaps the weirdest topping is found in Japan. It is squid. (A squid is a sea animal.) The next time you get bored with pepperoni, think about trying one of these unique varieties.

Write a topic sentence for this paragraph.

_____

_____

_____

HINT   What is the main idea of this paragraph? What sentence could sum up that idea?

Coached Example

Read the passage and answer the questions.

(1) Visiting Abuela, my grandma, in New York City is so much fun! (2) The <u>nieghborhood</u> she lives in has so many things to see and do. (3) For example, local artists have painted beautiful murals on some of the buildings. (4) We also like to visit different bodegas to find the most unusual one. (5) A bodega is a grocery store. (6) We like to look at the murals together. (7) As fun as all those activities are, my favorite one is playing street ball with the neighborhood kids while Abuela cheers me on. (8) I love visiting Abuela. (9) There is never a dull moment when I stay with her.

---

1. Read this sentence from the passage.

    The <u>nieghborhood</u> she lives in has so many things to see and do.

    What is the correct spelling of the underlined word in the sentence?

    A. nieghburhood

    B. neighborhood

    C. neighborhod

    D. neiborhood

     Words with a long *e* (rhymes with *me*) are spelled *ie*, and words that have a sound other than a long *e* generally are spelled *ei*. What sound do you hear in the first syllable of the underlined word?

2. What is the BEST way to reorder the passage?

    A. Move sentence 3 before sentence 2.

    B. Move sentence 9 before sentence 8.

    C. Move sentence 6 before sentence 4.

    D. Move sentence 4 before sentence 3.

    HINT Reread the part about the murals. Which sentence seems out of place?

Lesson Practice

This passage contains mistakes. Use the Reading Guide to help you find the mistakes.

Reading Guide

When does this story take place: the past, present, or future? Look at the action words in the sentences to help you figure it out. Now look at sentence 12. Is the tense of the verbs correct?

Suppose Jeremiah had been given more than one puppy in sentence 4. What is the plural of *puppy*? How do you spell it?

Look at sentences 8 and 9. The dad is speaking in both sentences. How would you correct the punctuation?

Look at sentence 19. The subject is Jeremiah. Does it agree with the verb that follows it?

Reread the last paragraph. Is there a sentence that does not seem to belong with the rest of the story?

A Dream Come True

(1) Jeremiah begged his dad for a pet again and again. (2) He was an only child, so he wanted a playmate. (3) A week ago, Jeremiah's wish was finally granted. (4) His dad came home with the cutest puppy Jeremiah ever saw. (5) Jeremiah could hardly believe it! (6) He named the puppy Linus.

(7) "Thanks, Dad!" Jeremiah exclaimed.

(8) It was my pleasure, buddy, his dad replied. (9) "But remember, you promised to take care of him all by yourself."

(10) Jeremiah nodded. (11) Minutes later, he raced outside to teach Linus how to fetch. (12) They run around in the yard together for what seems like forever. (13) Jeremiah couldn't remember the last time he was so happy.

(14) The next week was a blur for Jeremiah as he got used to his new responsibilitys. (15) These included playing, walking, and feeding. (16) He never realized owning a dog was so much work. (17) He had to take care of Linus every day.

(18) Linus was a great friend, though. (19) Jeremiah love to watch him run and play. (20) The best part was that Linus seemed to enjoy keeping Jeremiah company, no matter what he did. (21) Jeremiah had a lot of homework. (22) Linus was Jeremiah's dream come true. (23) He had a terrific new friend!

Answer the following questions.

1. Read this sentence from the passage.

   The next week was a blur for Jeremiah as he got used to his new responsibilitys.

   What is the correct spelling of the underlined word?

   A. responsibilities

   B. responsibilitees

   C. responsabilities

   D. responsabilitys

2. Read this sentence from the passage.

   It was my pleasure, buddy, his dad replied

   What is the correct way to write this sentence?

   A. "It was my pleasure, buddy, his dad replied."

   B. "It was my pleasure, buddy," his dad replied.

   C. "It was my pleasure," buddy, his dad replied.

   D. "It was my pleasure, buddy." his dad replied.

3. Which sentence has incorrect subject-verb agreement?

   A. He was an only child, so he wanted a playmate.

   B. Minutes later, he raced outside to teach Linus how to fetch.

   C. Jeremiah love to watch him run and play.

   D. Linus was Jeremiah's dream come true.

4. Which sentence does NOT belong in the last paragraph?

   A. He had a terrific new friend!

   B. The best part was that Linus seemed to enjoy keeping Jeremiah company, no matter what he did.

   C. Jeremiah had a lot of homework.

   D. Linus was Jeremiah's dream come true.

5. How does the writer use transitions in the passage to connect ideas? Give examples from the passage.

   _____

   _____

   _____

20 Research and Resources

W.4.7, W.4.8

Getting the Idea

Imagine you have to write a report for your social studies class. You know you want to learn more about Uganda, a country in Africa. So, where do you start? First you need to narrow your topic. What specifically about Uganda do you want to know?

Let's say you decide to research what school is like in Uganda. When you do **research**, you gather information about a topic. You can organize your research by looking at your topic from different angles. For example, you might ask questions such as: How are schools in Uganda similar to schools in the United States? How are schools in Uganda different from schools in the United States?

Now that you know *what* you want to find out, *where* are you going to find the information? There are several print and online **resources** to look at, such as the ones in the chart below.

Resources	
almanac	an online or print collection of information for a given year
atlas	an online or print collection of maps and geographical information
encyclopedia	an online or print collection of short articles about many topics, organized in alphabetical order by topic
newspaper	an online or print collection of articles about current events, usually published daily
Web site	an online page of information that can be published by almost anyone

Be sure that the information you find is reliable and accurate. One way to do this is to use more than one resource. Then, you can see if the information in your main resource is backed up by information in another. If it is not, check a third resource. When doing research on a computer, remember that not all Web sites are trustworthy. The most reliable Web sites have addresses that end in *.gov*, *.edu*, or *.org*.

Once you have located your resources, it is time to take notes. As you read, organize and label your notes based on the information they provide. For a report about schools in Uganda, for example, you might organize and label your notes into two categories: similarities and differences.

An important rule of research is never to copy what you read. Instead, **paraphrase**, or restate the information in your own words. Look at the examples below.

Original Source	Paraphrased Statement
The typical school day starts at 7:30 A.M. and does not end until 5:30 P.M.	Most students begin school at 7:30 in the morning and return home at 5:30 in the afternoon.
Sports are a popular after-school pastime.	Students like to play sports when the school day is done.

Though you are paraphrasing the author's original words, it is still important that you give credit to the authors whose information you used to write your report. As you work, keep a list of every resource you use. A **bibliography** is an organized list of resources on a topic. Each entry in a bibliography should include the book's title, author, and place and date of publication. A bibliography is alphabetized by the authors' last names.

The following is a partial bibliography that a student used when researching schools in Uganda. Notice that titles of articles are put in quotation marks. Titles of books are underlined.

Martin, Roger. <u>Education Around the Globe</u>. Chicago: World Press, 2009.

Smith, Leena. "Studying in Uganda." <u>Schools Throughout the World</u>. New York City: Smart Publishing, 2008.

Thinking It Through

Read the following paragraph, and then answer the question that follows.

People use many different kinds of transportation, or ways to get around. Cars, buses, and trucks are the most popular kinds of road transportation. Other ways to travel include jet planes and helicopters, railroad trains, and subways that run underground. In some cities, people ride in pedicabs, which are tricycles with passenger seats attached.

Paraphrase the information in the paragraph.

_____

_____

_____

_____

_____

 HINT   Remember to use your own words to paraphrase a source.

Coached Example

Read the passage and answer the questions.

The mantis is an insect. It gets the nickname "praying mantis" from the way it holds its front legs. They are bent up and pressed together, as if the insect were praying. Actually, the mantis uses these front legs to grab and hold its prey.

It takes a sharp eye to spot a mantis. This is because these insects look a lot like twigs, leaves, or blades of grass. Their thin brown or green bodies blend in with their environment. Their camouflage serves two purposes. It helps them hide from predators. It also helps them stay hidden until their prey gets close enough to grab and eat.

Like ladybugs, mantises are "good" garden insects. They do not eat plants. Instead, they eat the insects that would eat the plants. In this way, they can naturally help control pests in the garden.

---

1. Which of the following is the BEST way to paraphrase paragraph 3?

   A. Mantises can naturally help control pests in the garden.

   B. Like ladybugs, mantises are "good" garden insects.

   C. Mantises are good to have around because they eat other insects.

   D. Mantises are good in the garden because they eat insects that eat plants.

   HINT A paraphrase should include all the important information from the original text. Be sure it is in your own words.

2. Where would you look for more information about the mantis?

   A. almanac

   B. atlas

   C. encyclopedia

   D. newspaper

   HINT Choose a resource that contains short articles about a lot of different topics.

Use the Reading Guide to help you understand the passage.

Reading Guide

If you wanted to learn more about the Roman goddess Venus, which resource would you use?

As you read, think of how you would categorize the information in each paragraph. What is each paragraph mainly about?

What kinds of resources would provide the most reliable information about *Mariner 2*?

Earth's Bright Neighbor

by Janice Wheeler

Venus is the only planet with a female's name. It gets its name from Venus, the Roman goddess of love and beauty. The other planets, except for Earth, get their names from Greek or Roman gods. Venus is special in other ways, too.

Venus is worthy of a name meaning "beauty." For us on Earth, Venus is the brightest object in the night sky besides the moon. Venus shines brightest just before sunrise and just after sunset. For this reason, it has been called "the morning star" and "the evening star."

Why is Venus so bright? There are two main reasons. One is the blanket of clouds that surrounds the planet. These clouds reflect sunlight back out into space. Another reason is its closeness to Earth. Venus is the second planet from the sun, and Earth is third. Venus's brightness is close enough to dazzle us.

Until the mid-1900s, details of Venus's surface were a mystery. The cloud blanket blocked any view of the planet's surface. People wondered if Venus was suitable for human life, or if it had any life of its own. The possibilities were fascinating.

In 1962, the United States sent a robotic space probe to Venus. The *Mariner 2* measured the surface temperature of Venus. It was 797 degrees Fahrenheit! In contrast, Earth's surface temperature is just under 60 degrees Fahrenheit. We won't be living on Venus anytime soon.

Answer the following questions.

1. Which of the following is NOT related to the topic of the passage?

   A. the planets in the solar system

   B. Greek and Roman god names

   C. living conditions on planets

   D. ways to time travel

2. If you wanted to see a map of where the United States is on Earth, which resource would you use?

   A. almanac

   B. atlas

   C. encyclopedia

   D. newspaper

3. Which is the BEST way to label notes from paragraph 3?

   A. why Venus is so bright

   B. how Venus got its name

   C. what the surface of Venus is like

   D. why humans cannot live on Venus

4. Which is the correct bibliography entry for this passage?

   A. "Earth's Bright Neighbor" by Janis Wheeler, 2009.

   B. Janis Wheeler. "Earth's Bright Neighbor." Our Solar System.

   C. "Earth's Bright Neighbor." Wheeler, Janis. Boston" Science Times, 2009.

   D. Wheeler, Janis. "Earth's Bright Neighbor." Our Solar System. Boston: Science Times, 2009.

5. Paraphrase paragraph 1 of the passage on the lines below.

   _____

   _____

   _____

   _____

   _____

3 Cumulative Assessment for Lessons 16–20

This passage contains mistakes. Read the passage and answer the questions that follow.

Gandhi

(1) Mohandas K. Gandhi was a famous leader in India. (2) He helped India to become an <u>independint</u> nation. (3) India was not a free country from 1869 to 1948. (4) Indian food is delicious. (5) India was such an important part of the British Empire that it was called "the jewel in the crown." (6) Queen Victoria did not want to lose control of India because trade with India was a rich source of money for the British Empire.

(7) Gandhi was born in India. (8) He went to school in Great Britain. (9) Then he became a leader who wanted to have a free India. (10) He dressed like an Englishman there, and shortly afterwards he returned to India. (11) He dressed in a simple white wrap of Indian cotton. (12) He refused to wear cloth made in Britain.

(13) Gandhi believed that India should not try to become free by fighting. (14) He will want Great Britain to free India. (15) Gandhi felt certain that India could persuade the British peacefully. (16) Soon, he led his people on a 200-mile-long walk to protest the British tax on salt. (17) He led people all the way to the coast. (18) They reached the ocean and made salt from the seawater. (19) They showed the British that Indians did not need to use British salt.

(20) Gandhi planned and led many protests. (21) He was arrested many times for participating in these activities. (22) Sadly, he died before Great Britain freed India. (23) Most people gives Gandhi credit for India becoming free.

1. Which sentence does NOT belong in paragraph 1?

   A. Indian food is delicious.

   B. India was such an important part of the British Empire that it was called "the jewel in the crown."

   C. India was not a free country from 1869 to 1948.

   D. Mohandas K. Gandhi was a famous leader in India.

2. Which sentence is the BEST revision of sentence 16?

   A. Later, he led his people on a 200-mile-long walk to protest the British tax on salt.

   B. Once, he led his people on a 200-mile-long walk to protest the British tax on salt.

   C. Next, he led his people on a 200-mile-long walk to protest the British tax on salt.

   D. Finally, he led his people on a 200-mile-long walk to protest the British tax on salt.

3. Which sentence has incorrect subject-verb agreement?

   A. He dressed like an Englishman there, and shortly after, he returned to India.

   B. Then he became a leader who wanted to have a free India.

   C. He dressed in a simple white wrap of Indian cotton.

   D. Most people gives Gandhi credit for India becoming free.

4. Which is the correct spelling of the underlined word in sentence 2?

   A. indapendent

   B. independence

   C. indupendent

   D. independent

5. Which is the BEST way to reorder paragraph 2?

    A. Move sentence 8 before sentence 7.

    B. Move sentence 12 before sentence 10.

    C. Move sentence 10 before sentence 9.

    D. Move sentence 11 before sentence 10.

6. Which is the BEST way to paraphrase sentence 6?

    A. The British Empire made money from trading with India, so Queen Victoria wanted to keep India under her control.

    B. Queen Victoria wanted to keep India because the British Empire saw it as a rich source of money.

    C. The British Empire knew India was a rich source of money, so Queen Victoria did not want to lose control of the country.

    D. Losing control of India would be bad for Queen Victoria because the British Empire would lose a lot of money.

Informational Prompt

Write an informational piece about your favorite holiday. Tell what the holiday is, at what time in the year it falls, how you celebrate it, and why it is your favorite. Be sure to include facts and details about the holiday to support your writing. Use the checklist below to help you do your best writing.

Does your essay

- ❏ have a clear and focused subject?
- ❏ have a logical structure?
- ❏ present information clearly?
- ❏ use linking words and phrases to join ideas?
- ❏ use a style and vocabulary that is correct for the audience and purpose?
- ❏ have a solid conclusion?
- ❏ have good spelling, capitalization, and punctuation?
- ❏ follow the rules for good grammar?

Write your response on the page provided. You may use your own paper if you need more space.

CHAPTER

4 Language

Chapter 4: Diagnostic Assessment for Lessons 21–34

Chapter 4: Cumulative Assessment for Lessons 21–34

4 Diagnostic Assessment for Lessons 21–34

This passage contains mistakes. Read the passage and answer the questions that follow.

How to Pack for a Trip

(1) Have you ever gone on a trip somewhere? (2) It's so exciting to get ready for a trip away from home! (3) Whether it is a short weekend at a relative's house or an extended stay in a foreign <u>location</u>, traveling can be a great way to relax. (4) But what should you bring with you on your trip? (5) There are so many things to think about. (6) What will you <u>where</u>? (7) What kinds of personal items do you need? (8) Are there other things to bring along, too?

(9) The first thing to consider when planning what to pack is your Destination. (10) Are you going somewhere tropical and warm like Aruba, or someplace cooler like Alaska? (11) Be sure to pack clothing that is appropriate for the weather. (12) Even if you are going somewhere warm, bring at least one long-sleeved shirt in case the temperature drops at night. (13) Likewise, when traveling somewhere cold, bring a cotton, comfortable T-shirt in case the weather warms up. (14) Shoes are also an important part of your wardrobe. (15) Bring sandals for warm weather. (16) Heavy boots for the cold.

(17) Don't forget the following personal items soap, toothbrush, toothpaste, and shampoo. (18) You may also want to bring a book to keep you entertained. (19) Music may help you as well. (20) Some travelers bring a journal who they use to record all the details of their trip. (21) Keep your journal under your backpack. (22) If this is your first trip, you may want to think about writing down your experiences each day. (23) That way, you can remember your trip after you've come home. (24) You can also share your experiences with friends and family. (25) Try to bring a camera to snap some pictures of special things you see. (26) It's a wonderful way to remember your trip.

(27) Whatever corner of the world you're off to, happy travels! (28) Remember, the best part of traveling is whom you meet. (29) Especially when you were visiting a new place, people can be so helpful! (30) Have a great time on all your adventures!

1. Which word from paragraph 2 is NOT capitalized correctly?

   A. Alaska

   B. Aruba

   C. Destination

   D. Likewise

2. Which of the following is the correct revision of sentence 17?

   A. Don't forget the following personal items, soap, toothbrush, toothpaste, and shampoo.

   B. Don't forget the following personal items: soap, toothbrush, toothpaste, and shampoo.

   C. Don't forget the following personal items; soap, toothbrush, toothpaste, and shampoo.

   D. Don't forget the following personal items "soap, toothbrush, toothpaste, and shampoo."

3. The correct spelling of the underlined word in sentence 6 is

   A. ware.

   B. were.

   C. we're.

   D. wear.

4. Which of the following is a NOT a complete sentence?

   A. What will you wear?

   B. Heavy boots for the cold.

   C. Music may help you as well.

   D. Have a great time on all your adventures!

5. What is the correct way to write the verb in sentence 29?

   A. are visiting

   B. should visit

   C. will visit

   D. was visiting

6. What is the correct way to write sentence 13?

    A. Likewise, when traveling somewhere cold, bring T-shirt of cotton and comfortable in case the weather warms up.

    B. Likewise, when traveling somewhere cold, bring a T-shirt of more comfortable cotton in case the weather warms up.

    C. Likewise, when traveling somewhere cold, bring a comfortable and cotton T-shirt in case the weather warms up.

    D. Likewise, when traveling somewhere cold, bring a comfortable cotton T-shirt in case the weather warms up.

7. How could sentence 20 be corrected?

    A. Change *who* to *whom*.

    B. Change *who* to *which*.

    C. Change *they* to *we*

    D. Change *their* to *our*.

8. What is the BEST way to rewrite sentence 21?

    A. Keep your journal in your backpack.

    B. Keep your journal above your backpack.

    C. Keep your journal on your backpack.

    D. Keep your journal next to your backpack.

9. What is the suffix in the word <u>location</u>? What does the word <u>location</u> MOST LIKELY mean?

_____

_____

_____

_____

Read the passage and answer the questions that follow.

Matthew's Sunday

Matthew was not having a good day. It was Sunday morning and he was supposed to be going to the mall. But he couldn't find his running shoes anywhere, and his favorite jeans were dirty. Outside, clouds were gathering. But the biggest problem was that Matthew didn't want to go to the mall. He had a new puppy, Jasper, which his family had adopted from the animal rescue. Jasper's fur was as white as snow. Matthew already taught Jasper how to sit on command.

"Woof!" Jasper barked, at the foot of Matthew's bed. The puppy shivered with excitement, as if he knew that Matthew was thinking about him. Jasper bounced around Matthew's legs like a jumping bean. The thought of having to leave his pup to go to the mall was putting Matthew in a cranky mood. Just then, Sam, Matthew's older brother, popped his head in the doorway. He seemed as happy as could be.

"Ready, Jubilee?" Jubilee was Matthew's nickname.

"No," Matthew said, frowning, "I'm not."

Then Matthew hatched a plan. He clutched his stomach and stretched his mouth into a fairly fearsome-looking frown. "I don't feel very good. My stomach hurts," Matthew groaned. He got on his bed, stomach first. He stayed there, hoping Sam would go away. But Sam just stood there.

"Mom!" Sam hollered. "Matthew is being difficult."

Matthew heard his mother's footsteps as she walked down the hall toward his room.

"What's the deal, Matthew Timothy Jones?"

Matthew felt nervous. The only time his mother called him by his full name was when he was about to get into trouble. Matthew eyed his mother from the safety of his bed. She did not look pleased. Jasper was now in his dog bed, with his head between his paws. He looked as unhappy and <u>forlorn</u> as Matthew.

"Why are you in your pajamas?" his mother asked. "I told you last night at dinner that we were going shopping today."

"I don't think I should go to the mall," Matthew whined, rubbing his belly. "I don't feel well."

Matthew's mother walked over and put her hand to his forehead.

"You don't feel like you have a fever, Jubilee," his mother said.

"It's my stomach," Matthew complained, sitting up. "It's burbling inside. My stomach is like a battlefield. I'm afraid it will get worse if I don't rest."

Jasper jumped up beside Matthew, nudging his hand with his cold, wet nose. Matthew nearly laughed, but let out a burst of air that sounded like a half-cough, half-snort instead.

"See?" Matthew pointed to his throat. "It's getting worse already."

Matthew's mother eyed Sam, who was standing in the doorway, shaking his head.

"All right," she said. "Sam, let's go to the mall. Your brother should stay at home with Dad, as it seems that he needs to rest."

Before shutting the door, Matthew's mother turned back to look at him. He was now under the covers, and Jasper was underneath them, too, walking beside Matthew's legs like a lumpy ghost. Seconds after the door closed, Matthew whipped off the blankets.

"Hurray!" he whisper-shouted to Jasper, who was sniffing one of Matthew's pillows. "We did it! We get to spend the afternoon together!"

Jasper was just as excited as Matthew was, and jumped on the floor to do his jumping-bean dance again. Matthew danced in the middle of his room, hopping from one foot to another, trying to imitate Jasper. Right then, Matthew's door opened. Matthew's mother stood there, with Sam right behind her. She had her hands on her hips and looked <u>furious</u>. Without another word, Matthew walked to his dresser. He pulled out a pair of jeans and a shirt, and then he went to his closet and grabbed a pair of socks and shoes.

"Matthew, grow up. Meet us in the car in five minutes, please," his mother said, before turning to walk down the hallway.

"Yes, ma'am," Matthew answered. Then Matthew looked at Jasper and said, "Well, you win some, you lose some." And with those words, Matthew's Sunday was decided.

10. Read this sentence from the passage.

Jasper bounced around Matthew's legs like a jumping bean.

What does the simile in the sentence mean?

A. Jasper looked like a bean.

B. Matthew's legs were shaking.

C. Jasper ran in circles around Matthew's legs.

D. Jasper bounced energetically and quickly.

11. What is the BEST way to paraphrase the adage <u>you win some, you lose some</u>?

A. Sometimes things don't go your way.

B. The most important thing is winning.

C. Play the best game you can.

D. Listen to the advice of others.

12. What is a synonym for the word <u>furious</u>?

   A. worried

   B. waiting

   C. angry

   D. patient

13. Read this sentence from the passage.

> **He <u>got</u> on his bed, stomach first.**

Which word would make the underlined word more precise?

   A. was

   B. flopped

   C. stayed

   D. sat

14. Read this sentence from the passage.

He looked as unhappy and <u>forlorn</u> as Matthew.

What does the word <u>forlorn</u> mean? What context clue helped you figure out the meaning of the word?

_____

_____

_____

_____

21 Verbs and Verb Tenses

L.4.1.b, L.4.1.c

Getting the Idea

A **verb** is a word that expresses an action or state of being. A verb forms the main part of a sentence. An action verb tells what someone or something does. A state of being verb tells what someone or something is or is like. The verbs are underlined in the sentences below.

> Our parrot <u>whistles</u> loudly. (verb tells what the parrot does)
>
> Our parrot <u>is</u> loud. (verb tells what the parrot is like)

Some verbs work with main verbs. A **modal auxiliary verb** relates a possibility or necessity of an action. The words *can, may, must, should,* and *will* are some modal verbs. One way to use a modal verb is to express a level of certainty or a suggestion.

> You <u>may like</u> what you're about to hear.
>
> You <u>should have</u> more salad.

The first sentence expresses how much you like something. The second sentence suggests that you need to eat more salad.

Another condition for a modal is to express permission or a requirement.

> You <u>may have</u> more salad.
>
> You <u>may speak</u> only Spanish during the exam.

Tense is the time in which a sentence takes place—in the past, present, or future. The chart shows modals in different tenses.

Modal Auxiliary Verb	Past Tense	Present Tense	Future Tense
can	could	can	can
may	might	may	may
must	must	must	must
shall	should	shall	shall
will	would	will	will

Thinking It Through 1

Write sentences 1–8 correctly to express permission or a requirement on the lines provided, using the words "may," "must," or "can." If the sentence is correct, write "correct as is."

1.   You should brush your teeth twice a day.

_____

 The sentence expresses a recommendation. Replace *should* with a modal verb that expresses what you *need* to do.

2.   Kim will speak French only when she visits Quebec.

_____

 When you give someone permission to do something, which word do you use? For example, do you say "you *will* sit down," "you *can* sit down," or "you *may* sit down"?

3.   Charles might ride his bike after dinner.

_____

4.   Mattie must read three novels this semester.

_____

5.   Glen should eat more fruit.

_____

6.   Alice could practice piano Friday afternoon.

_____

7.   I must do my math homework first.

_____

8.   Dominic will clean the dishes after dinner.

_____

There are many kinds of verb tenses in the English language. The **progressive tense** expresses an ongoing action without a specific end time. Progressive tense verbs use a form of the verb *to be* followed by the main verb that uses the *–ing* ending.

> Dina <u>was jogging</u> in the park when it started to rain.

The word *was* is the past tense of *to be*. The action in the sentence is *jogging*. It is Dina's continuous action when the rain starts. The sentence, however, does not state whether or not Dina stopped jogging.

The verb *to be* is an **irregular verb**, which means it has different spellings when used in different tenses. Read the chart below.

Tense Forms of the Verb *To Be*

Subject	Past	Present	Future
I	was	am	will be
you	were	are	will be
he, she, it	was	is	will be
we	were	are	will be
they	were	are	will be

A progressive action can happen in the past, present, or future. The **past progressive tense** tells about an ongoing action that already happened.

> I <u>was talking</u> to Mom when the phone rang.

The **present progressive tense** tells about an ongoing action that happens now.

> Joel <u>is reading</u> a book about Albert Einstein.

The **future progressive tense** tells about an ongoing action that has not happened yet.

> Mark <u>will be waiting</u> for you on the front porch.

Thinking It Through 2

Read the following sentences. Write them using the correct progressive tense form on the lines provided. If the sentence is correct, write "correct as is."

1. Tomorrow we were going to the movies.

_____

> **HINT** Does the word *tomorrow* tell you that the action happened in the past, happens now, or will happen in the future?

2. We played basketball yesterday in gym class when the fire drill happened.

_____

> **HINT** The word *played* is written in the simple past tense. This should be expressed as a continuous action.

3. I going to the store now.

_____

4. James was dream about sharks when his father woke him up.

_____

5. You should try harder than that now.

_____

6. My uncle will be building a new skyscraper in Chicago next year.

_____

7. Jeff plays baseball at the park right now.

_____

8. Kristin was playing the saxophone when Josh was trying to study.

_____

This passage contains mistakes. Use the Reading Guide to help you find the mistakes.

Reading Guide

Find the progressive tense verb in sentence 1. Is it past, present, or future tense?

Which tense is the passage written in? The progressive verbs and the modal verbs should mostly be in the same tense.

What is the modal verb in sentence 13? Does it express a level of certainty, a suggestion, permission, or a requirement?

Is the progressive verb in sentence 22 correct?

The Audition

(1) Last month, I decided I was going to try out for the school play. (2) It seems that the same kids always get the parts. (3) I felt it was time for a new face on the stage. (4) I will be hoping that the teachers shall feel the same way.

(5) The play the teachers chose this year was *Oliver Twist*. (6) I knew it was about a poor boy in England, but that was about it. (7) On the day of try-outs, my hands started sweating. (8) I am regretting my decision to show up for the audition.

(9) One by one the students were called onto the stage. (10) Suddenly I heard my name called. (11) I felt butterflies in my stomach. (12) My friend Patrick sat next to me. (13) He told me not to worry, and that I would do fine.

(14) I stood on stage and looked at the script. (15) I was thinking about how the play takes place in England. (16) I guess that was why a strange voice came out of my mouth when I started to speak. (17) I sounded like those people in a British TV show, not a kid from America. (18) I may not stop myself. (19) Instead, I kept reading my lines.

(20) When I finished, everyone clapped! (21) Some people whistled and cheered. (22) "Well," one teacher said, "I guess you will be playing the part of Oliver."

Answer the following questions.

1. What is the correct way to write sentence 4?

    A. I am hoping that the teachers shall feel the same way.

    B. I was hoping that the teachers would feel the same way.

    C. I was hoping that the teachers can feel the same way.

    D. I will be hoping that the teachers will feel the same way.

2. What is the correct way to write the verb in sentence 8?

    A. was regretting

    B. will be regretting

    C. should regret

    D. may regret

3. How could you rewrite sentence 12 using the past progressive tense?

    A. My friend Patrick could sit next to me.

    B. My friend Patrick will be sitting next to me.

    C. My friend Patrick is sitting next to me.

    D. My friend Patrick was sitting next to me.

4. What is the correct way to write sentence 18?

    A. I might not stop myself.

    B. I could not stop myself.

    C. I cannot stop myself.

    D. I should not stop myself.

22 Adjectives and Adverbs

L.4.1.a, L.4.1.d

Getting the Idea

A **noun** is a person, place, or thing. An **adjective** tells more about a noun. The underlined words in the sentences below are adjectives.

> I like the <u>pink</u> flowers.

> We need <u>more</u> time to finish the project.

An adjective usually comes before the noun it describes. It can also be separated from the noun it describes by a verb, such as *is, are,* or *was*.

> The flowers are <u>pink</u>.

Up to three adjectives can be used with the same noun. The adjectives should appear in the following order, from left to right. Read the chart.

Opinion	Size	Age	Shape	Color	Origin (where something comes from)	Material
beautiful	big	new	round	blue	Italian	rubber

> My beautiful new Italian shoes got scratched. (opinion, age, origin)

> The big green rubber ball bounced into the street. (size, color, material)

Adjectives can be used to compare two or more things. The endings *-er* and *-est* are used with some adjectives. The words *more* and *most* are used with other adjectives. Still other adjectives are irregular. The forms need to be learned.

Adjective	Comparative: Used to Compare 2 Things	Superlative: Used to Compare 3 or More Things
tall	taller	tallest
famous	more famous	most famous
good	better	best

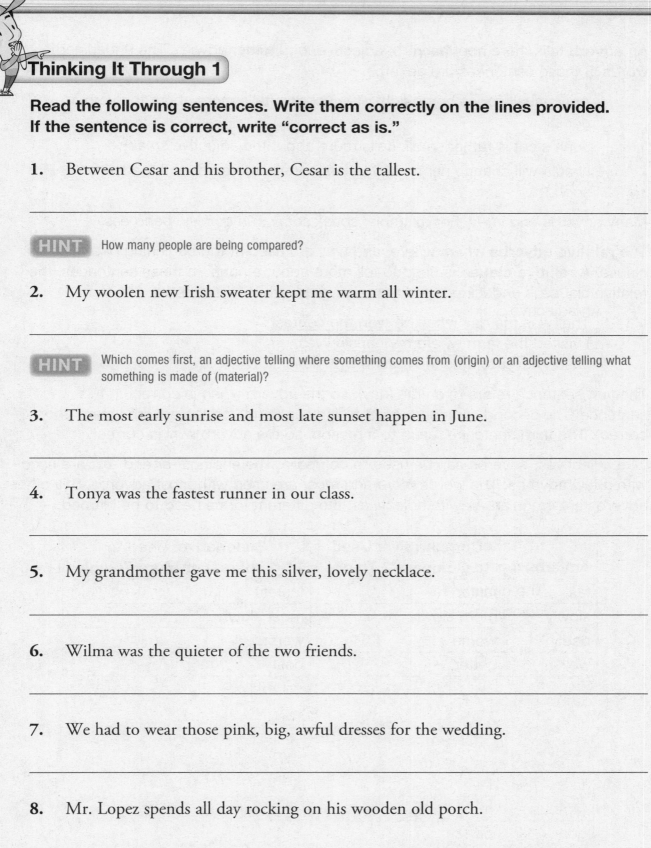

Thinking It Through 1

Read the following sentences. Write them correctly on the lines provided. If the sentence is correct, write "correct as is."

1. Between Cesar and his brother, Cesar is the tallest.

_____

HINT   How many people are being compared?

2. My woolen new Irish sweater kept me warm all winter.

_____

HINT   Which comes first, an adjective telling where something comes from (origin) or an adjective telling what something is made of (material)?

3. The most early sunrise and most late sunset happen in June.

_____

4. Tonya was the fastest runner in our class.

_____

5. My grandmother gave me this silver, lovely necklace.

_____

6. Wilma was the quieter of the two friends.

_____

7. We had to wear those pink, big, awful dresses for the wedding.

_____

8. Mr. Lopez spends all day rocking on his wooden old porch.

_____

An **adverb** tells more about a verb, adjective, or another adverb. The underlined words in these sentences are adverbs.

Amy <u>usually</u> goes home right after school. (tells more about the verb *goes*)

Juan's cat is <u>rather</u> small. (tells more about the adjective *small*)

Ursula will change her mind <u>very</u> soon. (tells more about the adverb *soon*.)

Many adverbs end in *-ly*. For example: *speak softly, run quickly, bend easily*.

The **relative adverbs** *when, where,* and *why* are used at the beginning of a relative clause. A **relative clause** is used to tell more about a noun. In these sentences, the relative clause is underlined, and the relative adverb is in *italic* print.

That was the day <u>*when* he won the contest</u>.
I visited the farm <u>*where* my cousin lives</u>.
Jason never told us the reason <u>*why* he left</u>.

The first sentence refers to a time (day), so the adverb *when* is correct in this sentence. The second sentence refers to a place (farm), so the adverb *where* is correct. The third sentence refers to a reason, so the adverb *why* is correct.

Like adjectives, adverbs can be used to compare. The endings *-er* and *-est* are used with a few adverbs. The words *more* and *most* are used with most adverbs. Still other adverbs are irregular. As with adjectives, the different forms need to be learned.

Adverb	Comparative: Used to Compare 2 Things	Superlative: Used to Compare 3 or More Things
fast	faster	fastest
slowly	more slowly	most slowly
badly	worse	worst
well	better	best

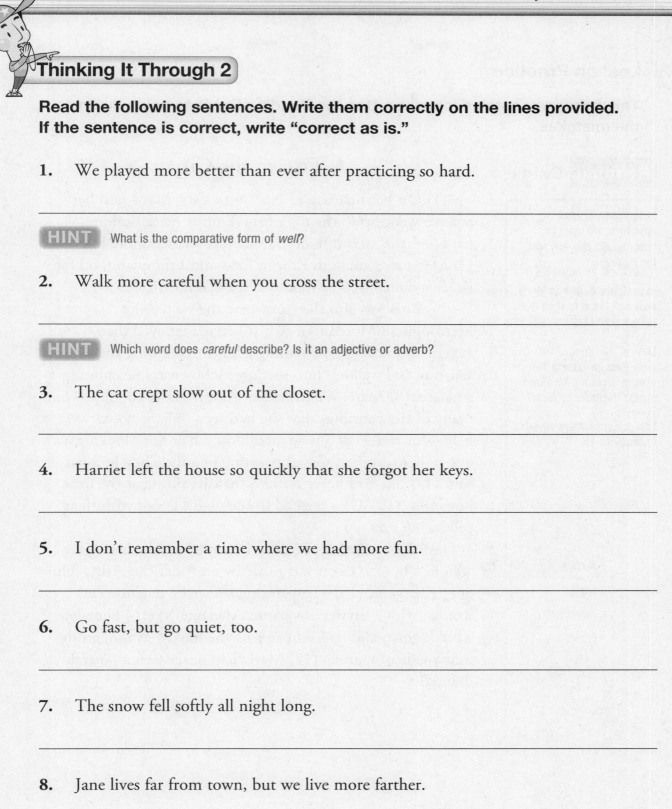

Thinking It Through 2

Read the following sentences. Write them correctly on the lines provided. If the sentence is correct, write "correct as is."

1. We played more better than ever after practicing so hard.

    _____

    HINT   What is the comparative form of *well*?

2. Walk more careful when you cross the street.

    _____

    HINT   Which word does *careful* describe? Is it an adjective or adverb?

3. The cat crept slow out of the closet.

    _____

4. Harriet left the house so quickly that she forgot her keys.

    _____

5. I don't remember a time where we had more fun.

    _____

6. Go fast, but go quiet, too.

    _____

7. The snow fell softly all night long.

    _____

8. Jane lives far from town, but we live more farther.

    _____

Lesson Practice

This passage contains mistakes. Use the Reading Guide to help you find the mistakes.

Reading Guide

In sentence 7, what adjectives are used to describe the stairway and the lobby?

In sentence 8, how is Maria walking? Is the form of the adverb correct?

Look at the order of the adjectives describing the eyes in sentence 12. How should the order be fixed?

Find the superlative adverb in sentence 13.

A Trip to the City

(1) On her first trip to New York City, Maria and her parents went up to the top of the Empire State Building. (2) From the 102nd floor, the sky just seemed more big. (3) Maria also ate both Korean food and Ethiopian food for the first time. (4) The food was spicy and delicious!

(5) This was also the trip where she visited the Metropolitan Museum of Art. (6) Maria enjoyed that experience more than anything else. (7) Climbing the wide stairway and walking into the huge lobby was like entering a palace. (8) Maria walked silent from room to room. (9) So many of the paintings that she had seen only in books were here—for real! (10) She spent almost a half hour looking at one of her favorites, Goya's painting of a little boy in a red suit. (11) She had never noticed the cats sitting at the little boy's feet. (12) They seemed to stare back at her with their yellow big eyes.

(13) The painting she liked best was one she had never seen in a book. (14) It was made by an American artist, John Singer Sargent. (15) The painting showed a magnificent woman with a mysterious name, Madame X. (16) She wore a black gown and had skin so pale she looked as though she were made of marble. (17) Maria had never seen a portrait so dramatic.

Answer the following questions.

1. How could sentence 2 be corrected?

   A. Change *more big* to *bigger*.

   B. Change *more big* to *most big*.

   C. Change *just* to *only*.

   D. Change *just* to *actually*.

2. What is the correct way to rewrite sentence 5?

   A. This was also the trip why she visited the Metropolitan Museum of Art.

   B. This was also the trip when she visited the Metropolitan Museum of Art.

   C. This was also the trip where she will visit the Metropolitan Museum of Art.

   D. This was also the trip during she visited the Metropolitan Museum of Art.

3. Read this sentence from the passage.

   Maria walked <u>silent</u> from room to room.

   Which is the correct form of the underlined adverb?

   A. with silence

   B. silenting

   C. silently

   D. silence

4. What is the correct way to rewrite sentence 12?

   A. They seemed to stare back at her with their yellow, bigger eyes.

   B. They seemed to stare back at her with their biggest yellow eyes.

   C. They seemed to stare back at her with their big, yellow eyes.

   D. They seemed to stare back at her with their eyes yellow and big.

23 Pronouns

L.4.1.a

Getting the Idea

A **noun** is a word that names a person, place, thing, or idea. The underlined words in these sentences are nouns.

> My <u>sister</u> works at that <u>restaurant</u>.
> The <u>cake</u> was delicious!

A **pronoun** is a word that takes the place of a noun. The underlined words in these sentences are pronouns.

> My sister works at a restaurant. <u>She</u> enjoys her job.
> The cake was delicious! Was <u>it</u> difficult to make?

An **antecedent** is the word that a pronoun replaces. In the first pair of sentences above, the antecedent of *She* is *sister*. In the second pair of sentences, the antecedent of *it* is *cake*.

Pronouns and antecedents need to match, or **agree**. If the antecedent is more than one, the pronoun needs to show more than one. If the antecedent is male, female, or neither, the pronoun also needs to be male, female, or neither.

> *Correct:* After <u>Jill</u> washed the car, <u>she</u> took a nap.
> *Incorrect:* <u>Drew and Sam</u> saw that movie, but <u>he</u> didn't like it.

The singular pronoun, *he*, does not agree with the antecedent. *Drew and Sam* is more than one. It needs a plural pronoun. The correct sentence is:

> Drew and Sam saw that movie, but <u>they</u> didn't like it.

Use the correct form of pronoun, depending on how it is used in a sentence.

Subject Pronouns	Object Pronouns	Possessive Pronouns
I, you, he, she, it, we, they *Example:* I throw the ball.	me, you, him, her, it, us, them *Example:* Throw the ball to me.	mine, yours, his, hers, its, ours, theirs *Example:* The ball is mine.

Thinking It Through 1

Read the following sentences. Write them correctly on the lines provided. If the sentence is correct, write "correct as is."

1. Kenya and then Maggie went down the slide. She laughed so hard!

_____

HINT Is the antecedent of *She* singular or plural?

2. Us fourth graders are faster than you might think.

_____

HINT Rewrite the sentence without *fourth graders*. Is *Us* being used as a subject or an object?

3. Weren't they the sweetest strawberries you've ever tasted?

_____

4. The girls on the volleyball team were stunned when it won the game.

_____

5. The students in the band practice hard, and so it deserves all the praise they get.

_____

6. The winner was always him.

_____

7. The Johnson family just moved next door, and they have already planted a garden.

_____

8. With she, you never know what is going to happen.

_____

The **relative pronouns** *who, whom, that, which,* and *whose* are used in relative clauses. Relative clauses are groups of words that tell more about the noun. The relative clauses in the sentences below are underlined, and the relative pronouns are in *italic* print.

> The runner *who* finished last was hurt.
> Ryan, *whom* I like, was voted president of our class.
> The book *that* Dan is reading has been made into a movie.
> Sofia lost my canvas bag, *which* was torn anyway.
> Do you know the student *whose* notebook this is?

The relative pronoun stands for the noun that comes before it. In the first sentence, *who* takes the place of *runner*. The words *who finished last* describes the *runner*. In the second sentence, *whom* takes the place of Ryan. The pronoun *whom* is used instead of *who* because the relative clause in this sentence has a subject (the word *I*). In the third sentence, the words *that Dan is reading* describe the *book*. In the fourth sentence, the words *which was torn anyway* describe the bag. The clause *whose notebook this is* tells what the student owns (a notebook).

Each relative pronoun is used with a different type of antecedent (the noun that comes before it), as shown in the chart below.

Relative Pronoun	Antecedent
who, whom	a person or group of people; never a thing
that	a thing; sometimes a person
which	a thing; never a person
whose	a person; a thing

Sometimes, a relative pronoun can be used with no antecedent. Examples are words such as *what, whatever,* and *whoever*.

> What he said just isn't true anymore.
> We can do whatever we want until dinnertime.

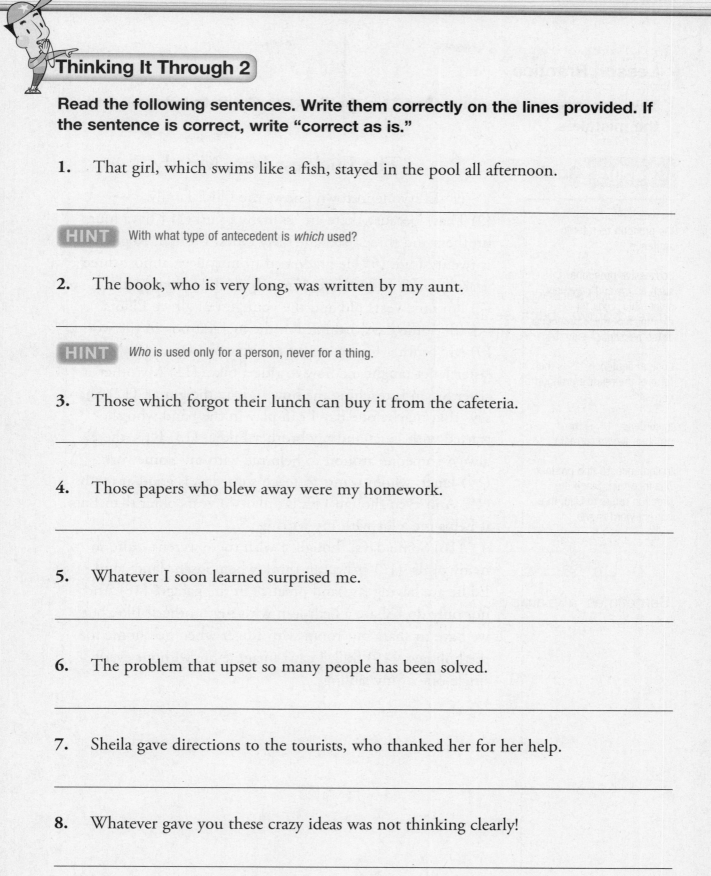

Thinking It Through 2

Read the following sentences. Write them correctly on the lines provided. If the sentence is correct, write "correct as is."

1. That girl, which swims like a fish, stayed in the pool all afternoon.

_____

HINT With what type of antecedent is *which* used?

2. The book, who is very long, was written by my aunt.

_____

HINT *Who* is used only for a person, never for a thing.

3. Those which forgot their lunch can buy it from the cafeteria.

_____

4. Those papers who blew away were my homework.

_____

5. Whatever I soon learned surprised me.

_____

6. The problem that upset so many people has been solved.

_____

7. Sheila gave directions to the tourists, who thanked her for her help.

_____

8. Whatever gave you these crazy ideas was not thinking clearly!

_____

This passage contains mistakes. Use the Reading Guide to help you find the mistakes.

Reading Guide

To which noun does the pronoun *us* refer in sentence 2?

Possessive pronouns such as *my* and *our* show ownership. Look for examples of these pronouns in the passage.

Look at sentence 12. Is the form of the relative pronoun correct?

In sentence 14, is the pronoun *whom* correct?

In sentence 15, the pronoun *it* is incorrect. Since the pronoun refers to Lisa, the correct word is *she*.

The Luckiest Boy, Mostly

(1) Everyone in town knows the Elliot family. (2) That's because there are so many of us! (3) I have four brothers and three sisters. (4) My oldest brother, Roger, is twenty-four. (5) He graduated from college almost three years ago. (6) Meanwhile, I'm only in the fourth grade. (7) I'm nine years old and the youngest of all we Elliots.

(8) Some days, I think I'm the luckiest boy in the world. (9) My brother Corey taught me how to swim. (10) My sister Janet taught me how to ride a bike. (11) My other sister Susan is teaching me how to play the guitar. (12) She says that maybe one day I can play in the band who she started with Janet and my brother Eddie. (13) Plus, there's always someone around to help me with my homework. (14) Janet, whom wants to teach someday, is good at math. (15) And even though Lisa is only two years older than I am, it helps me a lot with my writing.

(16) Some days, though, I wish there weren't quite so many of us. (17) Who can think when Susan, Janet, and Eddie are having its band practice in the garage? (18) And not only do I share a bedroom with my brother Mike, but we have to share our room with Roger when he's home for the holidays. (19) Still, I can't imagine life without every single one of my siblings.

Answer the following questions.

1. What is the BEST way to rewrite sentence 7?

   A. I'm nine years old and the youngest of all our Elliots.

   B. I'm nine years old and the youngest of all those Elliots.

   C. I'm nine years old and the youngest of all them Elliots.

   D. I'm nine years old and the youngest of all us Elliots.

2. In sentence 12, <u>who</u> should be changed to

   A. whose.

   B. that.

   C. what.

   D. whatever.

3. How could sentence 17 be corrected?

   A. Change *Who* to *Whoever*.

   B. Change *its* to *they*.

   C. Change *its* to *their*.

   D. Change *Who* to *What*.

4. Read this sentence from the passage.

   Janet, <u>whom</u> wants to teach someday, is good at math.

   The underlined word should be changed to

   A. who.

   B. which.

   C. that.

   D. whoever.

24 Prepositions and Prepositional Phrases

L.4.1.e

Getting the Idea

Prepositions are words that show relationships. The underlined words in the sentences below are prepositions.

> Wash your hands <u>before</u> dinner.
> Alicia's pencils fell <u>onto</u> the floor.

Prepositions are used to name a point in time.

> Maya's game begins <u>at</u> noon.
> We will return <u>on</u> Sunday.
> <u>In</u> August, they will visit their grandparents.

Notice that *at* is used with times, *on* is used with days, and *in* is used with parts of the day (*in the morning*), months, seasons, and years.

Prepositions are used to tell about longer periods of time.

> We went swimming <u>for</u> two hours.
> <u>During</u> the school day, Eric wears glasses.
> Wendy practiced <u>from</u> 9:00 <u>until</u> noon.
> The weather has been hot <u>since</u> last Saturday.

Notice that *for* is used with a specific length of time. *During* is used with a general period of time. *From* and *until* are used with a period with a specific beginning and ending. *Since* is used for a period with a specific beginning but no end.

Prepositions are used to tell about direction or to show where something is.

> Henry ran <u>past</u> the park and <u>to</u> the store.
> The milk belongs <u>in</u> the refrigerator.
> The cat is sleeping <u>on</u> the cool bathroom floor.
> Desiree hit the ball <u>over</u> the fence.
> The ground shook <u>beneath</u> our feet.
> We live <u>near</u> the beach.

Other prepositions that are used to show direction or location are *above, among, at, below, beside, between, by, inside, through, toward,* and *under.*

Thinking It Through 1

Read the following sentences. Write them correctly on the lines provided. If the sentence is correct, write "correct as is."

1. At Friday, we will go on vacation.

    _____

    HINT What preposition is used with days?

2. Freda has been working on this project from three weeks.

    _____

    HINT What preposition is used with a specific length of time?

3. Let's go in Shenandoah National Park this summer!

    _____

4. Robyn loves to see the cherry blossoms on the spring.

    _____

5. We like to sleep late in Saturdays.

    _____

6. At dinnertime, we talk about our day.

    _____

7. The birds flew high on our heads.

    _____

8. Tomas has gone to the park every day since last Wednesday.

    _____

A **prepositional phrase** is a group of words that begins with a preposition and includes its object. The **object of a preposition** is always a noun or pronoun. In these sentences, the prepositional phrase is underlined and the object of the preposition is in *italic* print.

> Why don't you come <u>with *me*</u>?
> <u>At *school*</u>, Nell is quiet, but <u>at *home*</u>, she has a lot to say.
> We hiked <u>up the *path*</u> and <u>through the *woods*</u>.

A prepositional phrase can act as an adjective. It can tell more about a noun or pronoun. In the sentences below, the prepositional phrase is underlined, and the noun it describes is in *italic* print.

> The *books* <u>on the table</u> do not belong there.
> The *birds* <u>in that tree</u> sing every morning.

A prepositional phrase can also act as an adverb. It can tell more about a verb. In these sentences, the prepositional phrase is underlined, and the verb it describes is in *italic* print.

> The mouse *disappeared* <u>under the porch</u>.
> Their mother *woke* <u>before dawn</u>.

Be sure to put a prepositional phrase near the word it describes. Read this sentence.

> Gene could see the wolf with his glasses on.

It sounds like the wolf is wearing glasses! That can't be right. The prepositional phrase needs to be closer to the noun it describes. The correct sentence is:

> With his glasses on, Gene could see the wolf.

Thinking It Through 2

Read the following sentences. Write them correctly on the lines provided. If the sentence is correct, write "correct as is."

1. They watched the birds fly with their binoculars.

    _____

    HINT A prepositional phrase can begin a sentence.

2. You may see fish from the boat under the water's surface.

    _____

    HINT Is it likely that the boat is underwater? Where are the fish?

3. Before the final game, the team met for practice.

    _____

4. On the table, Dave put the books back.

    _____

5. Place the cheese inside two slides of bread.

    _____

6. In the park on long leashes, we keep the dogs.

    _____

7. We found a wildflower growing in the forest.

    _____

8. I'm going by Gloria's house to play.

    _____

This passage contains mistakes. Use the Reading Guide to help you find the mistakes.

Reading Guide

In sentence 3, how would you correct the phrase *of the world*?

Find the prepositional phrase in sentence 4 that describes where the Arctic tern flies.

In sentence 9, how would you correct the phrase *over three weeks*?

Look at sentence 16. Where does the Arctic tern rest? Which prepositional phrases tell you?

Several sentences in the passage begin with prepositions that refer to time. Find those prepositions.

The Arctic Tern

(1) The Arctic tern does not look like an unusual bird. (2) It looks like a small seagull. (3) However, this small bird may be the strongest athlete of the world. (4) Every year it flies from the Arctic to Antarctica—and back again! (5) Together, the two trips take eight months and are about 50,000 miles long.

(6) Since the months of May and June, the Arctic tern breeds in the northern parts of North America, Europe, and Asia. (7) Both parents take care of the eggs, which are laid in nests on the open ground. (8) After the eggs hatch, the parents feed the babies for about three weeks. (9) Over three weeks, the young birds learn to fly. (10) The birds stay with their parents until another one month or two.

(11) The long journey to Antarctica begins at the late summer. (12) The birds fly far above the shore. (13) During this time, they mostly feed on fish. (14) Just below the surface of the water, they dive from the air to catch fish. (15) They also catch insects in flight.

(16) At the end of its journey, the Arctic tern rests on the ice off the shores of Antarctica. (17) While it is winter here in the North, it is summer in Antarctica. (18) The sun shines nearly all day long. (19) The Arctic tern enjoys not only two summers every year, but also more sunlight than most other creatures on Earth!

Answer the following questions.

1. How could sentence 6 be corrected?

    A. Change *Since* to *After*.

    B. Change *of* to *in*.

    C. Change *Since* to *During*.

    D. Change *in* to *under*.

2. What is the correct way to rewrite sentence 10?

    A. The birds stay with their parents after another month or two.

    B. The birds stay with their parents for another month or two.

    C. The birds stay near their parents until another month or two.

    D. The birds stay during their parents until another month or two.

3. How could sentence 11 be corrected?

    A. Change *to* to *into*.

    B. Change *at* to *with*.

    C. Change *to* to *above*.

    D. Change *at* to *in*.

4. What is the correct way to rewrite sentence 14?

    A. Just below the surface of the water, and they dive from the air to catch fish.

    B. They dive to catch fish just below the surface from the air of the water.

    C. They dive from the air to catch fish just below the surface of the water.

    D. Just below the surface of the water. They dive from the air to catch fish.

25 Sentences

L4.1.f

Getting the Idea

A **complete sentence** expresses a complete thought. It must have a subject, a verb, and proper punctuation. The **subject** is the person or thing doing the action. The **verb** is the action word.

A **simple sentence** expresses one thought. Read the example below.

> My friend and I will babysit my little brother tonight.

The subject is *My friend and I,* and the verb is *will babysit*. The sentence ends with a period.

A **compound sentence** contains two simple sentences. Each expresses a complete thought. They are joined by a comma and **conjunction** (such as *and, but,* or *so*) or a **semicolon** (;). Read the compound sentences below.

> My friend and I will babysit my little brother tonight, *and* we will make enough money to go to the concert.

> My friend and I will babysit my little brother tonight; we will make enough money to go to the concert.

In a **complex sentence**, one part of the sentence can stand alone, but the other part cannot. Read the complex sentence below.

> Even though we want to go to the movies, my friend and I will babysit my little brother tonight.

This sentence is made up of two parts, separated by a comma. Each part has a subject and a verb. However, the words before the comma do not make sense without the rest of the sentence. These words form a **dependent clause**. A complex sentence has at least one dependent clause. These clauses begin with words such as *after, although, because, if, since, when,* and *while*. The words after the comma can stand alone as a sentence. They form an **independent clause**.

Thinking It Through 1

Read the following sentences. In sentences 1–6, write the sentences correctly on the lines provided. If the sentence is correct, write "correct as is."

1.   When you go to the store remember to buy cat litter.

_____

HINT   The first part of the sentence (*When you go to the store*) is not a complete sentence. What punctuation belongs after it?

2.   My family and I love to go sledding in the winter

_____

HINT   This is a complete sentence. It needs punctuation at the end.

3.   Tomorrow I am going to the mall and I am going to Jan's birthday party.

_____

4.   This is a great time to go swimming I don't feel like it right now.

_____

5.   Since you don't like clowns, you probably shouldn't watch this movie.

_____

6.   I'm not going to buy that shirt although I really want it.

_____

For question 7, write your answer on the line below.

7.   Write a complex sentence using the word *because*.

_____

If a sentence is missing either a subject or a verb, it is incomplete. An incomplete sentence is called a **fragment**. You can fix a fragment by adding the missing subject or verb.

Fragment	Missing Piece	Corrected Sentence
Going to the beach.	The subject is missing. Who is going to the beach?	Tyrone is going to the beach.
Fred and his sister.	The verb is missing. What are Fred and his sister doing?	Fred and his sister are hiking.

Another mistake to avoid is writing run-on sentences. A **run-on sentence** combines at least two sentences without using conjunctions or a semi-colon. You should avoid run-on sentences because they confuse the reader. Here are three ways to fix a run-on sentence:

1. Split it into two separate sentences.

    Incorrect: I love surfing I also love skateboarding.
    Correct: I love surfing. I also love skateboarding.

2. Separate the two parts of the sentence with a semicolon.

    Incorrect: I love surfing I also love skateboarding.
    Correct: I love surfing; I also love skateboarding.

3. Separate the two parts of the sentence with a comma and a conjunction.

    Incorrect: I love surfing I also love skateboarding.
    Correct: I love surfing, and I also love skateboarding.

Finally, remember to check for repetition in your writing. The sentence above can be written in a shorter, simpler way by deleting the repetitious words.

    I love surfing and skateboarding.

Thinking It Through 2

Read the following sentences. Write them correctly on the lines provided. If the sentence is correct, write "correct as is."

1. Will watch the shuttle launch on TV.

    _____

    HINT What is the action in this sentence? Who is doing it?

2. The sun is shining the birds are singing.

    _____

    HINT Draw a line between the two parts of the sentence that can each stand alone.

3. Marissa is going on vacation with her family they are going to New York.

    _____

4. Victor, Leo, and I.

    _____

5. My aunt and uncle are two of my favorite people they are kind and understanding.

    _____

6. Are you going to take the bus, or are you going to walk instead?

    _____

7. Are happy that their project won first prize.

    _____

8. Before I go to bed, I brush my teeth.

    _____

This passage contains mistakes. Use the Reading Guide to help you find the mistakes.

Reading Guide

Can the first part of sentence 1 stand by itself? Then what kind of sentence is it?

Is sentence 5 a complete sentence? Does it have both a subject and a verb?

How do you know sentence 13 is a compound sentence? What mark of punctuation is needed before the word *and*?

My Great Idea

(1) When I found out how much paper our school throws out each day, I was annoyed. (2) That's a lot of paper going into our landfills all that paper could be recycled.

(3) I talked to my teacher about it, and she said that I should write a letter to our principal, Mrs. Swan. (4) My teacher said that if I researched and suggested ways to recycle the paper, Mrs. Swan might be willing to make this change.

(5) Spent hours researching online. (6) I wrote the letter, explaining why the school should be recycling paper. (7) Then I explained how the school could do this, and I even provided some resources for the principal. (8) Confident in my letter, I gave it to Mrs. Swan. (9) Waited for a few days. (10) Finally, Mrs. Swan called me into her office. (11) I hoped she would like my letter, but I was worried she might still say no to the idea.

(12) "Alice, this is a great idea!" she said. (13) "How would you feel about starting a recycling club and how would you like to be president?"

(14) I was so excited; I agreed. (15) I can't wait to get started.

Answer the following questions.

1. Which is the BEST way to revise sentence 2?

   A. That's a lot of paper going into our landfills: all that paper could be recycled.

   B. That's a lot of paper going into our landfills, all that paper could be recycled.

   C. That's a lot of paper going into our landfills. All that paper could be recycled.

   D. That's a lot of paper going into our landfills, and all that paper could be recycled.

2. Which of the following is NOT a complete sentence?

   A. Waited for a few days.

   B. Finally, Mrs. Swan called me into her office.

   C. I was so excited; I agreed.

   D. "Alice, this is a great idea!" she said.

3. Sentence 10 is a

   A. simple sentence.

   B. compound sentence.

   C. complex sentence.

   D. fragment.

4. Which of the following is a complex sentence?

   A. I talked to my teacher about it, and she said that I should write a letter to our principal, Mrs. Swan.

   B. My teacher said that if I researched and suggested ways to recycle the paper, Mrs. Swan might be willing to make this change.

   C. Then I explained how the school could do this, and I even provided some resources for the principal.

   D. I can't wait to get started.

26 Confusing Words

Getting the Idea

People often confuse words that are spelled alike or sound alike. **Homophones** are words that sound the same or similar, but have different spellings and meanings. Pay attention to these words when you write. The chart below lists some common homophones with examples of how they are used.

Homophones	
blew The wind blew hard today.	**blue** Danielle has blue eyes.
hear Did you hear that song?	**here** I live here.
knew Shane knew he had left his skateboard at home.	**new** Lenora bought a new pair of jeans.
principal The principal of our school is Mr. Jones.	**principle** Always stand up for your principles.
route I take the same route to school every day.	**root** The root of the tree poked out of the soil.
threw The player threw the ball to first base.	**through** That tunnel goes through a mountain.
week Celia swims once a week.	**weak** I feel weak when I don't eat breakfast.
write Write your name on the board.	**right** Jude figured out the right answer.

The following groups of homophones are the most commonly confused words:

> to = in the direction of
> too = also
> two = the number 2
> *Example:* Lucy will go <u>to</u> the store in <u>two</u> minutes. Ann will go, <u>too</u>.

> there = in a certain location
> they're = they are
> their = something belonging to *them*
> *Example:* <u>They're</u> headed to the trail over <u>there</u> with <u>their</u> backpacks.

> it's = it is
> its = something belonging to *it*
> *Example:* <u>It's</u> amazing that a turtle can shrink back into <u>its</u> shell.

Remember, a contraction is two words combined with an apostrophe. So, *they're* stands for *they are,* and *it's* stands for *it is*. This can be one way to help you know which homophone to use in a sentence.

The chart below lists a few more confusing words to learn.

affect	effect
How does the hot weather affect you?	Her hard work had a good effect on her grade.
conversation	**conservation**
Enid and I had a nice conversation on the phone today.	When there is little rain, conservation of water is important.
loose	**lose**
My dad keeps loose change in a jar.	The soccer team hates to lose.
of	**have**
Brian is a good friend of mine.	I should have brought an umbrella.
proceed	**precede**
Our team will proceed to the next level of the tournament.	The letter *b* precedes the letter *c* in the alphabet.
quiet	**quite**
We need to be quiet in the library.	That is quite a fancy hat you are wearing.

Thinking It Through

Read the following sentence, and then answer the question that follows.

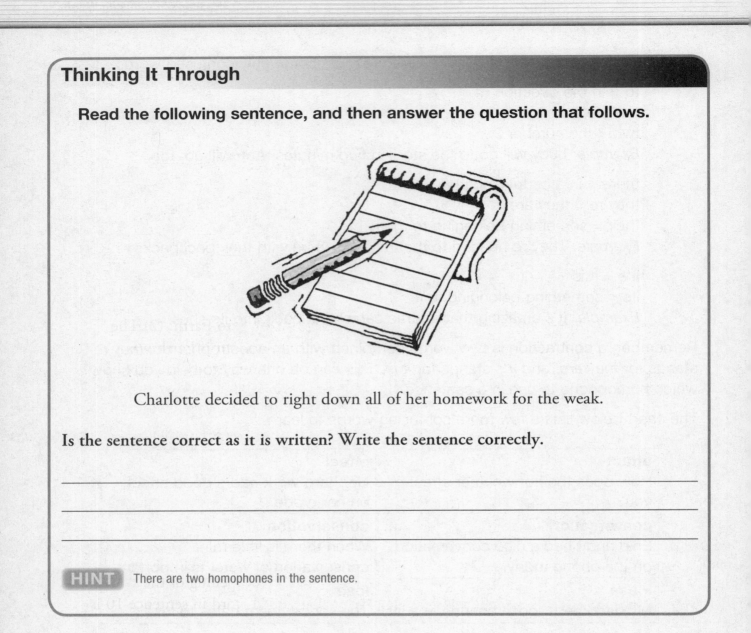

Charlotte decided to right down all of her homework for the weak.

Is the sentence correct as it is written? Write the sentence correctly.

_____

_____

_____

HINT There are two homophones in the sentence.

Coached Example

Read the passage and answer the questions.

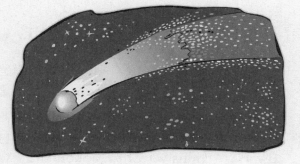

(1) Long ago, people were afraid that comets might crash into Earth. (2) The astronomer Edmund Halley decided to study comets to figure out if Earth was really in danger. (3) The planets in our solar system travel in paths around the sun called orbits. (4) Halley discovered that comets also travel in orbits around the sun. (5) That meant that people were safe from comets. (6) They would not crash into Earth because Earth is not in any comet's orbit. (7) He discovered that the comets he had been studying were actually only one comet that traveled in an orbit. (8) It is named Halley's Comet. (9) It travels <u>passed</u> Earth about every 76 years. (10) When Halley's Comet speeds <u>threw</u> a cloudless night sky, it is a thrilling, but no longer frightening, sight.

---

1. The correct spelling of the underlined word in sentence 9 is

   A. past.

   B. pased.

   C. passt.

   D. pass.

   HINT The word *passed* is a verb, but it is not used as a verb in sentence 9. The correct answer does not end in *-ed*.

2. The correct spelling of the underlined word in sentence 10 is

   A. thru.

   B. throw.

   C. through.

   D. throuh.

   HINT The word *threw* is an action word. Is that how the word is used in the sentence?

This passage contains mistakes. Use the Reading Guide to help you find the mistakes.

Reading Guide

In sentence 2, the words *do, fire,* and *great* are homophones. What are different meanings and/or spellings for these words?

When you see words like *to, too, two* and *there, their, they're,* check that the correct one is being used. In sentence 9, one of these homophones is used incorrectly. How should it be corrected?

In sentence 13, find the word that sounds right but is spelled incorrectly. How should the homophone be corrected?

Fire Lookout Towers

(1) A "fire lookout" is someone who spends months at a time searching for signs of forest fires. (2) To do this, a fire lookout must have shelter and a great view. (3) They live in small cabins built on mountains, usually on top of tall towers. (4) This way, fire lookouts can see clearly, sometimes for hundreds of miles. (5) When a lookout spots smoke, he or she immediately calls in firefighters.

(6) In 1910, after one of the largest forest fires on record, the U.S. Forest Service began building lookout towers all over the country. (7) Many of the most famous fire towers were built between 1910 and 1950. (8) In those days, when lookouts spotted fires, they alerted firefighters using carrier pigeons. (9) Over time, though, firefighters began too depend less on human lookouts and more on airplanes, radios, and satellites. (10) But more recently, manned fire towers have <u>maid</u> a comeback. (11) It seems <u>real</u> human eyes may be the best prevention!

(12) Being a lookout is one of the most important jobs <u>their</u> is, but it can be very lonely. (13) Some tower locations are sew remote that lookouts and supplies are dropped off and picked up by helicopter. (14) But other lookouts may get many visitors, whom they can educate about fire prevention and safety.

(15) Some old towers have been restored and are now official historic places. (16) Others have been renovated, and nature lovers can rent them for a <u>quite</u> week in the woods with terrific views!

Answer the following questions.

1. The correct spelling of the underlined word in sentence 16 is

   A. quit.

   B. quiet.

   C. quick.

   D. queit.

2. The correct spelling of the underlined word in sentence 10 is

   A. mayd.

   B. may'd.

   C. made.

   D. maide.

3. The correct spelling of the underlined word in sentence 12 is

   A. they're.

   B. ther.

   C. their.

   D. there.

4. As it is used in sentence 11, the meaning of <u>real</u> is

   A. a folk dance.

   B. a spool for thread.

   C. actual.

   D. to spin around.

27 Capitalization and Spelling

L.4.2.a, L.4.2.d

Getting the Idea

Following the rules of capitalization and spelling is important because it will help you write clearly. **Capitalization** is using capital (or uppercase) letters where necessary. The chart below lists rules for when to capitalize a word.

Capitalize	Examples
the first letter of the first word in a sentence	Everyone should read a mystery novel.
proper names	Heidi, James, Central Elementary School, Iowa, Los Angeles
titles that come before someone's name	Mrs. Chung, Dr. Jeffries, Principal Graziano
the main words in a title	*Charlie and the Chocolate Factory*
days, months, and holidays	Friday, June, Memorial Day
the greeting in a letter	Dear Jose
the first word in a letter's closing	Sincerely yours
the pronoun "I"	I love playing soccer.

Here are some common mistakes in capitalization to avoid.

Incorrect: My family visited my uncle in a nearby Town.
Correct: My family visited my uncle in a nearby town.
Why: Since the town is not a proper name, it does not need to be capitalized.

Incorrect: Julie went camping in Yosemite National park.
Correct: Julie went camping in Yosemite National Park.
Why: Yosemite National Park is the complete name, so all three words should be capitalized.

Incorrect: This year, independence day is on a sunday.
Correct: This year, Independence Day is on a Sunday.
Why: Always capitalize days, months of the year, and names of holidays.

Thinking It Through 1

Read the following sentences. Write them correctly on the lines provided. If the sentence is correct, write "correct as is."

1. the trees outside swayed in the breeze.

_____

HINT The first word of a sentence should be capitalized.

2. I asked maria for help with my homework.

_____

HINT Proper names should be capitalized.

3. Nathan brought the package to mrs. Boyce.

_____

4. Have you seen the movie *The Incredibles*?

_____

5. My mom and i love going to flea markets.

_____

6. Every year, we have a block party on memorial day.

_____

7. Mrs. Freeman took the class on a trip.

_____

8. We got ice cream last night at an ice cream parlor called scoop's.

_____

Here are some general rules that can help you know how to spell a word.

Spelling Rule	Examples
Put *i* before *e,* except after *c,* except when sounding like "ay" as in *neighbor* and *weigh*.	believe, field, receive, ceiling (*weird* is a word that breaks this rule)
Drop the silent *e* when adding a suffix that starts with a vowel.	bike—biking, wave—wavy
Don't drop the silent *e* when adding a suffix that starts with a consonant.	use—useless, state—statement
If a word ends with a consonant + *y,* change the *y* to *i* when adding a suffix (unless the suffix begins with *i*).	plenty—plentiful, happy—happiness
If a word ends with a vowel + *y,* just add the suffix.	play—playful, stray—strayed
If a one-syllable word ends in one vowel + one consonant, double the consonant before you add a suffix that begins with a vowel.	swim—swimming, bat—batter
If a word has more than one syllable where the accent is on the final syllable, double the final consonant.	control—controlled, prefer—preferred

Most nouns have plurals that follow regular rules. These nouns can be made plural by adding the suffix -*s* or -*es* (*star—stars, box—boxes*). Some nouns are irregular. They do not follow these rules. Here are some examples: *life—lives, wolf—wolves, tooth—teeth, mouse—mice, child—children, sheep—sheep*. If you are unsure of a noun's plural form, look it up in a dictionary.

Thinking It Through 2

Read the following sentences. Write them correctly on the lines provided. If the sentence is correct, write "correct as is."

1. The gooses ran around in the park.

_____

HINT The word *goose* forms a plural irregularly. It's similar to the word *foot* and its plural, *feet*.

2. She was decieved by her best friend.

_____

HINT Always remember to put *i* before *e* except after *c*.

3. I was very grateful for the help Julius gave me.

_____

4. The fury dog was soft to hold.

_____

5. The climbers hikked up the mountain.

_____

6. May I please have a piece of cake?

_____

7. The dentist told Ken that his two front tooths would grow back soon.

_____

8. Aaron beleives he can finish the race.

_____

This passage contains mistakes. Use the Reading Guide to help you find the mistakes.

A New Land

Reading Guide

In sentence 1, *America* is a proper noun. Proper nouns, including the names of places and holidays, are always capitalized.

Is the word *countrys* correct in sentence 2? Apply the rule: If a word ends in *y*, change the *y* to *i* and add *-es*.

In sentence 12, the word *people* is an irregular plural of the word *person*.

Find the word that is incorrectly capitalized in sentence 16.

In sentence 18, the word *stepped* was formed in the following way: The word *step* is a one-syllable word ending in a vowel, *e*, and a consonant, *p*. Doubling the consonant before adding a suffix that begins with a vowel, *-ed*, gives you *stepped*.

(1) In one hundred years, between 1824 and 1924, close to 35 million people came to America. (2) They left the countrys where they were born to find a new life. (3) It took courage to leave everything that was familiar.

(4) Until 1924, there were no strict laws about who could come into the United States. (5) New, stricter laws were passed in 1924. (6) The new laws made getting into our country more difficult.

(7) Many of the people who came here from Europe between 1824 and 1924 came on a ship, in steerage. (8) Steerage was in the bottom of a ship. (9) The people were jamed together. (10) They had a very uncomfortable voyage. (11) Many were seasick.

(12) Most of these people coming to America from Europe could only speak their own Language. (13) They would have to learn English as soon as they arrived.

(14) When the ships got to new york, the people in Steerage had to be examined at Ellis island. (15) Doctors looked at them to see if they had any diseases. (16) People from steerage had to answer questions about how they could take care of their Families. (17) They would have to be able to work and earn money.

(18) It is safe to say that when people first stepped into their new country, they were a little frightened. (19) They were also very hopful.

Answer the following questions.

1. The correct way to spell <u>jamed</u> in sentence 9 is

   A. jameed.

   B. jammed.

   C. jamd.

   D. jammd.

2. Which word in sentence 12 should NOT be capitalized?

   A. Most

   B. Europe

   C. Language

   D. America

3. Read this sentence from the passage.

   When the ships got to new york, the people in Steerage had to be examined at Ellis island.

   What is the correct way to rewrite this sentence?

   A. When the ships got to New York, the people in steerage had to be examined at Ellis Island.

   B. When the ships got to new York, the people in Steerage had to be examined at ellis island.

   C. When the ships got to New York, the people in steerage had to be examined at Ellis island.

   D. When the ships got to New york, the people in Steerage had to be examined at Ellis island.

4. The correct way to spell <u>hopful</u> in sentence 19 is

   A. hoppeful.

   B. hopiful.

   C. hopefull.

   D. hopeful.

28 Punctuation

L.4.2.b, L.4.2.c, L.4.3.b

Getting the Idea

Punctuation is the symbols that are used to organize sentences. Using the correct punctuation helps make your writing clear.

End marks show what kind of sentence you are writing. A **period** (.) is used to make a statement. Use a **question mark** (?) when you are asking a question. An **exclamation point** (!) is used to show excitement, surprise, or strong emotion.

> What are you doing for vacation this summer?
> I'm visiting my cousin in San Francisco.
> Wow, that sounds exciting!

A **comma** (,) is used to show a pause in a sentence or to connect ideas.

When to Use a Comma	Example
to separate items in a list	I need to buy milk, eggs, and bread.
to set off words people speak	My mom said, "Don't stay up too late."
after an introductory phrase	When I was your age, I didn't like spicy foods.
before a conjunction (*and, but*) in a compound sentence	I like most fruits, but my favorite is watermelon.
between the names of cities and states	My grandparents were married in Boston, Massachusetts.
between the day and year in a date	Renee's birthday is August 24, 2000.

Use **quotation marks** (" ") around dialogue, or the words that people say.

> "Where are you going?" Dad asked.
> "I need to get a book from the library," Tim replied.
> "On your way there," Dad said, "please mail this letter."

Thinking It Through 1

Read the following sentences. Write them correctly on the lines provided. If the sentence is correct, write "correct as is."

1. My best friend asked, What are you doing this weekend?

_____

HINT Remember that dialogue should be set off with quotation marks.

2. Barack Obama was inaugurated president on January, 20 2009.

_____

HINT Use a comma in a date to separate the day and the year.

3. My favorite sports are baseball swimming and surfing.

_____

4. When are you going camping.

_____

5. I want to make some popcorn and then I want to watch a movie.

_____

6. Watch out for that car.

_____

7. "Do we have any homework tonight?" Beth asked.

_____

8. It only took two days to drive from Dallas Texas to Louisville Kentucky.

_____

Another punctuation mark is a colon. A **colon** (:) appears before a list in a sentence. It is also used to introduce an explanation.

> There are three vegetables I don't like: parsnips, turnips, and asparagus.
> This test is really important: if I do well, I can get an A in the class.

A **semicolon** (;) is used to join together two sentences that are related.

> I love going to the mall; I could spend the entire day there.

There are two ways to use an **apostrophe** ('). First, an apostrophe is used in contractions. A **contraction** is two words joined to make one. The apostrophe takes the place of the missing letters.

> you + are = you're
> have + not = haven't
> he + will = he'll

An apostrophe and *s* is used to form possessive nouns. A **possessive noun** shows ownership. Be careful with singulars and plurals. If the noun is singular, the apostrophe goes before the *s*.

> Sharon's book
> the tree's leaves
> the baby's rattle
> the car's engine

If the noun is plural and ends with *s*, the apostrophe goes after the *s*.

> the sailors' ship
> the artists' studio
> the bears' den

If the noun is plural but does *not* end with *s*, the apostrophe goes before the *s*.

> the children's games
> the people's decision

Thinking It Through 2

Read the following sentences. Write them correctly on the lines provided. If the sentence is correct, write "correct as is."

1. Lee put three things in her bag a sweater, a magazine, and an apple.

_____

HINT Use a colon before a list in a sentence.

2. I can't wait for the weekend I'm going with my friends to see a movie.

_____

HINT Use a semicolon to join two complete sentences that relate to the same idea.

3. I asked to borrow Bens pencil because mine broke.

_____

4. Dont you just love that new dance competition show?

_____

5. I need to get some school supplies a notebook, three folders, and a box of markers.

_____

6. The babies' toys were scattered all over the room.

_____

7. I need to practice the clarinet tonight I have a concert tomorrow.

_____

8. I won't be able to go to your house after school today.

_____

This passage contains mistakes. Use the Reading Guide to help you find the mistakes.

Reading Guide

Notice the commas in sentence 1. A comma is used after the introductory phrase. A comma is also used before the word *but*.

Read sentence 2 aloud. Does it sound right to pause after the word *someone*? If not, then a comma is not necessary.

Look at the dialogue in sentence 7. Notice how the quotation marks go on either side of the speaker's words, and the end punctuation falls inside the closing quotation marks.

What punctuation marks belong around the speaker's words in sentence 8?

Planning the Perfect Party

(1) When my dad called a family meeting, I didn't know what to expect, but I feared the worst. (2) Family meetings usually meant someone, did something wrong.

(3) Hey, he said, "do you have any ideas of what we can do for your moms fortieth birthday."

(4) We considered a fancy dinner, but we'd already eaten in every nice restaurant in our town. (5) Toledo Ohio does have plenty of wonderful restaurants, but none of them would be really new or exciting for Mom. (6) I thought we should do something more original, since this was a big birthday for her.

(7) "What if we created a scavenger hunt around town that would lead her back here for a surprise party?" I asked.

(8) That's a great idea! my sister agreed.

(9) I explained that we would need to buy some party supplies balloons streamers candles and a cake. (10) My dad thought that was reasonable it shouldn't cost too much money.

(11) The next day, my dad, sister, and I began planning the perfect party for my mom.

Answer the following questions.

1. Which of the following is the correct revision of sentence 3?

   A. "Hey", he said, "do you have any ideas of what we can do for your moms fortieth birthday."

   B. "Hey," he said, "do you have any ideas of what we can do for your moms' fortieth birthday?"

   C. "Hey," he said, "do you have any ideas of what we can do for your mom's fortieth birthday?"

   D. "Hey", he said, "do you have any ideas of what we can do for your moms fortieth birthday!"

2. Why does sentence 5 need a comma added to it?

   A. to set off an introductory phrase

   B. to separate one place name from another

   C. to separate items in a list

   D. to go before a conjunction in a compound sentence

3. Which of the following is the correct revision of sentence 10?

   A. My dad thought that was reasonable. it shouldn't cost too much money.

   B. My dad thought that was reasonable and it shouldn't cost too much money.

   C. My dad thought that was reasonable, it shouldn't cost too much money.

   D. My dad thought that was reasonable; it shouldn't cost too much money.

4. Which of the following is the correct revision of sentence 9?

   A. I explained that we would need to buy: some party supplies balloons, streamers and candles, and a cake.

   B. I explained that we would need to buy some party supplies; balloons streamers and candles and a cake.

   C. I explained that we would need to buy some party supplies: balloons, streamers, candles, and a cake.

   D. I explained that we would need to buy some party supplies, balloons, streamers, and candles and a cake.

29 Style, Tone, and Word Choice

L.4.3.a

Getting the Idea

Have you ever heard the saying "Choose your words carefully"? This piece of advice holds true in writing. Your **word choice**, or the words you use to express your ideas, can greatly affect how your audience will respond to your writing.

Word choice is an important part of your **writing style**. Just like you have a unique speaking voice, you have your own writing style. In fact, it is often called a writer's "voice." Style is created not only through the individual words you use, but also through the kinds of sentences you construct.

Two of the most common styles are *formal* and *informal*. A **formal style** is characterized by language that is proper. Events are described in a serious way. The writer uses complete sentences, and they might be long and complex. For example:

> In 1776, the American colonists declared their independence from Great Britain.

An **informal style** is more personal, casual, and conversational. The writer might use slang, or colorful words and phrases from everyday speech. The writer might also use sentence fragments instead of complete sentences. For example:

> In 1776, the Americans were fed up with the Brits and decided to run things themselves.

Choose a style that suits the purpose of your writing. The **purpose** is your reason for writing. If you are writing a history report or a letter to a school official, use a formal tone. If you are writing a fictional story, an informal tone may be more effective or interesting.

Word choice also helps to create the writer's tone. **Tone** is the writer's attitude toward his or her subject. A writer's tone might be positive or negative, serious or funny. It is important to keep the same style and tone throughout your writing. This means that if you start your paper with a conversational style and a humorous tone, you should continue that style and tone throughout the paper.

Another thing to remember is to choose **precise**, or specific, words to express your ideas. Look at the following example.

It is bad to ride in a car without wearing a seatbelt.

Bad is a general word. Different readers could interpret it to mean different things. But what if you revised the sentence to make the word more specific? For example:

It is dangerous to ride in a car without wearing a seatbelt.

By using a specific word, such as *dangerous*, the reader gets a better understanding of why it is bad to ride in a car without a seatbelt. The reader now understands that safety is involved. The chart below lists examples of general and precise words.

General Words	Your Reader Wants to Know	Precise Words
The purse is *big*.	How big is it?	The purse is *gigantic*.
The painting is *pretty*.	Why is it pretty?	The painting is *colorful*.
My *dog* is playful.	What kind of dog is it?	My *poodle* is playful.
I am *sad*.	Why are you sad?	I feel *disappointed*.

Choosing precise nouns, verbs, adjectives, and adverbs will help you express your ideas more clearly to your reader. Using a dictionary or a thesaurus is a great way to select just the word you need!

Thinking It Through

Read the following passage, and then answer the question that follows.

Have you ever seen a toy ship in a bottle and wondered, "How do they do that?" I have. Last weekend, I interviewed a local artist about this craft. It turns out, there are more ways to get a ship through the itty-bitty neck of a bottle than you might think. The artist told me that some crafters build the ship in pieces, no bigger than the neck. Then, they use special tools to put the pieces together inside the bottle. I can't imagine how difficult that must be! Another way is to build the ship outside the bottle and put hinges on any pieces that are bigger than the neck of the bottle (like the mast). The artist folds the hinged parts and slips the ship inside the bottle. How cool is that?

How would you describe this writer's style? Give examples from the passage to support your response.

_____

_____

_____

_____

_____

HINT   Look at the choice of words. Does the passage sound like it's from a textbook, or does it sound as though the writer is having a conversation with you?

Coached Example

Read the passage and answer the questions.

Technology has come a long way. The problem is, a lot of today's electronic gadgets are making us lazy! Is flipping a switch to turn on the fan so tiring that you need a remote control? And don't even get me started on the voice-activated TV remote. Now your voice prompts alone can command your TV to change channels!

A gadget should be celebrated when it makes our lives better. However, it is a waste of money and talent when a gadget does nothing but encourage laziness. To all of you folks out there who have ideas for new inventions: Do me a favor and make sure they are worthwhile. The last thing we need is one more device that stops us from getting up off the couch.

---

1. What is the BEST way to describe the writing style and tone of this passage?

   A. The writing style is formal; the tone is negative.

   B. The writing style is formal; the tone is positive.

   C. The writing style is informal; the tone is negative.

   D. The writing style is informal; the tone is positive.

   HINT Does the passage sound like an article from a book, or like a conversation the writer is having with you? How does the word choice reflect the writer's overall feeling about technology?

2. Which of the following words does NOT contribute to the tone?

   A. lazy

   B. tiring

   C. waste

   D. worthwhile

   HINT If the tone is positive, the writer's word choice will express a positive feeling. If the tone is negative, the writer's word choice will express a negative feeling.

Use the Reading Guide to help you understand the passage.

Reading Guide

The passage is written in an informal style. But notice how the writer provides enough facts and information to make her point clearly.

What specific words does the writer use to describe what the potato chip company is doing?

Does the writer think this new potato chip bag is a good or bad idea? What evidence do you find in the passage to support your answer?

Leading the Way to a Healthier Environment

The average American town produces tons of garbage every week. Some of it is sent off to recycling centers. However, a lot of the trash is taken to landfills. It sits there for many years. This is harmful to our environment.

Imagine if we could reduce the size of our landfills. Imagine a world with no landfills at all! Some industries are working to make this dream a reality.

Many of the foods we buy are packaged in bags. Unfortunately, bags take a long time to break down in a landfill. The idea is to find materials that will break down more quickly. This would be better for our planet's land, oceans, and air.

One potato chip company is leading this effort. The company is developing packaging that is less harmful to the environment. Ninety percent of their new bag is made from plant-based materials. Even more exciting, it takes only fourteen weeks for this bag to break down and become part of the soil. All businesses should follow their example.

Hopefully, this big step forward is just the beginning. As people learn more about the new bags, maybe they will decide to buy the snacks that come in them. If this becomes a trend, it is sure to make more companies want to use this wonderful new technology.

Answer the following questions.

1. Read this sentence from the passage.

   Unfortunately, bags take <u>a long time</u> to break down in a landfill.

   Which phrase would make the underlined words more precise?

   A. a while

   B. many years

   C. a lot of time

   D. hundreds of years

2. Which concluding sentence would BEST fit with the writer's style?

   A. Don't buy products packaged any other way.

   B. You should keep a large supply of these potato chips in your home.

   C. I think this potato chip bag will be very popular.

   D. Everyone needs to work together to create a healthier planet.

3. Which word BEST describes the writer's tone?

   A. angry

   B. approving

   C. funny

   D. disappointed

4. Which sentence from the passage BEST supports the writer's tone?

   A. "Imagine a world with no landfills at all!"

   B. "Unfortunately, bags take a long time to break down in a landfill."

   C. "As people learn more about the new bags, maybe they will decide to buy the snacks that come in them."

   D. "Even more exciting, it takes only fourteen weeks for this bag to break down and become part of the soil."

5. How does the writer's word choice contribute to the tone of the passage? Give examples of specific words the writer uses to create this effect.

   _____

   _____

   _____

   _____

30 Determining Word Meanings

L.4.4.a, L.4.4.c

Getting the Idea

Sometimes, you may come across an unfamiliar word as you read. One way to figure out the meaning of the word is by using context clues. **Context clues** are the words, phrases, and sentences around an unfamiliar word that help you understand its meaning.

There are different kinds of context clues. Some context clues *define*, or give the meaning of, an unfamiliar word right in the same (or nearby) sentence. Read the sentence below.

> One way to <u>conserve</u>, or save, water is to take shorter showers.

The word *conserve* is defined in the sentence. It means "to save." Definition context clues are often set off with commas.

Another kind of clue is an *example* clue. This means the writer provides examples of something to help you understand what it is. Read the sentence below.

> The wolves were released into the <u>wilderness</u> in places such as Denali and Yellowstone national parks.

If you do not know what the word *wilderness* means, use the clues to figure it out. The sentence gives you two examples of wilderness environments—Denali and Yellowstone national parks. Since you know what national parks are like, you have a pretty good understanding of what the word *wilderness* means.

Some context clues *restate*, or sum up, information that tells you what a word means. Read the sentences below.

> The farmers began to cut the hay and put it up for the winter, and ripe vegetables would soon to be picked and stored away. The <u>harvest</u> had begun.

In the first sentence, the information about the farmers' work helps you to understand the meaning of the word *harvest*.

A context clue can provide a word's opposite, or antonym. If you are familiar with the antonym, you should be able to figure out the meaning of the new word.

>   While Milt is tall, Louise is quite <u>petite</u>.

The word *while* signals that a difference between Milt and Louise is being described. If Milt is tall, what does that tell you about the meaning of the word *petite*?

A word's position in a sentence can also be a clue to the word's meaning. Ask yourself, what part of speech is this word—a noun, a verb, or an adjective? This strategy is especially useful for homonyms—words that look the same but have different meanings.

>   How much weight can that bridge <u>bear</u>?

You know that a bear is an animal. An animal is a noun. But in this sentence, *bear* is used as a verb. It's an action word. Here, the word *bear* means "to support or hold up." That definition fits with what is being described: a bridge needs to be strong enough to support the cars and trucks that travel on it.

Besides using context clues, always remember to look up new words in either a printed or online dictionary. Dictionary entries include the word and its definition, part of speech, and pronunciation. Here is a typical dictionary entry:

> **fu•ture** /'fyü chər/ *noun* events that come at a later time

A thesaurus is another useful tool. Look up an unfamiliar word in a thesaurus to find its synonyms and antonyms.

Thinking It Through

Read the following passage, and then answer the questions that follow.

At the beginning of spring, Andy had trouble riding his new bike very far. He got tired quickly, and he had to walk the bike up hills. Then he began taking rides with his friend Evan. They took longer rides every weekend. By summer, Andy's <u>endurance</u> was much improved. He could ride for hours on end, and hills were no problem.

What is the meaning of the word <u>endurance</u>? How did you know?

_____

_____

_____

_____

_____

HINT   At first, Andy had trouble riding. But he worked at getting better. Soon, he was able to ride for longer.

Coached Example

Read the passage and answer the questions.

Yorkshire pudding is a popular English dish. Actually, Yorkshire pudding is not really a pudding at all. It is a light, puffy roll. Hundreds of years ago, roasted meat was a favorite dish in England. However, meat was very <u>expensive</u>. It cost so much that most people could only afford to eat it on special occasions.

When roasting meat, long tin pans were placed under the roast. These tins collected the meat drippings. Cooks made batter from eggs and flour, and they poured the batter into the tins with the drippings. The batter became a fluffy, delicious bread pudding. Cooks served these <u>savory</u> puddings as a first course. The puddings were cheap and flavorful. At times when there was not enough meat to go around, children would get Yorkshire pudding with gravy as their main meal.

---

1. What is the meaning of <u>expensive</u>?

   A. large

   B. hearty

   C. costly

   D. popular

    HINT Look for a context clue in the last sentence of paragraph 1.

2. Read these sentences from the passage.

   The batter became a fluffy, delicious bread pudding. Cooks served these <u>savory</u> puddings as a first course.

   The word <u>savory</u> means

   A. moist.

   B. tasty.

   C. nutty.

   D. sweet.

   HINT Read the two sentences carefully. *Savory* in the second sentence is a restatement of information in the previous sentence.

Use the Reading Guide to help you understand the passage.

Reading Guide

In paragraph 1, which words help you know what *liberty* means?

In paragraph 2, the word *colonists* is followed by its definition.

Look closely at paragraph 3. Use the first three sentences in the paragraph to help you figure out what *opposed* means.

The Path to Independence

In America, all people have the right to liberty. One person we can thank for this right to freedom is Patrick Henry.

Patrick Henry was a young man when the United States was made up of thirteen colonies. The king of England ruled the colonies. Many colonists, or people who had left England and settled in America, felt it was unfair for the king to make laws for them and impose harsh taxes. Many colonists felt they should be able to rule themselves. These people were called Patriots. Colonists who did not want to break away from England were known as Loyalists because they were loyal to the king of England. They still wanted to serve him.

In the spring of 1775, many of the Patriots got together to talk about what should be done. Some felt they should beg the king for permission to be free. Others were opposed to this idea because they had already asked the king and he refused. They wanted war. Patrick Henry stood up and interrupted the others, demanding to speak. "Give me liberty, or give me death!" he said. The men cheered and voted to be free.

Shortly afterward, the American Revolution began. The Patriots eventually won the war and created their own government. While England was a kingdom, the new country was not ruled by a king. In time, the United States became a nation where all people have the right to freedom and liberty.

Answer the following questions.

1. In the passage, the word <u>liberty</u> means

   A. rights.

   B. library.

   C. freedom.

   D. patriot.

2. Read this sentence from the passage.

   Others were <u>opposed</u> to this idea because they had already asked the king and he refused.

   The word <u>opposed</u> means

   A. against.

   B. excited.

   C. angry.

   D. tired.

3. What does the word <u>loyal</u> mean?

   A. frustrated

   B. helpful

   C. interested

   D. faithful

4. The word <u>interrupt</u> means to

   A. stand up straight and tall.

   B. stop a conversation suddenly.

   C. talk a lot to other people.

   D. bring freedom to new places.

5. Read this sentence from the passage.

   While England was a <u>kingdom</u>, the new country was not ruled by a king.

   What does the word <u>kingdom</u> mean? Which words help you understand what <u>kingdom</u> means?

   _____

   _____

   _____

   _____

31 Root Words and Affixes

L.4.4.b, RF.4.3.a, RF.4.4.c

Getting the Idea

Many common words in English came from other languages, such as Greek and Latin. For this reason, learning Greek and Latin roots can help you understand many words in English. A **root** is the base, or main part, of a word. A root needs to be joined with other word parts to make a complete word.

geo + graphy = geography

The root *geo*, meaning "Earth," is not a word. It cannot stand alone. Add *-graphy* to get the word *geography*, which means "the study of Earth's landforms, resources, and climate." The same root can appear in many different words. The following chart lists some common Greek and Latin roots.

Root	Meaning	Examples
astr	star	astronaut, astronomy
auto	same, self	automobile, automatic
bene	good	benefit
bio	life	biography, biology
eco	environment	ecology
graph	something written	autograph, paragraph
photo	light	photograph
port	to carry	export, import
scope	a tool for seeing	microscope
tele	far away	telephone, telegraph

Read the sentence below.

Computers designed to be <u>portable</u> in the 1980s look big and heavy now.

You can figure out the meaning of *portable* by looking at its root. The root of *portable* is *port*, which means "to carry." Something that is portable can be easily carried.

An **affix** is a word part added to the beginning or end of a word or root to change its meaning. An affix cannot stand alone as a word.

An affix added to the beginning of a base word is called a **prefix**. An affix added to the end of a base word is called a **suffix**. Read the charts below.

Prefix	Meaning	Examples
bi-	two	bicycle
co-	together, with	coworker
dis-	not, opposite	disagree, dishonest
ex-	out, away from	expand
extra-	outside, beyond	extravagant
in-	in, into	inside, infield
pre-	before	preview, prehistoric
re-	again	rewrite, resell
trans-	across, over	transmit
uni-	one	unicycle

Suffix	Function or Meaning	Examples
-able, -ible	forms adjectives, means "able to"	likable, reversible
-ation	forms nouns from verbs	imagination
-fy	forms verbs that mean "to make or become"	terrify, magnify
-logue	speech, to speak	dialogue
-ogy	science or study of	biology
-meter, -metry	a tool for measuring, a measure	kilometer, geometry
-ment	forms nouns from verbs	statement
-ty, -ity	forms nouns from adjectives	loyalty, purity

Read the following sentences. Figure out the meaning of the underlined word, based on the meaning of its affix.

> We stared at Ms. Hull in <u>amazement</u>. Did our teacher really just do cartwheels across the playground?

The affix in *amazement* is the suffix *-ment*. This suffix forms a noun from the verb *amaze*. To amaze is to surprise or astonish. *Amazement* means "surprise."

Thinking It Through

Read the following passage, and then answer the questions that follow.

Once upon a time, our cat was the most <u>adorable</u> kitten! He was skinny and fluffy and had big green eyes. His meow was so small and high that we named him Squeaky.

Now little Squeaky is a big cat. He roams around the neighborhood chasing birds, squirrels, and mice. He would be the most <u>extraordinary</u> hunter, if we did not put bells on his collar. The birds, squirrels, and mice hear Squeaky coming: *jingle, jingle, jingle.* They scatter as quickly as they can!

1. **What is the suffix in <u>adorable</u>? What does <u>adorable</u> MOST LIKELY mean?**

   _____

   _____

   _____

   HINT Find the suffix on the chart. Use its meaning, plus the meaning of the base word, to find the meaning of *adorable*.

2. **What is the prefix in <u>extraordinary</u>? What does <u>extraordinary</u> MOST LIKELY mean?**

   _____

   _____

   _____

   HINT What does *extra* mean? What does *ordinary* mean? What might these word parts mean together?

Coached Example

Read the passage and answer the questions.

In the early 1600s, the scientist Galileo Galilei used a telescope to study the white streak across the night sky called the Milky Way. He discovered that it is actually a large collection of stars. Our sun is just one of these stars.

For hundreds of years, people thought the Milky Way was the only galaxy in the universe. In 1923 and 1924, an astronomer named Edwin Hubble studied photographs of stars in the Andromeda Nebula. He found that the stars got brighter in a regular pattern. Because of this pattern, Hubble could measure their distance from Earth. To the <u>disbelief</u> of many, he found that these stars were so far away that they could not be in our galaxy. We now know that our galaxy is only one of many.

1. Read this sentence from the passage.

   To the <u>disbelief</u> of many, he found that these stars were so far away that they could not be in our galaxy.

   Based on the meaning of its prefix, the word <u>disbelief</u> probably means

   A. not true.

   B. the opposite of belief.

   C. the opposite of wish.

   D. not understood.

   HINT What is the meaning of the base word? How does the prefix *dis-* affect the meaning of the base word?

2. Which of these words has roots that together mean "a tool for seeing far away"?

   A. universe

   B. astronomer

   C. photographs

   D. telescope

   HINT Look back at the roots chart. Find the roots that mean "a tool for seeing" and "far away."

Use the Reading Guide to help you understand the passage.

Reading Guide

What prefix do you see in the word *cooperate*?

Based on its use in paragraph 2, what does *enjoyment* probably mean?

What are the roots of the words *ecology* and *transport*?

Community Supported Agriculture

The supermarket is only one place where you can buy fruits and vegetables. You can also go to a stand at a farm. If you live in a city, far from a farm, you might buy produce at a farmer's market. Now there is another way for people who live in cities to get fresh fruit and vegetables: through Community Supported Agriculture, or a CSA.

Members of a CSA <u>cooperate</u> with a farmer. In the spring, CSA members <u>prepay</u> the farmer for the food they will receive that year. This way, the farmer has money to get the farm ready. Then, each week from June until as late as November, each CSA member receives a share of food from the farm. The farmer brings the food right to the neighborhood where the CSA members live. To the <u>enjoyment</u> of CSA members, the shares often include surprises: vegetables they may never have heard of before, like purslane or callaloo.

There are many benefits to Community Supported Agriculture. One benefit is the delicious, nutritious food itself. The farm benefits, too. It can count on the support of the CSA members. Also, Community Supported Agriculture is good for the environment. Small farms that grow many different plants have a healthy <u>ecology</u>. Also, small farmers are less likely to use large amounts of harmful fertilizer and pesticides. Finally, trucks <u>transport</u> the food a short distance from the farm to the community. So, less pollution is created.

Answer the following questions.

1. Read this sentence from the passage.

   Members of a CSA <u>cooperate</u> with a farmer.

   Based on the meaning of its prefix, the word <u>cooperate</u> MOST LIKELY means

   A. to operate together.

   B. to practice under.

   C. to go opposite from.

   D. to come to.

2. Read this sentence from the passage.

   In the spring, CSA members <u>prepay</u> the farmer for the food they will receive that year.

   The word <u>prepay</u> means

   A. to pay too much.

   B. to pay after making a budget.

   C. to pay ahead of time.

   D. to pay in ways other than with money.

3. Which of the following BEST describes the meaning of <u>ecology</u>?

   A. study of logic

   B. study of sound

   C. study of the environment

   D. study of school

4. Which of the following BEST describes the meaning of <u>transport</u>?

   A. to drive a car

   B. to take the train

   C. to love sports

   D. to carry across

5. What is the suffix in the word <u>enjoyment</u>? What does this word MOST LIKELY mean?

32 Synonyms and Antonyms

L.4.5.c

Getting the Idea

Synonyms are words that have similar meanings. The following chart lists some common synonyms.

Word	Synonyms
bad	evil, wicked
beautiful	lovely, pretty
brave	bold, courageous, fearless
happy	cheerful, glad, joyful
little	small, tiny
difficult	tough, hard
dangerous	risky, hazardous
repair	fix, mend
shout	yell, scream
quickly	fast, speedily

Notice that the meanings of synonyms are similar, but they are not exactly the same. For example, read the sentence below.

I was a bad pianist until I learned to practice.

If you were to replace the word *bad* with *evil*, the sentence would not make sense.

I was an evil pianist until I learned to practice.

The word you choose depends on the idea you are trying to express.

Recognizing synonyms can help you understand the meanings of new words. Read these sentences.

We enjoyed the carnival. We especially <u>fancied</u> the jugglers.

You may not be familiar with the use of *fancy* as a verb. The word *especially* in the second sentence gives a clue that *enjoyed* and *fancied* have similar meanings. From this clue, you can draw the conclusion that the verb *fancy* means "to like" or "to enjoy."

Antonyms are words that have opposite meanings. The following chart lists some common pairs of antonyms.

Word	Antonym
bad	good
beautiful	ugly
brave	cowardly
happy	sad
little	big
difficult	easy
dangerous	safe
repair	break
shout	whisper
quickly	slowly

As with synonyms, recognizing antonyms can help you understand the meanings of new words. Read this passage.

> Cats come in all sizes. On the one hand, there are the <u>great</u> cats: the lions and tigers of Africa and India. On the other hand, there are our small housecats. Most housecats weigh 20 pounds or less.

You may not be familiar with the meaning of *great* as it is used in the second sentence. The phrases *On the one hand* and *On the other hand* give you a clue that *great* and *small* have opposite meanings. From this clue, you can draw the conclusion that *great* means "big."

Thinking It Through

Read the following passage, and then answer the questions that follow.

My grandfather and I are similar in many ways. For example, he sometimes calls me his "little librarian" because I like to read so much. But he enjoys reading, too. I sometimes call him the "giant librarian." After all, he has an entire room <u>packed</u> with books. Every shelf is crowded. I wish that I had one bookcase so full!

However, the books we like are mostly different. I enjoy lively stories and exciting tales of adventure. He likes to read <u>dull</u>, thick novels and history books. He says that one day I'll find his books interesting. We'll see about that!

1. **What synonyms of the word <u>packed</u> can you find in paragraph 1? List two synonyms of <u>packed</u>.**

   _____

   _____

   HINT Which words does the narrator use to describe his grandfather's collection of books?

2. **What antonyms of the word <u>dull</u> can you find in paragraph 2? List three of them.**

   _____

   _____

   HINT Which words does the narrator use to describe the books he likes?

Coached Example

Read the passage and answer the questions.

Louis Comfort Tiffany was a gifted artist. He began his career as a painter. However, he is now known best for his work in the decorative arts. The decorative arts include things made for the home. They can be <u>practical</u> things, like furniture, or <u>ornamental</u> things, like vases.

Tiffany worked with all kinds of materials: metal, textiles, pottery. But he was a master at working with glass. His stained-glass windows were unlike any seen before. He learned how to make glass in new colors. He also learned how to blend colors in a single piece of glass. With his <u>brilliantly</u> colored glass, he made beautiful landscapes.

Tiffany is also known for his unique lampshades. The lampshades were actually dome-shaped stained-glass windows. Lightbulbs lit up the lampshades from within.

---

1. Read this sentence from the passage.

   They can be <u>practical</u> things, like furniture, or <u>ornamental</u> things, like vases.

   If <u>practical</u> means "useful," then <u>ornamental</u> MOST LIKELY means

   A. boring.

   B. for decoration.

   C. sturdy.

   D. ugly.

   HINT The word *or* gives a clue that *practical* and *ornamental* are opposites.

2. Read this sentence from the passage.

   With his <u>brilliantly</u> colored glass, he made beautiful landscapes.

   Which word means the same as <u>brilliantly</u> in this sentence?

   A. smartly

   B. sharply

   C. quickly

   D. brightly

   HINT Replace the word *brilliantly* in the sentence with each answer choice. Which one makes the most sense?

Use the Reading Guide to help you understand the passage.

When the narrator says she likes "the roar of the waves," what sound do you imagine?

Find the word *bored* in paragraph 2. What are some words you might use to say that you are not bored?

Read the last sentence of the passage. What size is a sky that "stretches in every direction"?

To the Mountains Again

Before summer vacation, many of my friends look forward to trips to the ocean. Don't get me wrong. I don't dislike the ocean. I especially like the <u>roar</u> of the waves. But in the summer, I don't really want to sit out on a hot beach in the bright sunshine. I'd rather sit in the shade of a pine tree and feel a cool mountain breeze.

Luckily, in the summertime, my family goes to the mountains. We rent a small cabin next to a lake. There's not much to do inside the cabin. For example, there's no TV. I'm not <u>bored</u> at all. On a sunny day, I might swim from morning until sunset. Or, I might go on a hike with my family. On rainy days, we <u>usually</u> go to the movies. Or, we might even go on a hike in the rain. I like to listen to the sound of the rain in the trees.

At least once during every trip to the mountains, my family and I wake before dawn. We pack lots of sandwiches and water in our bags. We put on <u>sturdy</u> boots. Our goal is to reach the top of a mountain before anyone else gets there. There is nowhere in the world better to be than the top of a mountain. We stand above the tops of the trees. The <u>enormous</u> sky stretches in every direction above our heads.

Answer the following questions.

1. Read this sentence from the passage.

   I especially like the <u>roar</u> of the waves.

   Which word means the opposite of <u>roar</u>?

   A. noise

   B. whisper

   C. laughter

   D. anger

2. When the narrator says that she is not <u>bored</u>, she means that she is

   A. tired.

   B. dull.

   C. lonely.

   D. amused.

3. When the narrator says that the boots are <u>sturdy</u>, she means that they are

   A. strong.

   B. ugly.

   C. big.

   D. rubber.

4. Read this sentence from the passage.

   The <u>enormous</u> sky stretches in every direction above our heads.

   Which word means the same as <u>enormous</u>?

   A. blue

   B. far

   C. cloudy

   D. huge

5. Read this sentence from the passage.

   On rainy days, we <u>usually</u> go to the movies.

   Write a synonym or antonym for <u>usually</u>. Tell whether your word is a synonym or antonym.

   _____

   _____

   _____

33 Similes and Metaphors

L.4.5.a

Getting the Idea

Good writers use words in creative ways. They use figurative language. **Figurative language** does not mean exactly what it says. It is a way for writers to use words to paint a picture in the reader's mind. **Literal language** is language that means exactly what it says. Look at the difference between them.

> *Literal:* Abril dances gracefully.
> *Figurative:* Abril dances like a leaf in the wind.

Abril does not really dance like a leaf. The comparison to a leaf helps you understand how gracefully Abril moves.

This kind of figurative language is called a simile. A **simile** is a comparison of two unlike things using the word *like* or the word *as*. If you read a simile and think about what is being compared, you can understand and appreciate its meaning.

> At the pool, Jerome swims <u>like a fish</u>.

Jerome does not actually swim as a fish would. But by comparing him to one, the writer emphasizes Jerome's skill as a swimmer. Read another example.

> Darlene's suitcase was <u>as light as a feather</u>.

In this sentence, a suitcase is compared to a feather. You know how light a feather is. So you can imagine that the suitcase was very easy to carry.

Simile	Meaning
Nan's hair is like silk.	Nan's hair is soft and smooth.
By lunchtime, Dan was as hungry as a bear.	Dan was very hungry and wanted to eat lunch.
The cheetah ran like the wind.	The cheetah ran extremely quickly.

Like a simile, a **metaphor** compares two things in a sentence. The difference is that metaphors do not use the words *like* or *as*. A metaphor asks the reader to picture one thing as being another. It gives one thing the quality of another. Read the sentence below.

The <u>snow was a blanket</u> on the hills.

The snow is being compared to a blanket. When you think of a blanket, you imagine something thick and soft draping smoothly over a bed. Similarly, the snow provides the hills with a smooth white covering, hiding the frozen ground beneath. This metaphor gives the snow the qualities of a blanket. In that way, it helps you to picture the snowy hills in your mind.

Here's another example:

The king was cruel, and <u>his heart was a stone</u>.

The king's heart is compared to a stone. Stones are hard and cold, so the writer is expressing the idea that the king's personality has the same qualities. He is not open or understanding. The word *cruel* also helps you to understand the metaphor.

Metaphor	Meaning
Ravi is a volcano waiting to erupt.	Ravi will quickly lose his temper.
The baker is an artist when it comes to decorating cakes.	The baker creates beautiful designs with cake icing.
My bedroom is an oven.	The bedroom is very hot and uncomfortable.

Thinking It Through

Read the following passage, and then answer the questions that follow.

Bert woke up to the sound of a knock at the door. He opened the door to see a young boy standing in the rain.

"Would you like to buy a ticket for the Great Giveaway Raffle?" the boy asked. "It's my last one. You could win a new car. <u>The car is as bright as a shiny red apple</u>."

Bert bought the raffle ticket and went back to bed.

Later that day, Bert's phone rang. It was the Great Giveaway, telling him that he had won. <u>Bert's mind was a blank slate</u>. He had totally forgotten buying the raffle ticket that morning. Imagine his surprise!

1. What does the simile in paragraph 2 mean?

_____

_____

_____

HINT Look for two things being compared using the words *like* or *as*.

2. What does the metaphor in the last paragraph mean?

_____

_____

_____

HINT Bert has no memory of what happened that morning.

Coached Example

Read the poem and answer the questions.

The Big Game

The big game was here, and our team was ready,
<u>My knees shook like an earthquake</u>, but I held them steady.
I threw on my uniform and grabbed my baseball,
It was too late to run, too late to stall.

Mom said she'd be there, and Dad would be, too.
I got to the locker room, and <u>it was a zoo</u>!
The players ran around and panicked a lot,
But Coach said, "Don't worry; you've got a great shot."

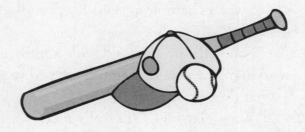

1. The simile <u>my knees shook like an earthquake</u> suggests that the speaker was very

   A. cranky.

   B. excited.

   C. happy.

   D. nervous.

   HINT If your knees are shaking, how do you usually feel?

2. Read the following line from the poem.

   I got to the locker room, and it was a zoo!

   What two things are being compared in this metaphor?

   A. the locker room and a zoo

   B. a locker and a room

   C. the speaker and the locker room

   D. the speaker and a zoo

   HINT Try to imagine what the locker room looked like.

Use the Reading Guide to help you understand the passage.

The Big Bass

How is figurative language used in paragraph 2?

In paragraph 4, how does Jay describe himself to his dad? Is the description a simile or a metaphor? How do you know?

Notice how the descriptions of things, such as the ocean and the flashlight beam, help you picture the events of the story.

Jay loved fishing. His dad had taught him all the basics. This included an important rule: If you don't plan to bring a fish home, you must return it to the water.

One day, after returning home from fishing with his friends at the canal, Jay saw his dad putting some line on a new fishing rod. Jay's dad fished for bass at night when the sky was as black as a crow's wing. Jay had always wanted to join him.

"How was fishing at the canal today?" his dad asked.

"I was a champion," said Jay proudly. "I caught five sea trout!"

"Not bad," his dad said with a smile. He continued working. The new fishing rod seemed to shine like glass. "What do you think?"

"Wow," Jay said. "It's really nice."

"I'm glad," said his dad, "because it's yours. You're big enough now to come bass fishing with me. Let's head down to the ocean after dinner."

That night at the beach, Jay and his dad waded out into the water. The ocean was a bottomless pit. They cast their lines. Suddenly, Jay felt a sharp jerk on his line. He managed to pull a large fish out of the water. The light from their flashlight shone as brightly as the sun as they took the hook out of the fish's mouth. It was an old fish—a king of the sea. At that moment, Jay decided to throw it back into the water. The entire night was as magical as a dream.

Answer the following questions.

1. What two things are being compared in the simile the sky was as black as a crow's wing?

   A. the color black and a crow's wing

   B. the sky and the color black

   C. the sky and a crow's wing

   D. the color black and all colors

2. What does the metaphor the ocean was a bottomless pit mean?

   A. The ocean was blue.

   B. All pits are oceans.

   C. The ocean was deep.

   D. All pits are bottomless.

3. The simile the light from their flashlight shone as brightly as the sun suggests that the light was

   A. very bright.

   B. very hot.

   C. yellow in color.

   D. gold in color.

4. Which sentence from the passage contains a metaphor?

   A. "The new fishing rod seemed to shine like glass."

   B. "At that moment, Jay decided to throw it back into the water."

   C. "'You're big enough now to come bass fishing with me.'"

   D. "It was an old fish—a king of the sea."

5. Read this sentence from the passage.

   The entire night was as magical as a dream.

   Is the sentence a simile or a metaphor? How do you know? What does the sentence mean?

   _____

   _____

   _____

   _____

   _____

34 Idioms, Adages, Proverbs, and Allusions

L.4.5.b, RL.4.4

Getting the Idea

An **idiom** is a phrase whose meaning is different from the individual words that make it up. Idioms are a kind of figurative language. They do not make literal sense, yet most people know exactly what they mean. Read this example.

> Mom told Jeff, "It's time to <u>hit the sack</u>!"

The idiom *hit the sack* does not actually mean to take a sack and hit it. It means "it's time to go to bed."

> "You're <u>driving me up a wall</u>!" the babysitter cried.

No one is traveling up a wall. This idiom means "you are annoying and upsetting me."

> Since the quiz is tomorrow, we're all <u>in the same boat</u>.

The idiom *in the same boat* means the whole class is facing the same thing.

When you come across an unfamiliar idiom, use context, or the words and phrases nearby, to figure it out. You can then **paraphrase** the idiom, or put it into your own words. For example, someone might say: "It's a surprise party for Kara, so *don't let the cat out of the bag*." You use the context to understand that the idiom means "don't let Kara know."

An **adage** is a statement that expresses some kind of truth about human nature, or how people behave. For example:

> Birds of a feather flock together.

This adage means that people with similar interests tend to spend time with one another.

Proverbs are very much like adages. A **proverb** is a saying that offers advice or instruction about how to live your life. Read these examples.

Don't judge a book by its cover.

This proverb teaches that it's not fair to judge someone or something at first glance.

Treat others as you would have them treat you.

This proverb teaches that if you want others to be fair and friendly to you, you must be fair and friendly to them.

You may also come across allusions in reading or speaking with others. An **allusion** is a reference to a person or event from literature, history, or mythology. Here are some allusions based on Greek myths.

Allusion	Meaning
Achilles' heel	Achilles was a great warrior whose only weak spot was his heel. Today, someone's Achilles' heel means his or her area of weakness.
Midas touch	King Midas had the power to turn everything he touched to gold. If someone has the Midas touch, it means what he or she does turns out well or makes money.
Pandora's box	Pandora had a box filled with all the evils of the world, like war, disease, and death, which she was forbidden to open. She eventually did open it, which is how those things came to be in the world. Today, a Pandora's box means a tempting opportunity that could be disastrous.
Odyssey	*The Odyssey* is a very long poem about Odysseus's journey home after the Trojan War. Today, the word *odyssey* means any long trip or adventure.

Thinking It Through

Read the following passage, and then answer the questions that follow.

Today was unbelievable! Troy, Gary, and I were just sitting on the school steps, telling jokes and <u>cracking up</u>. Suddenly, a car driving way too fast nearly hit a dog! The driver blasted his horn and leaned out the window shouting. Not just at the dog, but at us, too. And we hadn't done anything wrong!

We had an assembly lecture on traffic safety last week, and it was great. Maybe the adults in this town need to have a traffic safety lecture of their own. We all have to work together to be safe. It's like they say: <u>better safe than sorry</u>!

1. Is the phrase <u>cracking up</u> an idiom, an adage, or a proverb? Explain your answer and tell the meaning of the phrase in your own words.

_____

_____

_____

_____

HINT   Use the context to help you. The writer and his friends were telling jokes.

2. What does the adage <u>better safe than sorry</u> mean? Paraphrase the adage in your own words.

_____

_____

_____

_____

HINT   Think about what advice this adage offers.

Coached Example

Read the passage and answer the questions.

George was really excited about the class assignment: to create a new game. It could be a board game or a sport. That afternoon, George went home and brainstormed ideas. He thought about games for what seemed like hours. Finally, he realized he needed some help, so he called his friend, Louise. After all, George thought, two heads are better than one!

"Hello? Louise?" George said. "I'm working on that new project, and I was hoping you could give me a hand."

"Oh, I've started the project, too," Louise replied. "I've been sitting here forever trying to think of ideas! I'll be right over."

Together, Louise and George managed to come up with two great games. Teamwork, they agreed, was the best strategy.

---

1. What is the BEST paraphrase of the adage two heads are better than one?

   A. It's important to use your mind to solve problems.

   B. Thinking is the best thing you can do.

   C. Working together is better than working alone.

   D. It's always better to think about everything twice.

    Read the sentences around the phrase. What is George hoping to do?

2. What does the idiom give me a hand mean?

   A. Please help me.

   B. Please wash your hands.

   C. Handle with care.

   D. Think of using your hands.

   HINT George is having trouble coming up with ideas for his project.

Use the Reading Guide to help you understand the passage.

Reading Guide

Reread the words in paragraph 4 that Jen's mom tells her to remember. Think about why Mom says this. What idea is she trying to express?

Jen's mother tells her to *take it easy* in paragraph 6. Is this an idiom or an adage? How do you know?

Allusions can refer to legends, stories, or real events. When Shawn says *the sky is falling* in paragraph 12, to what well-known tale is she referring?

Stage Fright

Jen could hardly believe it. She had let her friend Shawn talk her into trying out for the school play. Now it was the night of the show, and Jen was really scared! Jen was good at many things, but speaking in public had always been her Achilles' heel.

Jen's mother came into her room. "Hey, Jen," she said with a smile. "Ready for the big night?"

"Not really. I'm so nervous. Maybe I bit off more than I can chew."

"Oh, honey. I know it's hard. But remember: It's always darkest before the dawn!"

"Yeah, I guess." Jen frowned.

"Try to take it easy. I'm sure you'll knock their socks off!" She kissed Jen's head and left the room.

Jen wasn't so sure. What if she forgot her lines? What if no one clapped? Jen got up from her bed and stared into the mirror.

"Okay, Jen," she said out loud. "Cut it out! You can *do* this!"

With that, she grabbed her costume and walked out the door.

At school, Shawn gave her a big hug. "Jen," she said, "I know you're nervous. But you know what? I am, too!"

"You are?" Jen asked.

"Sure! Everyone gets a little stage fright," Shawn said. "But really, it's not like the sky is falling! Okay, Chicken Little?"

Jen laughed. With a friend like Shawn by her side, she knew she would do just fine.

Answer the following questions.

1. Read this sentence from the passage.

   "Maybe I bit off more than I can chew!"

   What does this idiom mean?

   A. to eat too much and feel sick

   B. to take on a job you can't finish

   C. to worry about starting something

   D. to avoid seeing your friends

2. Read this sentence from the passage.

   "But really, it's not like the sky is falling!"

   What is the figurative meaning of the sky is falling?

   A. The world is coming to an end.

   B. Everything is new again.

   C. You can accomplish anything.

   D. It's about to start raining.

3. What does the idiom knock their socks off mean?

   A. to make people undress

   B. to change someone's socks

   C. to disappoint an audience

   D. to impress and thrill an audience

4. The adage it's always darkest before the dawn means

   A. the sky is very dark early in the morning.

   B. try your best and don't be discouraged.

   C. things look the worst just before they improve.

   D. the sky is light before dawn.

5. In the passage, Jen feels that speaking in public has always been her Achilles' heel. What does this allusion mean?

   _____

   _____

   _____

   _____

   _____

4 Cumulative Assessment for Lessons 21–34

This passage contains mistakes. Read the passage and answer the questions that follow.

Carmen Salva: Protector of the Land

(1) Carmen Salva is a teacher that grew up in a City called Tilcara in Argentina. (2) It has a rich history and wonderful views. (3) However, Salva felt troubled when she walked around Tilcara. (4) She knew that people were not giving the land the respect it deserved.

(5) On her way to school in the mornings, Salva saw trash nearly everywhere she looked. (6) She saw broken bottles and tin cans. (7) Old tires and bits of plastic. (8) Seeing this did not make Salva feel proud about where she lived. (9) But Salva did not <u>loose</u> hope. (10) Instead, she began to think. (11) She knew that with a plan, she could help make a difference.

(12) A lot of people did not understand the importance of clean water or caring for the land. (13) Many believed that someone else would take care of the litter problem. (14) But Salva knew that everyone needed to be responsible. (15) Salva <u>reviewed</u> her ideas and shared them with her students. (16) Most agreed that litter was a problem. (17) Salva and some of her students began volunteering. (18) A government program gave the students plastic large green trash bags and threw away the litter they collected. (19) Salva and her students started small. (20) They cleaned the area around their school first. (21) Then they moved to other neighborhoods. (22) From the first day, they saw what a difference they made.

(23) Salva created a youth environmental group. (24) She named this group *Esperanza de Vida*. (25) This means "Hope for Life" in English. (26) She knew that teaching people while they were still young was important. (27) There were many things Salva hoped to teach. (28) The country around them was a beautiful place. (29) It deserved to be protected. (30) These were all lessons Salva knew would last a lifetime.

(31) Salva has become a well-known person at her country. (32) Her group is always adding volunteers and working on new projects. (33) Many parents and other adults have become involved, too. (34) Slowly, the community changes. (35) Carmen Salva is proud of the progress that has been made. (36) As she says, It's never too early to start caring for the land you live in and grow up in.

1. Which word from paragraph 1 is NOT capitalized correctly?

   A. Argentina

   B. City

   C. However

   D. Tilcara

2. Which sentence is the correct revision of sentence 36?

   A. As she "says," It's never too early to start caring for the land you live in and grow up in.

   B. "As she says," It's never too early to start caring for the land you live in and grow up in.

   C. As she says, "it's never too early to start caring for the land you live in and grow up in."

   D. As she says, "It's never too early to start caring for the land you live in and grow up in."

3. The correct spelling of the underlined word in sentence 9 is

   A. lose.

   B. loos.

   C. luse.

   D. lews.

4. Which of the following is NOT a complete sentence?

   A. sentence 5

   B. sentence 6

   C. sentence 7

   D. sentence 8

5. What is the correct way to write the verb in sentence 34?

   A. was changing

   B. is changing

   C. changed

   D. will be changing

6. What is the correct revision of sentence 18?

   A. A government program gave the students green large plastic trash bags and threw away the litter they collected.

   B. A government program gave the students large plastic green trash bags and threw away the litter they collected.

   C. A government program gave the students large green plastic trash bags and threw away the litter they collected.

   D. A government program gave the students trash bags of large green plastic and threw away the litter they collected.

7. How could sentence 1 be corrected?

   A. Change *that* to *which*.

   B. Change *that* to *whom*.

   C. Change *that* to *who*.

   D. Change *that* to *she*.

8. What is the correct revision of sentence 31?

   A. Salva has become a well-known person in her country.

   B. Salva has become a well-known person of her country.

   C. Salva has become a well-known person on her country.

   D. Salva has become a well-known person with her country.

9. What is the prefix in the word <u>reviewed</u>? What does the word MOST
LIKELY mean?

_____

_____

_____

_____

Read the passage and answer the questions that follow.

Pearly Whites

Amanda had a dentist appointment, and she was not happy about it. She did not want to go. Her mother, however, would not let her back out.

"It's been six months," Amanda's mom said. "You need to have a check-up."

"Come on, Mom," Amanda <u>pleaded</u>. "Can't I go some other time? My teeth feel fine."

Her mom shook her head and went back to making dinner. It was clear Amanda was not going to be convinced otherwise. Amanda's appointment was scheduled for that Friday after school. On Thursday night, Amanda stood in front of the bathroom mirror after brushing and flossing her teeth. She opened her mouth wide so she could <u>inspect</u> every tooth. She examined each one very closely. Moments later, Amanda's older brother Owen walked by and saw her.

"What are you doing?" Owen asked.

"Nothing, Owen," Amanda replied. "Mind your own business, please."

Owen smiled. He knew about Amanda's appointment, and he knew that she hated going to the dentist. He decided to have a little fun with his sister.

"It's no surprise that Mom is making you go to the dentist," Owen began. "You haven't been there in years."

"It's only been six months," Amanda said, annoyed that her brother was still standing there. "Plus, I brush twice a day. And I floss, too."

"I don't know," Owen continued, shaking his head. "Six months is a pretty long time. Think of how much can happen in six months. You might need to have some of your teeth pulled. Or, you might have a cavity. A lot of kids our age get cavities. If you have one, the dentist might have to use one of his instruments on you. Maybe an old, rusty drill!" Owen sighed dramatically. "I'm sorry, sis," he said. "It looks like you might be in big trouble."

Amanda tried to ignore her brother. Unfortunately, while he talked, she thought she saw something in the mirror—was that a tiny brown spot on one of her teeth? She scraped at it with a fingernail. She hoped it was a shadow, but she was uncertain. What if it was a cavity?

"Ugh! When it rains, it pours. Maybe Owen is right," thought Amanda to herself. "Maybe the dentist is going to have to pull one of my teeth. Maybe I have a cavity, and he's going to use one of his old, rusty drills on me." Amanda's heart sank.

The next day, Amanda sat in the backseat of the car after school. Her appointment with Dr. Boucher was at 4:00. The clock in the car read 3:45. Amanda's palms were sweaty. She could feel a lump rising in her throat. Her stomach ached as her mom drove. She considered asking her mom if she would cancel the appointment, but instead she sat there in silence. Owen's <u>words</u> from the day before rang in her ears.

"Hey, Mom," Amanda said. "How often does Dr. Boucher use his rusty drill?"

"What rusty drill?" Mom asked with a laugh. "Who put that idea in your head?"

Amanda's face became as red as a stoplight. "A little bird told me," she said with a frown. They arrived at Dr. Boucher's office right on time. Amanda was in the dentist's chair at 4:01.

Dr. Boucher spoke softly. He asked Amanda about school and quickly set to work on her teeth. For twenty minutes, Amanda waited for him to open a drawer containing a pair of pliers and a rusty drill. She imagined how she would look with false teeth like Grandpa's.

Before Amanda knew it, Dr. Boucher was finished. He removed his rubber gloves. Amanda wiped her mouth with a paper towel and felt her teeth with her tongue. They were all there. Amanda breathed a sigh of relief. Dr. Boucher smiled broadly.

"Great work, Amanda," said Dr. Boucher. "Now, if only your brother took such good care of his teeth."

10. Which sentence from the passage is a simile?

   A. "Amanda's face became as red as a stoplight."

   B. "They arrived at Dr. Boucher's office right on time."

   C. "Amanda was in the dentist's chair at 4:01."

   D. "Before Amanda knew it, Dr. Boucher was finished."

11. What is the best way to paraphrase the adage when it rains, it pours?

   A. The weather is always hard to predict.

   B. When things are bad, sometimes they can get even worse.

   C. Always be prepared for the worst.

   D. Nature is sometimes on your side.

12. What is a synonym for the word pleaded?

   A. begged

   B. asked

   C. requested

   D. discussed

13. Read this sentence from the passage.

   Owen's words from the day before rang in her ears.

   Which word would make the underlined word more precise?

   A. joke

   B. threat

   C. stories

   D. warning

14. Read this sentence from the passage.

   She opened her mouth wide so she could inspect every tooth.

   What does the word inspect mean? What context clues helped you figure out the meaning of this word?

   _____

   _____

   _____

   _____

**Crosswalk Coach for the
Common Core State Standards,
English Language Arts, Grade 4**

SUMMATIVE ASSESSMENT
FOR CHAPTERS 1–4

Name: _____

Session 1

Read the passage and answer the questions that follow.

Earth Shake!

It was four o'clock in the morning on February 10, 2010. In Chicago, everyone in Kim's family was sleeping. Suddenly the walls began to shake! Her room was a gigantic rattle! Kim's eyes snapped open. At first she didn't know what was going on. Then her mom and dad ran into her room.

"It's an earthquake!" her dad said.

He pulled Kim out of bed. They stood near the wall on the opposite side of the room from the window. Kim's mom put her arms around her daughter and held her close. After about six seconds, the shaking stopped.

"Is everyone OK?" her father asked. Kim and her mom were fine. They went into the living room and turned on the TV to get news about what had happened. As they watched the news, they learned more and more about the earthquake. One thing was clear—they were not the only people who felt it.

After the earthquake hit, more than 10,000 people sent reports to the U.S. Geological Survey, or USGS. That's the government agency that tracks natural hazards like earthquakes, wildfires, floods, hurricanes, landslides, and volcanoes.

Kim and her family learned more facts about the earthquake. The U.S. Geological Survey reported that it shook an area about 45 miles from Chicago. The earthquake measured 3.8 on the Richter scale.

"What's the Richter scale?" Kim asked.

"The Richter scale is how we measure earthquakes," her mom told her. "It's named for Charles Richter, the man who developed it."

"This wasn't a very strong earthquake," her dad said. "The walls shook, but earthquakes this size don't cause much damage. Usually, it takes an earthquake of 5.0 or more on the Richter scale to cause damage."

"It sure felt strong to me," said Kim.

"Earthquakes are very powerful," her mom said, nodding. "This one was felt by millions of people. The USGS is saying that people felt it in Georgia, Tennessee, Kentucky, Ohio, Indiana, Michigan, Iowa, and Wisconsin, as well as here in Illinois."

"Wow!" Kim's eyes opened wide. "You mean people in all those states felt the same thing we did?"

"They may not have felt the exact same thing," her dad answered. "Their walls didn't shake like ours did because they were farther from the place where the earthquake happened. That's called the epicenter. The USGS is saying that the epicenter of this quake was between the towns of Virgil and Sycamore. That's about 50 miles from here."

"Will there be another one?" Kim wanted to know.

"Probably not," her mother told her. "Earthquakes are very common in places like California. They're much less common in Illinois and other parts of the Midwest."

"But what if there is another one?" Kim asked.

"That's a good question," said her mom. "Let's talk about earthquake safety. If you're indoors during an earthquake, you should find a safe place in the room. That could be under a strong desk or table, or along a wall."

"Is that why we all stood next to the wall?" asked Kim.

"Yes," her mom replied. "But it wasn't just any wall. We stood near the wall that was far from the window."

"During an earthquake, things might fall or break," her dad added. "So you don't want to be near a window or large mirrors. And you don't want to be near heavy furniture, hanging objects, or anything else that might fall."

"OK," said Kim. "But what should I do next?"

"Hold on to something solid and wait until the earthquake stops," her mom said. "They're kind of scary while they're happening, but they don't last very long."

"And remember—they don't happen here very often," her dad added.

"I'm glad about that!" said Kim. "But if there is another earthquake, I know what to do."

1. You know the family did not lose electricity during the earthquake because

    A. they turned on the television and listened to the news.

    B. Kim's mom turned on the lights in her room.

    C. the telephone rang.

    D. they were 50 miles from the epicenter of the earthquake.

2. According to the passage, what did the earthquake measure on the Richter scale?

    A. 1.1

    B. 3.8

    C. 5.0

    D. 10.0

3. Which sentence from the passage is a metaphor?

    A. "One thing was clear—they were not the only people who felt it."

    B. "'The walls shook, but earthquakes this size don't cause much damage.'"

    C. "After about six seconds, the shaking stopped."

    D. "Her room was a gigantic rattle!"

4. Write a one-sentence summary of this story. What is the major event in this story?

    _____

    _____

    _____

    _____

    _____

Your Friend the Bat

Have you ever seen a bat? They kind of look like rats with wings. Many people think that bats are creepy. This reputation is undeserved—they are actually not bad. In fact, bats are no more dangerous than house flies. People may have these wrong ideas because bats are not familiar to most of us. Many people rarely see bats in person. But in photos, they can look frightening. Their lips are often curled back, showing their teeth. Bats do this when they sense danger, such as when someone comes close to take a picture.

Bats live in most parts of the world. There are about 900 kinds of bats. Many are small, though each species looks different from the others. They are the only mammals that can truly fly. (You have probably heard of flying squirrels, but these animals glide rather than fly.)

Bats are mammals, so they grow inside their mothers. Baby bats are called pups. They are usually born between the months of May and July. When pups are first born, they rely on their mothers to feed them. When bats are about three or four weeks old, they can find food on their own. If they do not have any diseases or get in any accidents, bats can live to be thirty years old.

If insects bug you, you'd be glad to hear this: most bats eat insects, sometimes in very large amounts. Some small bats can eat hundreds, or even thousands, of insects in one night. Most bats eat larger insects such as moths, but will also eat smaller insects such as flies and mosquitoes. So, if you have bats around, you might not be swatting as many flies away. Some bats eat ripe fruit, nectar, small fish, frogs, birds, or rodents. Some bats even eat other bats!

Have you ever heard the expression "blind as a bat"? Well, that's not actually correct. All bats *can* see. But some also are able to use sounds to find their way in the dark. These bats make special noises. Then they listen for sounds that bounce back from things around them. The bats can "see" the sounds just as people can see pictures from light reflected into their eyes. In this way, bats are able to escape dangers and catch food in complete darkness. This lets them hunt and feed at night and sleep during the day.

When sleeping or just resting, bats hang upside down. This may seem strange, but their bodies allow them to do this. This ability lets bats roost in places where other animals—predators in particular—could not. These places include the ceilings of caves and the rafters of old buildings. Caves can be very popular with bats. A large cave in Texas has twenty million bats living in it!

Sometimes people build bat houses out of wood hoping to attract bats to their yards and give them a safe place to live. Bats will often not move into the bat houses unless some other animals take them over first. The bats eat mosquitoes and other insects that may be in the yard. In this way, they can help the people and the plant life around them. If you would like to help out a family of bats, look for library books or Web sites that tell how to build a bat house and where to place it. You might just be able to have a "pet" bat of your own!

5. Bats are known to eat all of the following EXCEPT

   A. flies.

   B. bats.

   C. birds.

   D. turtles.

6. Which sentence from the passage BEST supports the idea that bats can be helpful to humans?

   A. "They are usually born between the months of May and July."

   B. "These places include the ceilings of caves and the rafters of old buildings."

   C. "The bats eat mosquitoes and other insects that may be in the yard."

   D. "You might just be able to have a 'pet' bat of your own!"

7. What do bat pups do right after they are born?

   A. stay with their mothers

   B. fly around and look for food

   C. get into accidents

   D. get a disease

8. According to the passage, bats

   A. should all travel together.

   B. are scary animals that do not like people.

   C. would not make good pets.

   D. are interesting creatures that can help people.

9. Write the main idea of paragraph 4.

   _____

   _____

   _____

   _____

Crow and the Pitcher
adapted from a fable by Aesop

Crow was a bird who lived a long time ago in a beautiful place. During the day, Crow would fly about and listen to the people in the town below. He heard their stories and loved their laughter. The wind carried Crow around each day, and he flew about in peace. He lived a happy life and was as <u>content</u> as a bird could be.

One day, Crow decided to take a trip and travel to a distant land. He did not know much about the land he was visiting, but he was eager to see it. Crow flew for days and days to the new place. When he finally arrived, he was very tired. He was also very hungry. Most of all, after all that flying, Crow was very, very thirsty.

The sun blazed in the sky above the land. The air was dry, and the soil was cracked. The rays of the sun beat down on Crow as he walked along the road, looking for water. The heat was so strong that Crow began to feel weak. Crow looked east and west, north and south, but he could find no river, lake, or pond in sight. He had to find water—and fast!

Finally, Crow came to the end of a long road. In the small alley nearby, Crow saw a tall pitcher—the kind used to hold water. At last Crow could have a drink of water! He excitedly went to the pitcher and pointed his beak into the top of it. He opened his beak, then closed it. "No water!" Crow thought. He sighed with sadness. He was so very thirsty. How could this be? Then Crow looked deep into the pitcher. He saw water at the very bottom! But how would he be able to reach it? His beak was short and the pitcher was tall. It seemed impossible!

Crow thought and thought. He knew that he needed to figure out a way to reach the water at the bottom of the pitcher. Then Crow looked down on the ground and saw a small pebble. He reached down, picked up the pebble with his beak, and dropped it into the pitcher. Next, he hopped over to the other side of the road, where he saw another pebble. He picked up that pebble and put it into the pitcher as well. Crow continued walking around picking up pebbles. As he dropped each pebble into the pitcher, the water rose higher and higher.

Now Crow knew what he needed to do. He began to fly here and there, picking up pebbles and bringing them back to the pitcher. Finally, after all of his hard work, Crow dropped the last pebble into the pitcher. Just as he did, the water rose close enough to the top for him to stick his beak in and take a long, cool drink.

The water was crisp and refreshing. Crow <u>gulped</u> it down and smiled. He had learned an important lesson: Hard work pays off in the end. Crow finished his drink and flew back home.

10. Who is the narrator of "The Crow and the Pitcher"?

  A. Crow

  B. the pitcher

  C. someone outside of the story

  D. another crow

11. What BEST describes the conflict in this passage?

  A. Crow is bored and travels to a new land.

  B. Crow is thirsty but can't find any water.

  C. Crow is lost and must find a way home.

  D. Crow is looking for a pitcher to hold his water.

12. Which sentence BEST states the theme of this passage?

  A. Traveling is a learning experience.

  B. Haste makes waste.

  C. Endings are better than beginnings.

  D. Working patiently brings rewards.

13. Which word means the same as gulped as it is used in this passage?

  A. drank

  B. sipped

  C. tasted

  D. sniffed

14. Read this sentence from the passage.

  He lived a happy life and was as <u>content</u> as a bird could be.

  Write two synonyms for the word <u>content</u> as it is used in the sentence. Explain why your words are synonyms.

  _____

  _____

  _____

  _____

  _____

Read the passage and answer the questions that follow.

SUMMATIVE ASSESSMENT

The Story of Tantalus
adapted from a Greek myth

Once there was a man named Tantalus who ruled a place called Sipylos, in the country of Greece. Tantalus was the son of the god Zeus and a woman who was mortal, or not a god. Zeus adored his son. One day, he decided to give Tantalus something very special. Zeus and the other Greek gods told Tantalus that he was allowed to dine with them on Mount Olympus, where they lived.

This privilege was indeed rare. No other mortals were allowed to dine with the gods. This meant that no one had ever tasted what the gods ate and drank. Still, everyone knew that the food of the gods must be more delicious than any other food. Zeus took Tantalus to Mount Olympus. There, he was able to enjoy ambrosia, the food of the gods, and nectar, their special drink. He expected the food would be good, but this was better than anything anyone had ever tasted on Earth!

Back home, Tantalus could not help but tell the people in Sipylos about the ambrosia and nectar. He was not bragging, but his enthusiasm soon made everyone want to taste the food of the gods. Yet this was the only rule that Zeus had made when he had invited Tantalus to Mount Olympus: He could never share the food he had there with other mortals.

At first, Tantalus was happy with the arrangement. Before long, though, he realized that people were jealous of his special relationship to the gods. Even worse, they began to pressure him to share some of the ambrosia and nectar. Tantalus explained that this was not allowed. The people replied that he was just being selfish and greedy. They told him that he was afraid to bring a tiny bit of the food down from Mount Olympus.

Tantalus was a good king, and his people liked him. However, when he saw their jealousy and heard their grumbling, he became upset. He worried and worried about his <u>predicament</u> until it upset his stomach. "How can I enjoy this wonderful food with a stomachache?" he wondered. Tantalus finally decided that the love of his people was more important than the trust of the gods. He began taking small portions of ambrosia and nectar with him when he left Mount Olympus.

301

Before long, he was very popular indeed! Everyone was demanding a bite or a sip of the heavenly treats. Tantalus found he had to steal more and more of the food to avoid a riot. Eventually, of course, the gods discovered what Tantalus was up to. They were furious. The most furious of all was Zeus.

"We give you this great privilege," Zeus roared, "and you thank us with your greed and stealing? You have betrayed us, Tantalus! You have done the one thing that we asked you never to do!"

Tantalus knew that he was guilty, and he agreed to accept his punishment. The gods agreed that the punishment should fit the crime. Because Tantalus had been greedy and selfish with their food and drink, he should be hungry and thirsty for the rest of his life. They summoned Tantalus to Mount Olympus.

"For your crime against us," Zeus began, "you must stand up to your neck in water at the edge of a lake, with the branches of fruit trees hanging above you. Forever."

"Well," thought Tantalus, "this could be worse. At least I can eat and drink!"

The gods brought him to the lake. They placed him in it, beneath the branches full of ripe, tempting fruit. When he felt a bit hungry, Tantalus reached up for an apple. But the branch rose up out of reach. He tried reaching for sweet grapes, and those vines also pulled away from him. He bent to sip from the water all around him. But when he did, the water level went down. He couldn't get a single drop of water!

This was Tantalus's sad fate. He would be forever thirsty and hungry, and tempted by food and water just beyond his reach.

15. Which point of view is used in "The Story of Tantalus"?

    A. first-person

    B. second-person

    C. third-person limited

    D. third-person omniscient

16. The climax of the passage is when

    A. Tantalus is invited to Mount Olympus.

    B. Zeus announces the punishment.

    C. Tantalus first tastes ambrosia.

    D. Tantalus tells people about ambrosia and nectar.

17. Read this sentence from the passage.

    He worried and worried about his <u>predicament</u> until it upset his stomach.

    The word <u>predicament</u> means

    A. a difficult situation.

    B. a special privilege.

    C. a poor decision.

    D. a painful illness.

18. Based on what happens to Tantalus at the end of the story, what do you think the word <u>tantalize</u> means?

    A. to tease by holding something back

    B. to prepare delicious foods

    C. to behave dishonestly

    D. to rule a land fairly

Use "Crow and the Pitcher" and "The Story of Tantalus" to answer questions 19–20.

19. How are the motivations of Crow and Tantalus MOST different?

    A. Tantalus wants to please his father, while Crow wants to see a new place.

    B. Tantalus wants to deceive the gods, while Crow wants to steal food

    C. Tantalus wants to travel the world, while Crow wants to stay at home.

    D. Tantalus wants to be popular with everyone, while Crow wants to quench his thirst.

20. Compare and contrast the characters of Crow and Tantalus. What lesson do you think each of them learned?

    _____

    _____

    _____

    _____

    _____

    _____

    _____

    _____

Read the poem and answer the questions that follow.

My Shadow
by Robert Louis Stevenson

I have a little shadow that goes in and out with me,
And what can be the use of him is more than I can see.
He is very, very like me from the heels up to the head;
And I see him jump before me, when I jump into my bed.

The funniest thing about him is the way he likes to grow—
Not at all like proper children, which is always very slow;
For he sometimes shoots up taller like an India-rubber ball,
And he sometimes goes so little that there's none of him at all.

He hasn't got a notion of how children ought to play,
He can only make a fool of me in every sort of way.
He stays so close behind me, he's a coward you can see;
I'd think shame to stick to nursie as that shadow sticks to me!

One morning, very early, before the sun was up,
I rose and found the shining dew on every buttercup;
But my lazy little shadow, like an errant sleepy-head,
Had stayed at home behind me and was fast asleep in bed.

21. Which version shows which syllables are stressed in line 2?

A. <u>And</u> what <u>can</u> be <u>the</u> use <u>of</u> him is more <u>than</u> I <u>can</u> see

B. And <u>what</u> <u>can</u> be the <u>use</u> <u>of</u> him is <u>more</u> <u>than</u> I can see

C. And <u>what</u> can <u>be</u> the <u>use</u> of <u>him</u> is <u>more</u> than <u>I</u> can <u>see</u>

D. And <u>what</u> <u>can</u> <u>be</u> the use of him <u>is</u> <u>more</u> than I <u>can</u> <u>see</u>

22. Which word BEST describes the poet's tone?

A. serious

B. playful

C. frightened

D. miserable

23. Which line from the poem contains a simile?

A. One morning, very early, before the sun was up

B. For he sometimes shoots up taller like an India-rubber ball

C. He stays so close behind me, he's a coward you can see

D. And I see him jump before me, when I jump into my bed

24. How does the speaker feel about his shadow? Provide examples from the poem.

_____

_____

_____

_____

_____

_____

_____

Read the passage and answer the questions that follow.

The United States Coast Guard

The United States has five armed services: the Army, the Navy, the Marine Corps, the Air Force, and the Coast Guard. One way to think of the Coast Guard is as the police officers of the nation's coastline. They patrol the water near the United States. They make sure that the laws are followed at sea. They also make sure that people on boats are safe. The U.S. Coast Guard provides an <u>essential</u> service for our country.

The Coast Guard is the oldest sea service in our country. It used to be called the Revenue Cutter Service. It was formed on August 4, 1790. It started with only one hundred people and ten fast ships called cutters. The Revenue Cutter Service was formed to enforce the law at sea. The cutters made sure ships from other countries did not enter the United States without permission.

In the 1790s and 1800s, Congress passed laws to stop slave ships from coming into the United States. The cutters stopped ships carrying enslaved Africans and freed them. They also tried to stop pirates from attacking other ships. For a while, the cutters were the country's only armed force on the water. The Navy was not formed until 1798. So, sometimes the cutters fought in battles. Even today, the Coast Guard helps out in wars.

The Coast Guard as we know it today was formed in 1915. This happened when the Revenue Cutter Service joined with the Life-Saving Service. Later, other services were also joined with the Coast Guard. The Coast Guard now performs many jobs. One of its biggest jobs is to help people in trouble. If something bad happens to a boat, the Coast Guard finds the boat and tries to save the people onboard. Even in very stormy seas, the Coast Guard will do everything it can to rescue people.

Accidents at sea are a major problem. To solve this problem, the Coast Guard tries to stop accidents from happening. One way it does this is by making sure lighthouses are working properly. Lighthouses are built at specific places on the coasts. They help sailors stay out of danger by showing where it is not safe to go. The Coast Guard makes sure all the country's lighthouses are working at all times.

In 1912, a ship called the *Titanic* sank after hitting an iceberg. Because of this accident, it was decided that ships needed to be more aware of dangerous icebergs. The Coast Guard now tracks the locations of icebergs. It tells sailors where icebergs are so that they can stay away from them. This helps prevent accidents like the one that happened to the *Titanic*. With this <u>precaution</u>, the Coast Guard helps to save lives every year.

The Coast Guard works to stop people from importing illegal items into the country. The Coast Guard has the authority to stop and search any boat at sea that they believe might be bringing things into the country illegally.

The Coast Guard doesn't just protect people. It also protects the environment. When ships or offshore oil rigs are damaged, oil spills into the sea. This can be very <u>harmful</u> to fish and other animals. The Coast Guard tries to stop oil from spreading. It also helps animals that have been hurt by spilled oil.

U.S. Coast Guard Timeline

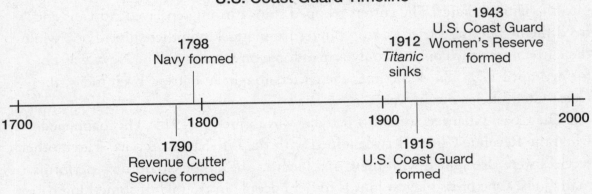

25. Which text structure is used in paragraphs 3 and 4 of the passage?

A. cause and effect

B. problem and solution

C. compare and contrast

D. chronological order

26. Read this sentence from the passage.

The U.S. Coast Guard provides an essential service for our country.

The word essential means

A. necessary.

B. complicated.

C. expensive.

D. fair.

27. What information can readers get from the timeline that they cannot get from the passage?

A. when the Reserve Cutter service was formed

B. when the U.S. Coast Guard Women's Reserve was formed

C. how the U.S. Coast Guard helps with oil spills

D. when the *Titantic* sank

28. Which text structure is used in paragraph 5 of the passage?

A. cause and effect

B. problem and solution

C. compare and contrast

D. chronological order

29. What is the root of the word harmful?

A. armful

B. ful

C. harm

D. har

30. Based on the meaning of its prefix, the word precaution MOST LIKELY means

A. care taken after.

B. care taken before.

C. care not taken.

D. care taken again.

In the Army

The United States Army is a <u>division</u> of the five United States armed forces. Just as the U.S. Navy protects the country on the high seas, the Army protects it on land. The soldiers in the Army must go through months of training. There are army bases in our country where soldiers are trained. Sometimes, a soldier's family will stay on or near an army base so they can remain together.

The Army was first formed in 1775, and George Washington was the commander, or the person in control. Back then, it was called the Continental Army. At that time, America was still a part of Great Britain and not an independent country. The people of America wanted to be a free nation, free from the rule of Great Britain. So they banded together under George Washington to fight for their freedom. George Washington went on to become the first president of the United States. Today, our president is also the commander-in-chief of all of the armed forces.

In the 1800s, the Army played an important role in the growth of America. As a result of the Mexican War, the Texas Revolution, and the Louisiana Purchase, the territory of the United States increased. The Army was involved in gaining and settling all of the new land. In the last century, the United States Army fought in World War I and World War II, and the wars in Korea and Vietnam.

The Army helps to protect the citizens of the United States. It is divided into three parts: the regular Army, the Army Reserve, and the National Guard. There are many different ranks, or levels, that a soldier can serve in during his or her career. Here are some Army titles: private, corporal, sergeant, lieutenant, captain, major, colonel, and general. The longer a soldier serves in the Army and the more he or she accomplishes, the higher he or she can rise in the ranks. Soldiers of a higher rank command lower-ranking soldiers.

Soldiers in the Army must protect themselves from danger. There is a special uniform that soldiers wear. This is called the Army Combat Uniform (ACU). This uniform has a camouflage pattern on it. The pattern has green and brown swirls and shapes that blend easily into the natural environment. Different types of camouflage patterns are used for different environments. The uniform includes a helmet and strong boots to help protect soldier's feet. The uniform is fire-resistant as well. It is important that soldiers have uniforms that allow them to do their many difficult jobs as safely as possible.

There are two holidays when everyone can honor the people in our armed forces. Every November 11, we observe Veterans Day by honoring living military <u>veterans</u>. Memorial Day is celebrated on the last Monday in May each year. On this day, we remember the soldiers who have died while on duty.

Some soldiers are stationed very far from their families. Many of them work in very dangerous and stressful conditions. It can be difficult, but they know that their jobs are extremely important. As George Washington himself said, "To be prepared for war is one of the most [effective] means of preserving peace."

By celebrating Memorial Day and Veterans Day, we say "thank you" to the brave men and women who are responsible for preserving peace.

31. Look at the dictionary entry below.

> **di·vi·sion** *noun* **1.** a term in mathematics that describes dividing a number by another number **2.** the act of dividing something into parts **3.** a part of the military **4.** an argument that separates people

Which definition tells you what <u>division</u> means as used in the passage?

A. definition 1

B. definition 2

C. definition 3

D. definition 4

32. What does the word <u>veteran</u> mean?

A. the commander-in-chief of the armed forces

B. a person who has served in the military

C. specially patterned clothing for soldiers

D. a place where soldiers are trained

33. Which part of "In the Army" is a primary source?

A. the exact date of Memorial Day

B. the quote from George Washington

C. the list of U.S. Army ranks

D. the description of the Army Combat Uniform

34. Claire is taking notes on paragraph 5 of "In the Army." What should her notes look like? Write them on the lines below.

_____

_____

_____

_____

_____

_____

_____

35. Which statement BEST describes how "The United States Coast Guard" and "In the Army" are alike?

   A. Both passages are about American culture.

   B. Both passages are about U.S. armed services.

   C. Both passages are about military training.

   D. Both passages include timelines.

36. One difference between the two passages is that

   A. the first passage talks about the U.S. Coast Guard, while the second passage talks about the U.S. Army.

   B. the first passage describes the U.S. Navy, while the second passage describes the U.S. Army.

   C. the first passage focuses on America, while the second passage focuses on other countries.

   D. the first passage tells the history of the U.S. Coast Guard, while the second passage tells the history of the U.S. Navy.

SUMMATIVE ASSESSMENT

Support Public Art!

I believe that everyone should support public art projects. Works of public art include statues, murals, and fountains. These are usually works done by artists hired by the town or community. They are always in public spaces, for everyone to enjoy. This can mean the art might appear in a park or a town square, but also in other public places, such as hospitals, train stations, post offices, and schools. Anyone would agree that this kind of art is so much better than limiting art to museums, where people have to pay to see it, or private homes, where practically no one ever gets to enjoy it!

Public art is important because, sometimes, it has a message. For example, sometimes art honors something. It could be a statue of a well-known storybook character, or a mural of a famous event or person from history. Some people object to public art because of this. For example, these people say that a statue of a famous general from a war could insult or upset some people. Just because this person was a hero for one side of the war, he could have been responsible for a lot of suffering to the other side. Some of these people even say that any kind of art relating to war is bad, because war is bad. But this is silly! Everyone knows war is bad, but that might be the best reason of all to choose it as a subject for public art—so that we never forget what happened and hopefully never repeat it. Just because there is public art that has to do with war, it doesn't mean you can't make art celebrating peace!

Sometimes public art has nothing to do with history. This art is sometimes called "art for art's sake." It is the most beautiful of all. It can be things from nature, like animals, or statues of people. People have been making art like this for centuries. Even the ancient Greeks and Romans did it, and if they made public art like this back then, we certainly should do the same today.

Some people argue that public art is a wasteful way to use public money, which comes from the taxes that working people pay. They feel that this money should be spent on fire departments, schools, and hospitals. Now, those sorts of things are very important, and need to be paid for. But I'm saying that public art is just as important and also deserves funding. Public art makes people happy! It improves the lives of everyone who sees it.

Best of all, some public art is "interactive." This means it is art that you can work with, play with, and even learn from. A famous example of this is a fountain called a "hydraulophone" outside the Ontario Science Centre in Canada. This fountain is also a musical instrument that anyone can play by blocking the flow of water from different pipes. Who would object to a beautiful cooling fountain that everyone can play with, listen to, and learn from? Could any public art be better than that?

I hope I have helped you see that public art is important for every community. It needs all of our support. Some people say, "Beauty is in the eye of the beholder." I say, when beauty is in public, every one of us gets to behold and enjoy it.

37. Which of the following sentences from the passage is an opinion?

    A. "It is the most beautiful of all."

    B. "Works of public art include statues, murals, and fountains."

    C. "This means it is art that you can work with, play with, and even learn from."

    D. "These are usually works done by artists hired by the town or community."

38. What do the facts in paragraph 5 provide evidence for?

    A. Interactive art should include music.

    B. Interactive art is the best kind of art.

    C. Everyone should learn to play the hydraulophone.

    D. We should build more fountains.

39. Where would you look to learn more about interactive public art projects?

    A. almanac

    B. atlas

    C. Internet

    D. dictionary

40. Read this sentence from the passage.

    Some people say, "Beauty is in the eye of the beholder."

    What is the meaning of the adage <u>beauty is in the eye of the beholder</u>?

    _____

    _____

    _____

    _____

    _____

    _____

Help Save Animals!

(1) I am sitting in class yesterday when something interesting happened. (2) Our teacher gave us a new colorful magazine about nature. (3) We read an article about some of the endangered species on our Planet. (4) An endangered species is a group of animals that are becoming extinct, or no longer living on Earth. (5) I really love animals. (6) It made me angry and sad to hear about what is happening to them. (7) There are endangered species in many different parts of the world, including Asia, Africa, and South America. (8) But there are also endangered species right here in the United States! (9) A few of the animals that are currently endangered is certain types of bats, bears, foxes, seals, and sheep, to name only a few.

(10) In many cases, the reason that these animals have become endangered is because of what humans have done. (11) For example, when people move into a new area and build homes and buildings, they often have to destroy the places where animals live, like nests and trees. (12) Pollution caused by humans can hurt animals, too. (13) If we dump garbage on land or in the sea, the animals that live there are in trouble.

(14) One way to help save endangered species is through conservation of wildlife. (15) Wildlife <u>conversation</u> usually means setting aside preserves, or large areas of land, and protecting them. (16) No one is allowed to build homes or other buildings on a preserve. (17) Instead, the land is saved for the animals that live there I asked my teacher how we could help. (18) She said we could get in touch with our local state office to learn how to help preserve wildlife. (19) Another thing we could do is organize a clean-up in our local park. (20) Neighbors, friends, and others in the community. (21) A final thing we can do to help nature in general is to always recycle at home and in school.

(22) People which love animals usually own pets, such as a cat or a dog. (23) Among all the animals in the world, they are the most important to some people (24) Endangered species are animals, too. (25) They deserve to have our care and respect? (26) The animals on this world need our help!

41. How should sentence 22 be corrected?

    A. Change *which* to *that*.

    B. Change *which* to *who*.

    C. Change *love* to *loves*.

    D. Change *which* to *whom*.

42. What is the BEST way to rewrite sentence 26?

    A. The animals or this world need our help!

    B. The animals at this world need our help!

    C. The animals of this world need our help!

    D. The animals about this world need our help!

43. Which of the following words from paragraph 1 is NOT capitalized correctly?

    A. Planet

    B. Asia

    C. South America

    D. United States

44. What is the correct way to write the verb in sentence 1?

    A. had been sitting

    B. were sitting

    C. was sitting

    D. will be sitting

45. What is the BEST way to write sentence 2?

    A. Our teacher gave us a new magazine about colorful nature.

    B. Our teacher gave us a new but colorful magazine about nature.

    C. Our teacher gave us a new, colorful magazine about nature.

    D. Our teacher gave us a colorful new magazine about nature.

46. Which word should replace the underlined word in sentence 15?

    A. conserve

    B. conservation

    C. conversant

    D. condensation

47. Which sentence below uses incorrect punctuation?

    A. They deserve to have our care and respect?

    B. Endangered species are animals, too.

    C. One way to help save endangered species is through conservation of wildlife.

    D. But there are also endangered species right here in the United States!

48. Which of the following is a run-on sentence?

    A. Wildlife conservation usually means setting aside preserves, or large areas of land, and protecting them.

    B. No one is allowed to build homes or other buildings on a preserve.

    C. Instead, the land is saved for the animals that live there I asked my teacher how we could help.

    D. I really love animals.

49. Which of the following is a sentence fragment?

    A. People who love animals usually own pets, such as a cat or a dog.

    B. Neighbors, friends, and others in the community.

    C. I am sitting in class yesterday when something interesting happened.

    D. Another thing we could do is organize a clean-up in our local park.

50. Which sentence has incorrect subject-verb agreement?

    A. sentence 4

    B. sentence 6

    C. sentence 9

    D. sentence 13

STOP

Session 2

Persuasive Prompt

Many students bring their lunches from home every day. Others prefer to eat the food provided in the cafeteria. Do you think schools should continue to provide lunches for students, or would it better for students to bring their own lunches from home? Write a letter to your school principal explaining your views. Be sure to use reasons and details to support your opinion.

Does your letter

- ❑ have a clear topic?
- ❑ show a point of view about that topic?
- ❑ have a logical structure?
- ❑ support reasons with details?
- ❑ connect reasons and details with the right words or phrases?
- ❑ use a style and vocabulary that is correct for the audience and purpose?
- ❑ have a solid conclusion?
- ❑ have good spelling, capitalization, and punctuation?
- ❑ follow the rules for good grammar?

Write your response on the page provided. You may use your own paper if you need more space.

Glossary

adage a statement that contains some kind of truth about human nature (Lesson 34)

adjective a word that describes a person, place, or thing (Lesson 22)

adverb a word that describes a verb, an adjective, or another adverb (Lesson 22)

affix a prefix or suffix that is added to a root word (Lesson 31)

agree to match in gender (male, female, or neither) and number (singular or plural) (Lesson 23)

allusion a reference to a person or event from literature, history, or mythology (Lesson 34)

antecedent the word a pronoun replaces (Lesson 23)

antonym a word that means the opposite of another word (Lesson 32)

apostrophe a punctuation mark used to create a contraction or a possessive noun (Lesson 28)

argument a written piece that states and defends an opinion (Lesson 16)

bibliography an organized list of resources used to write an article or a report (Lesson 20)

capitalization using capital (or uppercase) letters where necessary (Lesson 27)

cast of characters a list of characters who appear in a play (Lesson 5)

cause a reason why something happens (Lesson 11)

characters the main actors in a story. They can be people, animals, or other creatures. (Lessons 3, 5, 18)

character trait a quality possessed by a character (Lesson 3)

chart a graphic aid that uses columns and rows to organize information (Lesson 14)

chronological order the sequence in which events happen (Lessons 9, 11)

claim a statement that something— an idea, event, or observation—is true (Lesson 13)

climax the part of a story where the conflict reaches its most exciting point (Lesson 3)

colon a punctuation mark used to introduce a list or an explanation in a sentence (Lesson 28)

comma a punctuation mark used to show a pause in a sentence or to connect ideas (Lesson 28)

compare to examine and consider the similarities between two or more objects, ideas, or people (Lessons 6, 11, 15)

complete sentence a sentence that contains both a subject and a verb (Lesson 25)

complex sentence a sentence made up of two sentences: one that can stand on its own and one that cannot (Lesson 25)

compound sentence a sentence that is made of two sentences that can both stand on their own (Lesson 25)

concluding statement the closing statement in an argument (Lessons 16, 17)

conflict a problem that the main character in a story must solve (Lesson 3)

conjunction a word that joins two complete sentences to make a compound sentence (Lesson 25)

context clues the words, phrases, or sentences around an unfamiliar word that help you understand its meaning (Lesson 30)

contraction two words joined to make one; an apostrophe takes the place of the missing letters (Lesson 28)

contrast to examine and consider the differences between two or more objects, ideas, or people (Lessons 6, 11, 15)

dependent clause a group of words that include a noun and a verb, but do not make sense on their own as a sentence (Lesson 25)

description descriptive words that help to paint a picture in the reader's mind (Lesson 18)

detail a specific piece of information (Lesson 1)

diagram a drawing with labels that shows the different parts of an object or how something works (Lesson 14)

dialogue the words characters say to each other (Lessons 5, 18, 28)

dictionary a book that lists words and their definitions (Lesson 10)

drama a play that is written in dialogue and performed on stage (Lessons 2, 5)

editing correcting grammar, punctuation, and spelling errors in a piece of writing (Lesson 19)

effect a result of a cause (Lesson 11)

evidence information used to support a claim (Lesson 13)

exclamation point a punctuation mark used to show excitement, surprise, or strong emotion (Lesson 28)

expert opinion the opinion of an expert or someone who knows a lot about a topic (Lesson 13)

eyewitness account a first-hand description of an event (Lesson 13)

fact a statement that is always true and can be proved (Lesson 13)

fiction writing that describes made-up people and events (Lesson 3)

figurative language language that does not mean exactly what it says; two examples are similes and metaphors. (Lesson 33)

first-person the point of view expressed by a narrator who is part of the story; uses the pronoun *I* (Lesson 4)

flowchart a graphic organizer that shows the order of events in a story from start to finish (Lesson 18)

formal style a writing style characterized by language that is proper and impersonal. (Lesson 29)

fragment a sentence that is missing either a subject or a verb (Lesson 25)

future progressive tense a form of a verb used to express an ongoing action that has not happened yet (Lesson 21)

glossary a section at the end of a book that lists alphabetically all the technical words and key words in the text with their definitions (Lesson 10)

graphic a visual tool such as a chart, graph, diagram, or timeline that is used to convey information (Lesson 14)

heading a title in bold print at the top of a section of text or column of a chart that says what the section or column is about (Lessons 14, 17)

homophones words that sound the same or similar, but have different meanings (Lesson 26)

idiom a phrase whose meaning is different from the individual words that make it up (Lesson 34)

independent clause a group of words with a noun and a verb that can stand alone as a sentence (Lesson 25)

inference an educated guess about a passage based on the author's clues and the reader's prior knowledge (Lessons 1, 7)

informal style a writing style characterized by language that is casual or conversational (Lesson 29)

informational text nonfiction text that provides information about a topic (Lesson 17)

irregular verb a verb that has different spellings when used in different tenses (Lesson 21)

literal language language that means exactly what it says (Lesson 33)

main idea what a story or article is mainly about (Lesson 8)

metaphor a comparison of two unlike things without using the word *like* or the word *as* (Lesson 33)

meter the pattern of rhythm in a poem (Lesson 5)

modal auxiliary verb a verb such as *can, may, must,* and *will* that relates a possibility or necessity of an action (Lesson 21)

motivations the reasons for the ways characters act (Lesson 3)

narrative text a text that entertains the reader with a story (Lesson 18)

narrator the person who tells the story (Lesson 4)

nonfiction writing that describes factual information about people, places, and things (Lesson 7)

noun a word that names a person, place, thing, or idea (Lessons 22, 23)

object of a preposition the noun or pronoun in a prepositional phrase (Lesson 24)

opinion a personal belief that cannot be proven true (Lessons 13, 16)

outline a plan or "skeleton" of an essay in list form (Lesson 16)

paraphrase to restate information from a resource in your own words (Lessons 20, 34)

past progressive tense a form of a verb that tells about an ongoing action that has already happened (Lesson 21)

period a punctuation mark used at the end of a sentence to show that it is a statement (Lesson 28)

perspective the attitude or feeling of the author toward the topic (Lesson 15)

plot a series of events that happen in a story (Lessons 3, 18)

poetry a genre of writing that is separated into lines and stanzas, in which an author uses sound devices such as rhyme and rhythm to create meaning and evoke emotion in the reader (Lesson 5)

point of view the perspective, or view, from which the narrator tells the story (Lessons 4, 15)

position statement a statement of the writer's opinion in an argument (Lesson 16)

possessive noun a noun that shows who or what owns an object (Lesson 28)

precise a word used to describe something that is specific or exact (Lesson 29)

prefix an affix added to the beginning of a root word (Lesson 31)

preposition a word that shows relationship in time or space (Lesson 24)

prepositional phrase a phrase that begins with a preposition and ends with a noun or pronoun; can act as an adjective or adverb (Lesson 24)

present progressive tense a form of a verb used to express an ongoing action that is happening now (Lesson 21)

primary source a source written at the time of an event by someone who was there (Lesson 12)

problem and solution a way of organizing a text by presenting a problem and describing how it is solved (Lesson 11)

progressive tense a form of a verb used to express an ongoing action without a specific end time (Lesson 21)

pronoun a word that takes the place of a noun in a sentence (Lesson 23)

prose a form of writing in which one sentence follows another, with sentences arranged into groups called paragraphs (Lesson 5)

proverb a short, well-known saying that often gives advice (Lesson 34)

punctuation the symbols used to organize sentences (Lesson 28)

purpose an author's reason for writing (Lesson 29)

question mark a punctuation mark used at the end of a sentence to show that it is a question (Lesson 28)

quotation marks punctuation marks used to show someone's exact words (Lesson 28)

relative adverb an adverb, such as *when, where* and *why*, that introduces a relative clause (Lesson 22)

relative clause a group of words that tells more about a noun (Lesson 22)

relative pronoun a pronoun, such as *which, that, who, whom,* and *whose,* that is used in a relative clause (Lesson 23)

research to gather information about a topic (Lesson 20)

resolution how the conflict or problem in a story is solved (Lesson 3)

resources print and online texts that provide information about a topic (Lesson 20)

revising deleting, reordering, and organizing sentences to make your writing better (Lesson 19)

rhyme words that end with the same sound (Lesson 5)

rhythm the pattern of stressed and unstressed syllables in a poem (Lesson 5)

rising action the events in a story that lead to a conflict (Lesson 3)

root the base, or main part, of a word (Lesson 31)

run-on sentence two or more complete sentences that are joined together without proper punctuation (Lesson 25)

scene a part of a drama (Lesson 5)

secondary source an account of an event that was not witnessed by the writer (Lesson 12)

second-person the point of view expressed by a narrator who speaks directly to the reader, using the word *you* (Lesson 4)

semicolon a punctuation mark used to join sentences that are related (Lessons 25, 28)

sequence the order in which things happen (Lesson 18)

setting where and when a story takes place (Lessons 3, 5, 18)

simile a comparison of two unlike things using the word *like* or the word *as* (Lesson 33)

simple sentence a complete sentence that expresses one main thought (Lesson 25)

sources materials that provide facts, details, and other information about topics (Lesson 12)

stage directions instructions written in a play that tell the actors what do to (Lesson 5)

stanza a group of lines in a poem (Lesson 5)

subject the person or thing doing the action in a sentence (Lessons 19, 25)

subject-verb agreement the use of a singular verb for a singular subject, and a plural verb for a plural subject (Lesson 19)

suffix an affix added to the end of a root word (Lesson 31)

summary a brief description of a longer work; a summary states only the most important ideas and details (Lessons 2, 8)

supporting detail a fact, example, or other piece of information that strengthens or backs up the main idea (Lesson 8)

synonyms words that have the same or similar meanings (Lesson 32)

tense the time in which a sentence takes place (Lessons 19, 21)

text structure the way in which an article or passage is organized (Lesson 11)

theme the central idea or message of a story, poem, or drama (Lessons 2, 6)

third-person the point of view expressed by a narrator who tells the story without actually being in it (Lesson 4)

third-person limited the point of view expressed by a narrator who knows only the thoughts and feelings of a single character (Lesson 4)

third-person omniscient the point of view expressed by a narrator who knows all of the characters' thoughts and feelings (Lesson 4)

timeline a graphic organizer that shows the dates when important events happened (Lesson 14)

tone a writer's attitude toward his or her subject (Lesson 29)

topic sentence a statement of the main idea in a paragraph (Lessons 17, 19)

transitions words or phrases that connect ideas to make writing flow better (Lessons 16, 19)

verb a word that expresses an action or state of being (Lessons 19, 21, 25)

verse a group of lines in a poem (Lesson 5)

web a graphic organizer that shows the main idea of a story or article in the center and details in connected circles (Lessons 1, 17)

word choice the words a writer chooses to convey his or her ideas (Lesson 29)

writing style a writer's unique way of writing; also called a writer's "voice" (Lesson 29)

Mechanics Toolbox

➤ Subject-Verb Agreement

The **subject** tells who or what a sentence is about. The **verb** tells what the subject does. Some subjects are singular. Other subjects are plural.

Examples:

The <u>sun</u> shines.

The <u>dogs</u> bark.

The sun is a singular subject. There is just one sun. *The dogs* is a plural subject. There is more than one dog. The verbs *shines* and *bark* tell what each subject does.

A subject and verb need to match in number, or **agree**.

Examples:

<u>Franklin runs</u> up the hill. (correct)

<u>The little boy run</u> to catch up with his big sister. (incorrect)

The plural verb, *run*, does not agree with the singular subject, *The little boy*. The correct sentence is:

The little boy runs to catch up with his big sister.

➤ Pronoun-Antecedent Agreement

A **pronoun** is a word that takes the place of a noun. An **antecedent** is the word that a pronoun replaces.

Example:

The ducklings followed their mother in a line along the shore. Then they plopped into the lake after her.

In the second sentence, the words *they* and *her* are pronouns. The antecedent of *they* is the plural noun *ducklings*. The antecedent of *her* is the singular noun *mother*.

Pronouns and antecedents need to agree. If the antecedent is more than one, the pronoun needs to show more than one. If the antecedent is male, female, or neither, the pronoun also needs to be male, female, or neither.

Examples:

<u>Geoff</u> read another chapter of the mystery before <u>he</u> went to bed. (correct)

<u>Jessica and Stacey</u> walked to the park. <u>She</u> had a picnic there. (incorrect)

The singular pronoun, *She,* does not agree with the antecedent. *Jessica and Stacey* is more than one. It needs a plural pronoun. The correct sentence is:

Jessica and Stacey walked to the park. They had a picnic there.

Words for Effect

Good writing uses vivid words. Compare these examples:

The girls <u>went happily</u> across the lawn. (weak word choices)

The girls <u>skipped</u> and <u>giggled</u> across the lawn. (strong word choices)

The words *skipped* and *giggled* are strong and vivid. They help the reader "see" the girls.

Using more words is not always better. Vivid words can say a lot on their own. Compare these examples:

The crowd <u>made a lot of noise</u>. (weak word choices)

The crowd <u>roared</u>. (strong word choice)

Adjectives and Adverbs

An **adjective** tells more about a noun. The underlined words in these sentences are adjectives.

Jasmine's bicycle is <u>blue</u>.

Artie ate his <u>favorite</u> meal of spaghetti and meatballs.

The adjective *blue* tells more about the noun *bicycle*. It tells about the color of the bicycle. The adjective *favorite* tells more about the noun *meal*. It tells that the meal is the one Artie likes best.

An **adverb** tells more about a verb, adjective, or another adverb. It answers the question *How?* The underlined words in these sentences are adverbs.

The cat slinked <u>quietly</u> out of the room.

We were happy to go swimming on that <u>very</u> hot Saturday.

The adverb *quietly* tells how the cat slinked. The adverb *very* tells how hot that Saturday was.

Complete Sentences

A sentence tells a complete thought. It has a subject and a verb.

Example:

We laughed.

This sentence is short, but it is complete. It has a subject, *We*. The verb, *laughed*, tells what the subject does.

Some sentences tell two or more complete thoughts. Words like *and*, *but*, and *or* are used to connect the thoughts. In the following sentence, the complete thoughts are underlined.

<u>Dark clouds covered the sky</u>, and <u>rain began to fall</u>.

In other sentences, a less important idea is added to a complete thought. Words like *when*, *because*, *if*, and *after* are used to connect the less important idea to the main thought. In the following sentences, the less important idea is underlined once and the main thought is underlined twice.

<u><u>My father wakes up</u></u> <u>when the birds begin to sing</u>.

<u>Because he leaves for work so early</u>, <u><u>my father also comes home early</u></u>.

A **run-on sentence** tells two or more thoughts without using any connecting words.

Example:

The sirens grew louder and louder, the fire trucks rushed down the avenue.

You can correct a run-on sentence by splitting it into two complete sentences. You can also correct it by adding a connecting word.

Examples:

The sirens grew louder and louder. The fire trucks rushed down the avenue.

The sirens grew louder and louder, <u>and</u> the fire trucks rushed down the avenue.

A **sentence fragment** does not tell a complete thought.

Example:

The panda that was just born at the zoo.

The subject, *The panda*, does not have a verb. You can correct a sentence fragment by completing the thought. The fragment is completed by adding a verb.

Example:

The panda that was just born at the zoo <u>is</u> still too young for visitors to see.

► Confused Words

Homophones are two or more words that sound alike but are spelled differently and mean different things. They are easy to confuse. Here are some homophones.

Homophones and Meanings	Examples
A lot: many **Allot:** to give out	Janice used <u>a lot</u> of fruit to make a big salad for the party. We will <u>allot</u> five cards to each player.
Board: a plank **Bored:** uninterested, dull	We need just one more <u>board</u> to complete our tree house. On the second day of the car trip, Terrence was <u>bored</u>.
Hear: to take in sounds **Here:** at this place	We could <u>hear</u> the children shouting before we saw them. We keep a spare key <u>here</u>, under this rock.
It's: it is **Its:** belonging to it	<u>It's</u> not likely to snow in June. The garden is famous for <u>its</u> prize-winning roses.
Knew: past tense of *know* **New:** opposite of *old*	Johnny <u>knew</u> the name of every student at his school. Angela wore her <u>new</u> bracelet the day after her birthday.
Their: belonging to them **There:** at that place **They're:** they are	<u>Their</u> house has a big porch, whereas ours has none. If you go <u>there</u> to visit, they will ask you to stay for lunch. <u>They're</u> friendly and enjoy company.
Weak: Opposite of *strong* **Week:** A series of seven days	The baby birds were still too <u>weak</u> to fly. In one more <u>week</u> our vacation will begin.

Other words are also commonly confused. Some of them are nearly homophones. Some of them are similar in both sound and meaning. Here are some examples.

Commonly Confused Words and Meanings	Examples
Accept: to agree **Except:** not including	I hope that you <u>accept</u> our invitation to play in the recital! Everyone had fun at the game <u>except</u> for Russell, who was too tired.
Affect: to cause a change **Effect:** result	I cried, but the end of the movie did not <u>affect</u> my mother. The floods were not the only <u>effect</u> of the heavy rains.
Close: to shut **Clothes:** garments, such as a shirt or pants	Mrs. Lee asked me to <u>close</u> the door behind me. I wore my best <u>clothes</u> to the wedding, including the red tie my grandfather gave me.
Loose: opposite of *tight* **Lose:** opposite of *win*	My shoelaces were <u>loose</u>, and I almost tripped on them. It never feels good to <u>lose</u>.
Than: in comparison with **Then:** at that time	My sister likes playing soccer much more <u>than</u> I do. We did not know as much <u>then</u> as we do now.
Weather: the state of the atmosphere in a place **Whether:** shows a choice	The <u>weather</u> here changes quickly, from sunshine to snow in moments. <u>Whether</u> or not you come with me, I am going swimming.

The verbs *lie* and *lay* are also commonly confused. Their meanings are similar. Also, the past tense of *lie* is *lay.* However, *lie* never has an object. *Lay* always has an object. Here are some examples.

Lie: to rest, recline	Go <u>lie</u> on the bed until you feel better.
Lay: past tense of *lie*	Thomas <u>lay</u> there until dinner was ready.
Lay: to put down	I <u>lay</u> the flowers on the table.
Laid: past tense of *lay*	Irma <u>laid</u> the tools she needed on the counter.

 ## Word Choice

Good writing uses exact words. Compare these examples:

The boy was <u>tired</u>.

The boy was <u>sleepy</u>.

The boy was <u>worn out</u>.

Sleepy and *tired* have similar meanings. The word *sleepy* gives more information than the word *tired*. It tells the way the boy is tired: he needs sleep. The word *sleepy* is a more exact word than *tired*.

Worn out and *tired* also have similar meanings. *Worn out* is also more exact than *tired*. It tells that the boy is tired from playing or working hard.

Like vivid words, exact words can say a lot on their own. Compare these examples:

The class <u>had a good time</u> at the farm. (weak word choice)

The class <u>enjoyed</u> the farm. (strong word choice)

Here are some weak words and some stronger words you can use in their place.

Weak Words	Strong Words
Cold	• chilly • frozen • wintery
Warm	• boiling • burning • tropical
Big	• huge • giant • vast
Small	• puny • slight • tiny
Happy	• delighted • pleased • thrilled
Sad	• depressed • gloomy • miserable

Punctuation

Every sentence ends with a punctuation mark. A sentence that tells a statement ends with a **period** (.). For example:

> We go to the farmers' market on Saturday mornings.

A sentence that gives a command also ends with a period. For example:

> Please get me a pound of apples when you are there.

A sentence that asks a question ends with a **question mark** (?). For example:

> Does anyone sell fresh eggs at the market?

A sentence that shows excitement ends with an **exclamation point** (!). For example:

> That pumpkin weighs 300 pounds!

A **quotation** shows the exact words that someone said. A quotation begins and ends with **quotation marks** (" "). For example:

> Rami said, "Those cider doughnuts are the best."

Notice that a **comma** (,) is used before the quotation. In the following example, a comma is used at the end of the quotation.

> "I like the doughnuts from our bakery better," Allison said.

If the quotation asks a question, a question mark is used. If the quotation shows excitement, an exclamation point is used.

> Examples:
>
> "Is the market also open on Wednesdays?" Rami asked.
>
> "I wish it were open every day!" Allison exclaimed.